Stephen Chambers

1986

OSTIA

ASPECTS
OSTIA OF
ROMAN
CITY
LIFE

GUSTAV HERMANSEN

 The University of Alberta Press

First published by
The University of Alberta Press
Edmonton, Alberta, Canada
1981

ISBN 0-88864-066-8 (hardcover)
ISBN 0-88864-072-2 (paperback)
copyright © The University of Alberta Press 1981

Canadian Cataloguing in Publication Data

Hermansen, G., 1909-
  Ostia

  ISBN 0-88864-066-8 (bound).—ISBN 0-88864-072-2 (pbk.)

  1. Ostia (Italy)—Antiquities. 2. Ostia (Italy)—Social conditions. 3. Ostia (Italy)—
Economic conditions. I. Title.
DG70.08H47   937.6   C81-091193-0

Printed by
John Deyell Company
Willowdale, Ontario

Contents

Abbreviations

AC	*Archeologia Classica. Rivista della Scuola Nazionale di Archeologia Classica.* Rome 1949 ff.
AE	*L'Année Epigraphique.* Paris 1888 ff.
AJA	*American Journal of Archaeology.* Archaeological Institute of America. 1885 ff.
Bloch	Herbert Bloch, "Iscrizioni rinvenute tra il 1930 e il 1939," *NSc* VIII, 7 (1953) 239-306.
Bloch, *Bolli*	Herbert Bloch, *I bolli laterizi e la storia edilizia romana.* Rome 1938.
Brunt	P.A. Brunt, *Italian Manpower.* Oxford 1971.

Buck	C.D. Buck, *A Grammar of Oscan and Umbrian*. Boston 1928.
Casson	Lionel Casson, *The Ancient Mariners*. N.Y. 1959.
CIL	*Corpus Inscriptionum Latinarum*.
Cod. or *Cod. Just.*	*Codex Justinianus* of the *Corpus Juris Civilis*.
Cod. Theod.	*Codex Theodosianus*.
de Robertis	Francesco M. de Robertis, *Storia delle corporazioni e del regime associativo nel mondo romano* I-II, Bari, s.a.
Dig. or *Digesta*	*Digesta* of the *Corpus Juris Civilis*.
Excavation Diary	in the office of the Superintendency of the Scavi di Ostia, Ostia Antica.
Gismondi's Plan	"Ostia. Pianta delle regioni e degli isolati," in 14 sheets, attached to *ScO* I.
Instit.	*Institutiones* of the *Corpus Juris Civilis*.
Itinerari	*Itinerari dei musei, gallerie e monumenti d'Italia*, publ. by Ministero della pubblica istruzione. Rome.
JRS	*Journal of Roman Studies*. London 1911 ff.
Kleberg, *Hôtels*	Tönnes Kleberg, *Hôtels, restaurants et cabarets dans l'antiquité romaine*. Uppsala 1957.
Kleberg, *Wirtshäuser*	Tönnes Kleberg, *In den Wirtshäusern und Weinstuben des antiken Rom*, Darmstadt 1963.
MAAR	*Memoirs of the American Academy in Rome*. Rome 1917 ff.
Meiggs	Russell Meiggs, *Roman Ostia*, Oxford 1960; 2d edition Oxford 1973.
Mélanges	*Mélanges d'archéologie et d'histoire de l'Ecole française de Rome*. Rome 1881 ff.
Mommsen, *Staatsrecht*	*Römisches Staatsrecht* I-III von Theodor Mommsen, in *Handb. der Römischen Alterthümer von J. Marquardt und Theodor Mommsen*, 3rd ed. Leipzig 1887-88.

Monumenti Antichi	*Monumenti Antichi pubblicati per cura della Reale Accademia dei Lincei.* Milan 1892 ff.
Nash, *Pictorial Dictionary*	Ernest Nash, *Pictorial Dictionary of Ancient Rome* I-II, revised edition, London 1968.
NSc	*Notizie degli Scavi di Antichità, comunicate alla Accademia Nazionale dei Lincei,* Rome 1876 ff.
Packer	*The Insulae of Imperial Ostia* by James E. Packer, *MAAR XXXI,* Rome 1971.
PBSR	*Papers of the British School at Rome.* London 1902 ff.
Reynolds	P.K. Baillie Reynolds, *The Vigiles of Imperial Rome.* London 1926.
Rickman	Geoffrey Rickman, *Roman Granaries and Store Buildings,* Cambridge 1971.
Rodger	Alan Rodger, *Owners and Neighbours in Roman Law,* Oxford 1972.
ScO	*Scavi di Ostia. A cura della Soprintendenza agli Scavi di Ostia Antica,* I and following volumes, Rome 1953 ff.
SHA	*Scriptores Historiae Augustae*
Tengström	Emin Tengström, *Bread for the People. Studies of the Corn Supply of Rome During the Late Empire. Skrifter utg. av Svenska Institutet i Rom.* Stockholm 1974.
Testaguzza	Otello Testaguzza, *Portus,* Julia Editrice. Rome 1970.
Thes.	*Thesaurus Linguae Latinae.*
Waltzing	J.-P. Waltzing, *Etude Historique sur les Corporations Professionelles chez les Romains* 1-4, Louvain 1895-1900.

Preface

Ostia has many enemies: sun, rain, weeds, hay cutting, vandals, and marauding souvenir hunters. Owing to these enemies, many of the delicate details that can tell about past activities carried out in the excavated houses are in full decay. Several interesting details that could be observed earlier have now disappeared completely. Unfortunately, this humble ephemeral material of Ostia does not appeal to scholars as much as things that are here forever, such as marble sculptures, mosaics, and capitals, and consequently, Ostia is only sparingly published. Yet this material needs faster attention than anything else.

The excavations from 1938-42 were a kind of archaeological blitzkrieg, of which the records and observations, contained in the *diari di scavo*, necessarily became extremely scanty. Some bits and pieces are preserved in an oral tradition, which goes back to Calza, Gismondi, and other members of the excavating teams; Gismondi would, in a casual way, give information about important but unrecorded details. But most of that is gone with the wind. A few remarks in Raissa Calza's guide to Ostia reflect the excavators' otherwise unpublished thoughts and interpretations. Obviously, Ostia is begging for our attention to save the vanishing testimony.

Some of the subjects that are discussed in this book have been presented in a preliminary way in lectures, seminars, and articles in festschrifts and journals, and some of the sins therein I hope to have corrected here. To Professor Denis Saddington I am thankful for the permission to repeat a passus from *Proceedings of the African Classical Associations* XIV (1978).

This is a work of interpretation, not an archaeological report; descriptions of the ruins mostly emphasize the features that have a bearing on the interpretations. Regrettably, it was impossible to offer a detailed, large-scale map of Ostia. However, the map in figure 2 will indicate the locations of the main sites under discussion. The ruins are mostly called by their Italian names, which now have become international. The locations of the ruins are identified by numbers of region, city block (isolato), and individual house.

I owe thanks to many people. First of all to The University of Alberta, which in 1966 accepted my idea of a summer school of archaeology in Rome, and to The British School at Rome and its former director, the late Professor J. B. Ward-Perkins, who was my host during my years as director of the summer school.

I owe great thanks to the people of the Scavi di Ostia Antica. Foremost to Ostia's valiant protectress, the Soprintendente Dr. Valnea Santa Maria Scrinari, who so generously helps those who want to work there. I also remember the former Soprintendente, Dr. Maria Floriani Squarciapino. Professor Guido Barbieri and Dr. Antonio Licordari have helped with the unpublished inscriptions. Professor Maria Antonietta Ricciardi drew the plans for figures 33, 41A, and 41B, and the reconstruction in figure 40.

The Technical Services of The University of Alberta and Shelagh Rixon, Rome, have drawn plans. A number of plans have been reproduced, or adapted, from Gismondi's big map in *ScO I*. Most of the plans were redrawn by Linda Porter, who designed this book. Bill Barazzuol and Professor Martin Kilmer contributed photographs. The photograph, figure 132, I owe to the courtesy of the Soprintendenza agli Scavi di Ostia Antica.

I thank Professor Alastair M. Small, who read an early version of the manuscript, and Professor Lionel Casson, with whom I on many occasions have discussed ancient shipping problems.

These studies were mainly finished in 1976; for their publication in 1982 I am grateful to The University of Alberta Press.

Westerose, July 1981   G. H.

Acknowledgement

This book has been published with the help of a grant from the Canadian Federation for the Humanities, using funds provided by the Social Sciences and Humanities Research Council of Canada.

Introduction

Ostia is one of the very few ancient cities whose development can be followed from the very start till the day when it dies from natural causes. After its death the whole ruin was, by and large, left alone, because the whole district was rendered uninhabitable.

The start of Ostian history is, of course, the construction of the Castrum. Equally important is the civilian settlement west of the Castrum, where three roads met and where one finds facilities for urban life such as a market-place, a *macellum*. That the spontaneous settlement happened west of the Castrum has never been properly pointed out, but the subsequent building program of permanent houses confirms that observation.

The Golden Age of Ostia is the time through the second and the beginning of the third centuries when all of Ostia was magnificently rebuilt, just after the time when Claudius's and Trajan's new harbours, Portus, took much of the usefulness away from Ostia. The paradoxical fact of this lavish building activity in Ostia, when Portus would seem to be the place where construction was required, has never been discussed or explained, and neither has the ensuing communication and administration problem between Ostia and Portus.

Finally, all the evidence and material provided by Ostia to illustrate a city in decay have never received the attention they deserve.

It may be useful, as a short introduction, to outline these developments and their possible causes.

The Castrum. To be realistic about it, we hardly know anything about Ostia before the Castrum was built. All reports about Aeneas and Ancus Marcius are a mixture of mist and poetry. The Castrum is the only fact, and it was built on virgin sand.[1]

The date of 338 B.C. for its foundation is acceptable, if one does not follow Säflund's idea that the tufa-block walls were erected during the third century as a defence against Carthage, replacing older earthen walls[2]—a view which was rejected by Richmond[3] and has not won many followers since.

Ostia was a fortification, a military establishment, and a military establishment is placed where it is militarily correct to place it; this is the overriding consideration. The original purpose was to defend the mouth of the Tiber and the coastline at Rome's doorstep.

At an early stage there must have been a lot of activity at the mouth of the river. People south of the river (Laurentum) and east of the river mouth needed roads to get there. There is no real controversy about old Ostia till the question about the choice of location is asked. The controversy started with Becatti's explanation that there were two roads which led to the mouth of the river, one from the Laurentum area, the other from Rome, and the place where the two roads crossed each other was chosen for the Castrum.[4] C.C. van Essen, however, thought that the two roads were both salt roads; they did not

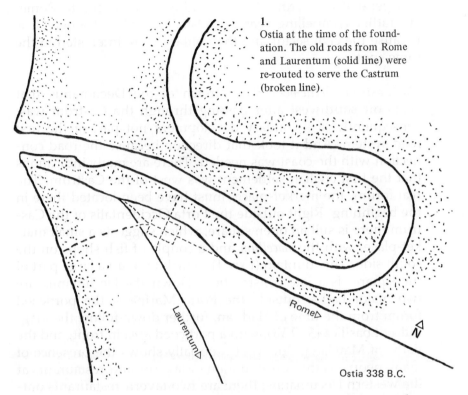

1.
Ostia at the time of the foundation. The old roads from Rome and Laurentum (solid line) were re-routed to serve the Castrum (broken line).

Laurentum△

Rome△

△
N

Ostia 338 B.C.

cross each other but converged, and both wound up in the *salinae* at the river mouth.[5] Van Essen made a real contribution in pointing out that the old road comes in from Rome south of Julius II's fortress, passes into Ostia at the Porta Romana, but then turns north at the location where later the Castrum was built. The line of this road is preserved in the oblique line showing in Region I iii 6; iv 5; xix; and xx. This salt road merged with the one from the southeast (fig. 1).

Russell Meiggs accepts van Essen's criticism of Becatti's theory but rejects his salt road for the reason that there could not be salt beds at the river mouth: "the firm sands in this area were not suited to the production of salt."[6]

Van Essen's correction should be accepted because the population of that district might have wanted to go to the mouth of the river for reasons other than salt. Fishing, trade, especially by merchant vessels that were run up on the beach, and general communication, including river traffic to Rome, are rather compelling reasons. Ostia was placed where it is because the civil sector and the military were interested in the same spot.

The Castrum Settlement. The stretch of the Decumanus that veers off southwest after passing through the Castrum was, consequently, a secondary development not part of the first road system. And it took that direction because the road connection with the coast was needed. There are many indications that the first civilian settlement was west of the Castrum. The real forum, the market-place, must have been located there in the beginning. Right outside the Porta Occidentalis of the Castrum there is still an open square, which suggests a small market-place, with the *macellum* and a couple of fish shops on the south side. The fountain (I xiv 1), which took up a large part of the square, is a late construction. Down the Decumanus are two major baths; outside the Porta Marina is the porticoed forum from the time of Hadrian; further down follow the magnificent basilica (*ScO* VI), with a porticoed area in front, and the Baths of Marciana. But what especially shows the presence of many people is the concentration of taverns and restaurants at the western Decumanus: there are two tavern-restaurants outside the Porta Marina and nine more inside the Porta Marina—nearly one-third of the identifiable taverns of Ostia. "Downtown" Ostia was west of the Castrum.

Furthermore, there are signs that the west end was developed a long time before the east end or, rather, the southeast end of the city. The settlement until the first century was basically the Castrum and the area west of it. There was nothing in Region II until the first century B.C. and Augustus; in Region V there is, for instance, nothing under the Baths of the Swimmer till the time of Domitian. Old Ostia was a compact unit.

For a fast survey of the development, here are the traces of the more permanent buildings that can be dated to the first four centuries B.C., distributed *regionatim* (fig. 2):

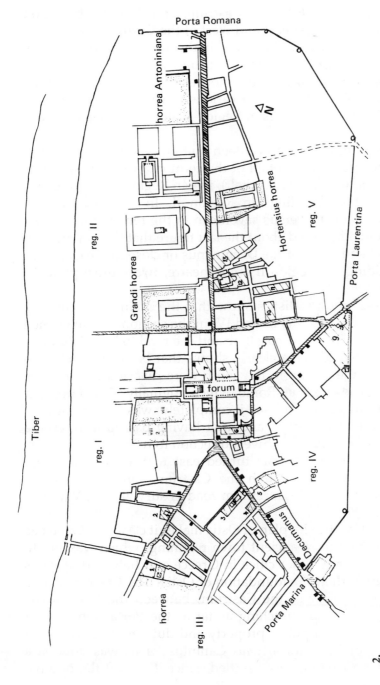

2.

Ostia. The map shows the ancient river bed of the Tiber. The hatched streets indicate the borders of the five regions. The locations of the Ostian taverns are marked by dark squares. The grain horrea are distinguished by dotted borders. The guild sites and guild property are hatched in an open pattern and numbered; starting from the west they are: 1. The Serapeum. 2. *Mensores frumentarii.* 3. *Fabri navales.* 4. Guild seat with Mars altar. 5. Schola del Traiano. 6. *Stuppatores.* 7. *Lenuncularii.* 8. *Fabri tignuarii.* 9. Campus of Magna Mater. 10. Guild seat in the Baths of the Philosopher (Terme del Filosofo). 11. Unnamed guild seat, with guild property. 12. Augustales. 13. The Themistocles Block. Scale 1:7500.

Porta Romana

horrea Antoniniana

reg. II

Grandi horrea

Tiber

reg. I

forum

reg. IV

horrea

reg. III

Porta Marina

Decumanus

Hortensius horrea

reg. V

Porta Laurentina

N

Fourth century B.C. The Castrum; a few building blocks on the Decumanus right east and west of the Castrum.

Third century B.C. Buildings in the northwest corner of the Castrum; *tabernae* outside the Castrum wall on the east side.

Second century B.C. Three houses inside the Castrum (last half of the century); thirteen various constructions in Regions III and IV; three buildings in Region V along the eastern Decumanus.

First century B.C. Seventeen buildings in Regions III and IV (seven from the first half of the century, two from the middle, and eight from the last half); five in Region V, and eight in Region I; four buildings in Region II. In all, seventeen in Regions III and IV versus seventeen in the remaining regions, but it should be noted about the last figure that the buildings in Regions I and V are at the Decumanus or close to the Castrum. The buildings in Region II are a theatre, two temple projects, and *horrea*.[7]

These crude statistics show that the main early building activity was in Regions III and IV, in the section of Ostia which is located between the coastline and the road to Laurentum.

The plan of Ostia clearly shows that both the road from Rome and the one from the south were diverted to serve the Castrum. The one from Rome, which originally turned north of the Castrum site and missed it completely, was turned south to become the Decumanus, and after having passed through the Castrum it bent in a southwest direction to reach the coast. The one from Laurentum was turned east to become the Cardo Maximus, passing through the Castrum; outside the Porta Occidentalis the old Laurentum road is surviving in Via della Foce (fig. 1).

A look at the city plan of Ostia makes it clear that Ostia has not benefitted from ancient town planning, which was put to work in so many other cities in Greece and Italy and at times much earlier than the foundation of Ostia. The Castrum is laid out squarely. East of the Castrum, between the Decumanus and the river, and stretching as far as the Porta Romana, an area was declared public property and duly marked with *cippi* set up by one praetor *urbanus* Caninius.[8] This was done at a time when Ostia was well settled, since it cut off the original road through Ostia, which was replaced by the Decumanus. The property lines, to which allusion was made previously, had already been established north of the Castrum, and houses had already been built when this proclamation of *ager publicus* was made.

The Castrum and the *ager publicus* seem to be the only areas where some planning, or at least a look into the future, has been applied. Otherwise, there is not a trace of the grid system known in so many other colonies. The southeast corner of the colony, especially, shows that expediency has determined where the streets should point. They fan out from a gate in the Sullan Wall. Via delle Ermette, Via degli Augustali, and Via del Sabazeo meet the Decumanus at an oblique angle, and the areas on which the various buildings are built have an irregular plan. The streets all communicate with farm land southeast of the colony. This is where the *coloni* had their land. No centuriation has been found there, but five roads, including Via Laurentina (the extension of the Cardo), were studied on air photographs and on the ground by Russell Meiggs and John Bradford. [9] The plan of this part of the city and the lack of older constructions shows that the southeast corner of the city must have been open land for a long time.

The Seasonal Character of Ostia. Or was it really open land? Russell Meiggs reminds us that much of Ostia, especially pre-Sullan Ostia, must have been built with perishable material like wood and mud brick. [10] Lugli has pointed to the same situation in Rome where evidence of early *insulae* and *case strette* has disappeared. [11] The flimsy houses of Ostia were replaced by sturdier ones in some order of priority: the sections of the city where there was much business and activity were built up sooner than the quieter parts. In terms of our statistics it means that Regions III and IV were built up sooner than the southeast Region V, because the former were the first centres of urban life. Regions III and IV were where the business was at that time.

It all makes sense in a different respect: it is obvious that Ostia, which depended so much on seasonal work, must have had a fluid population. Ostia was closely tied in with the season of navigation, which was the summer only, about two hundred and forty days a year.[12] During that period the big supplies for Rome were brought in; after the navigation period the shipping and travelling must have been much reduced. Cassius Dio reports (60, 11: 2) that one of the reasons for building Claudius's new harbour was that it might make it possible to maintain some grain import during the winter. Before the Portus was built, that was considered too hazardous. Later legislation, however, proves that this winter navigation was not accepted.[13] It took a smaller crew for the reduced winter workload and for the maintenance of the existing facilities. Much of the trade group and the service industry remained, but a group of migratory workers, peddlers, and caterers, free or unfree, must have been engaged in the moving of grain and other goods, in the catering to travellers, and in the extra jobs deriving from these activities. When the season was over, they were idle and could go elsewhere. Ostia had prepared herself for an influx of people in the summer: travellers from Africa and the western Mediterranean and the merchantmen's crews, who often would lie over for a considerable time: the travellers waiting for passage to a specific place, the seamen waiting for favourable weather or permission from the bureaucracy to go home.[14] Just the number and size of the baths would exceed the capacity needed for the permanent population, who in summer would also swim in the sea behind the rock barriers of the *balneae*, the *marina lavacra* of Minucius Felix (*Octavius* II, 3). The restaurant and hotel facilities will be discussed in a later chapter. Among the facilities must be counted a number of temporary shelters; not much was needed to shelter a humble worker during the summer season, and a combination of a shack town with very basic facilities and of densely packed dormitories may have met those needs.

During the time that interests us here, civilians in Ostia did not have to compete for space with the Roman navy. The navy's impact was not felt much at Ostia after the Punic wars, especially after the transfer of the navy to Misenum by Augustus. And before that time it is probable that the naval shore facilities all were located in Caninius's *ager publicus* (cf. Meiggs[2], 580).

The Golden Age of Ostia. The leap forward in the development of Ostia begins with Domitian. It was inspired by the expansion of imported goods to Rome, which increased in volume during the second century B.C. as Rome grew. In the beginning of the first century A.D. the expansion had completely outgrown all existing facilities. Out of bitter necessity Claudius added his new harbour, and a generation later Trajan added another harbour. The growth of the harbours necessitated a corresponding growth of the city of Ostia.

The number of *horrea* that were built during the century following the construction of Claudius's harbour is interesting. From the time of Claudius we have the partly excavated *horrea* V i 2 at the south end of the city and the Grandi Horrea II ix 3 and 7, the biggest of the ones excavated so far. Trajan added the Horrea Mensorum I xix 4, the small *horrea* III ii 6, and the Horrea of Artemis V xi 8. Most of the *horrea*, however, were built during the years of Hadrian: I vii 2, I viii 1, I viii 2, I xiii 1, I xx 1, III xvii 1, IV viii 5. After that only two plants are constructed: the Horrea Epagathiana I viii 3, A.D. 145-150, under Antoninus Pius and the large but unexcavated Horrea Antoniniana II ii 7 under Commodus. Only two, maybe three, *horrea* are pre-Claudian: V xii 2 from the first century B.C.; IV v 12, a minor plant from the beginning of the first century A.D.; and the impressive Horrea of Hortensius on the eastern Decumanus V xii 1, dated to A.D. 30-40.[15] It is clear that the important part of the storage space in Ostia was built as an immediate consequence of the new port facilities, at a time when the importance of Ostia was declining (see p. 17).

The big, important *horrea* that were built after the time of Commodus all went up at Portus. But we need archeological probes before we can form concrete ideas of what exactly went on in Portus. (On the *horrea* and their importance see also p. 227.)

As said before, Domitian started the building activity in Ostia or, rather, the complete transformation of Ostia. At the east end of the city the Porta Romana was rebuilt in marble, along with two baths toward the centre of the city, and in the centre the Curia and the basilica were major innovations. In this period the level of most of Ostia was brought up as much as five feet—a metre and a half—presumably to keep streets and ground floors dry in an area where swamps and stagnant water were not far away but not in order to create better building foundations. [16] It has taken an enormous amount of fill to raise the level of Ostia, and it would not be too far out to guess that some of this fill was brought down from Rome after the Great Fire of A.D. 64, although it may be assumed that much of the rubble was used as aggregate in the Roman cement when Rome was rebuilt under the Flavians. Tacitus's *Ann.* XV 43 reports that Nero ordered the grain vessels that had brought the wheat up to Rome to bring rubble from the ruins as a return cargo down to the Ostian swamps: "ruderi accipiendo Ostienses paludes destinabat" ("the swamps of Ostia were designated as rubble dump").

There followed now the period up to Commodus during which Ostia changed appearance. We see the modern city, the city of our time, rise from the ground. The new architecture is created by new material, Roman concrete, whose strength and versatility makes it possible to span wider areas and build to greater elevations than before. The noblest creations are from the day of Hadrian, when we see the highly civilized apartment houses, spacious and full of air and light, reaching up three, four, or five storeys, with a sophisticated utilization of space that is only matched in modern times. The Ostian apartment will be studied in detail in a later chapter. By now, Ostia is served by sewer, water, baths, and other amenities. We see the solid burghers consolidated in their guilds, *collegia*, which are in the good grace of the emperors, especially when they do what the emperors want. In a later chapter the guilds of Ostia will be surveyed, and five guilds will be scrutinized.

This period of Ostia's development is particularly interesting, because it coincides with the building of New Rome, the Rome that rose from the ashes of the Great Fire. When studying Ostia one studies Imperial Rome of the same period, with minor differences. The Forma Urbis and Roman legislation show that the two cities have everything in common but that the dimensions differ: residences in Rome are on average smaller and more crammed than in Ostia. Ostia's twenty-two domus and 228 *insulae* and *caseggiati* cover 181,405 square metres for an average 726 square metres.[17] Lugli has studied six fragments of the Forma Urbis, the Severan marble plan of Rome.[18] Shown on these fragments are thirty-eight potentially residential houses whose outlines have been preserved completely. Their average area is 249 square metres.[19] Lugli compares the Forma Urbis with the older districts of modern Italian cities and finds the average size of houses to be: Rome, 232 square metres; Naples, 162 square metres; Turin, 240 square metres; Trieste, 187 square metres; and Verona, 281 square metres. These figures are confirmed elsewhere. In Herculaneum, for instance, the group of houses which Maiuri called "case con più abitazioni" ("houses with several residences"), and which constituted one-third of the houses in Herculaneum, average 185 square metres.[20]

City-Roman laws can be used to interpret Ostian buildings. Ostian architecture complies with the Roman building code. The Roman prohibition against communal walls (Tacitus *Ann.* XV 43) is observed in Ostia; the *porticus* is a standard feature in Ostia, with exceptions for which rules may be given; and the various servitudes, described in Roman legislation, are observed here, all of which will be discussed later.

The Rise of Portus. The period of Ostia's growth described above constitutes the highest point in the development of Rome. As far as Ostia was concerned, there was a nemesis built into the whole course of events. In a way all of Ostia of the second century A.D. was doomed before it was finished.

By building the two harbours, Claudius and Trajan had taken away the foundation for Ostia's existence. Ostia originally served the port facilities in the mouth of the river and also took care of the merchantmen who were riding at anchor off the beach or who ran their vessels up on the sandy shore (if the vessel had a ram in the bow). The immense expansion of port facilities four kilometres from Ostia moved the greater part of the operation away from Ostia. With Claudius's and Trajan's canals open for navigation, most of the supplies destined for Rome did not have to go through Ostia, and the natural consequence would have been to move the administration and the supporting services to Portus. But this did not happen. Trajan,

Hadrian, and the Antonines kept building in Ostia as if Portus had not been created; all Ostia was built in the grand style after the twin harbours had been constructed. Some basic services went up at Portus, but it was not until the third century that Portus could compete with old Ostia. There was no direct link between Portus and Rome except by river traffic. We do not hear about a direct road to Rome, Via Portuensis, until the fourth century.[21] There may have been some road before that time, but an indication of the close link between Ostia and Portus and of the heavy traffic is Via Flavia, which at 10,5 metres in width is twice the width of ordinary Roman highways.

It seems that the emperors had created a very laborious piece of bureaucracy by retaining so many vital functions in Ostia. There must have been constant communications between Portus and Ostia and from there further to Rome. The distance from some place in Portus, across Trajan's bridge, down the Via Flavia, across the Tiber in a ferry boat, to some place in Ostia, or maybe all the way to Porta Romana to catch a ride on a *cisium* to Rome, could be five to six kilometres.[22]

The Decay. The Romans put up with this inconvenience for a long time, but before the middle of the third century A.D. a spontaneous correction slowly began. By that time the Piazzale delle Corporazioni was dying, the *navicularii* apparently were moving to Portus, and early in the century they had already stopped erecting statues in Piazzale delle Corporazioni.[23] At the end of the third century Ostia was decaying: a big milling plant and bakery burned down in the middle of that century and was left in ruins; an apse built on to the Forum Baths was allowed to block a street; the same happened at the Baths of Mithras; an inscription on the base of a statue in the Forum tells that it has been brought up there, away from grime and decay; sixteen inscriptions are taken from the Piazzale delle Corporazioni to repair the theatre; in the beginning of the fourth century a public latrine was built at the Forum, the seats made with marble slabs taken from sarcophagi, tombstones, and other architecture; in Via del Sole after a fire they did not rebuild the house but simply barricaded it; garbage and rubble was piled up in some buildings; and inscriptions (marble slabs) were used to repair floors or pavements or for water basins.[24] In the beginning of the fourth century—the exact date is unknown—Constantine granted independence to Portus and so reduced the importance of Ostia drastically. The martyr deaths of St. Aurea, St. Quiriacus, and their companions on 24 August 296 must have been a great event in a half-dead city.[25] The deep silence of Ostia breathes through St. Augustine's description of his conversation with his mother, while they, all by themselves and withdrawn from the crowds, rest their elbows on the window-sill and look into the garden of their hotel. The year was A.D. 387 (*Confessiones* IX 10, 23).[26]

Notes

1. *ScO* I, 93.
2. *Le Mura di Roma Repubblicana* Lund (1932), 239; Meiggs,[2] 23.
3. *JRS* (1932), 236, in a review of Säflund's book.
4. *ScO* I, 93-95.
5. In *Collection Latomus* 28 (1957), 509-513.
6. Russell Meiggs, *Roman Ostia* (1960; 2d edition, Oxford, 1973).
7. The figures gathered from *ScO* I, 233-234; compare 93-114. Grave constructions are excluded, temples included.
8. *ScO* I, 99.
9. Meiggs, 2d edition, 473-474, 580.
10. *Ibid.*, 127-28; compare 123.
11. *Atti della Pontifica Accademia Romana di Archeologia, Rendiconti* 18 (1942), 193, n. 7 (hereafter cited as *Rend. Pont.*).
12. Vegetius, *De re mil.* IV, 39: "ex die igitur tertio Idus Nouembres usque in diem sextum Idus Martias maria clauduntur."
13. Emin Tengström, *Bread for the People: Studies of the Corn Supply of Rome During the Late Empire.* Skrifter utg. av Svenska Institutet i Rome (Stockholm, 1974), 39-41, 44-45.
14. See Irenaeus's letter in Hunt and Edgar, *Select Papyri,* vol. I (London, 1934), no. 113; compare Casson, 237, with note on p. 261.
15. All dates from *ScO* I, 233ff.; about V xii 2, see Meiggs, 122.
16. This is claimed by F.H. Wilson in *PBSR* 13 (1935), 53, and by Meiggs, 64-65. Fills, however, make for poor foundations, and fills would have been unnecessary since Roman cement kept its strength and was unaffected by water. The cement would set under water, and for that reason one of the first applications of Roman *terra Puteolana* was for making piers. Vitruvius II 6, 1: "commixtum cum calce et caemento non modo ceteris aedificiis praestat firmitates, sed etiam moles cum struuntur in mari sub aqua solidescunt." Soundings in Ostia under the mosiac floors confirm the massive fills in the decennia following the Great Fire in Rome. See Fausto Zevi in *NSc* 24 (1970), supplement, 43ff., about the 1,50-metre fill in stratum A4 under the Insula delle Pareti Gialle; the fill contains coins and brick fragments dating to Vespasian—Trajan. Zevi refers to other soundings, to which could be added unpublished soundings in V iii 1 and I x 4 in Ostia, both of which give the same result.
17. Becatti in *ScO* I, 170-71.
18. *Rend. Pont.* 18 (1942), 191ff.
19. See G. Hermansen, "The Population of Imperial Rome: The Regionaries," *Historia* 27 (1978), 129ff.
20. A. Maiuri, *Ercolano. I nuovi scavi* (1927-58), vol. I (Rome, 1958).
21. Meiggs, 62.
22. From the Tiber to the Fiumicino canal was three and a half kilometres; from the canal to the pier between the two harbours was one kilo-

metre; and through Ostia to Porta Romana was about one and a half kilometres, for a total of about six kilometres.

23. Meiggs, 308-09.

24. *ScO* I, 159ff.

25. It should be noted that their execution took place at the theatre, not in an amphitheatre, which gives conclusive proof that Ostia had no amphitheatre.

26. In *Confessiones* IX 10, 23, St. Augustine's words are: "Impendente autem die, quo ex hac vita erat exitura. . . . provenerat . . . ut ego et ipsa soli staremus incumbentes ad quandam fenestram, unde hortus intra domum, quae nos habebat, prospectabatur, illic apud Ostia Tiberina, ubi remoti a turbis post longi itineris laborem instaurabamus nos navigationi" ("When the day drew near, when she was to leave this life . . . it happened that she and I, all by ourselves, were leaning on a sill from the window where one looked into the garden of the house, where we stayed, over in Ostia by the Tiber, where we, far from the crowds, after our long and exhausting travel, prepared ourselves for the sea voyage"). The location of St. Augustine's hostel is unknown. That St. Monica died in Ostia is borne out by the fact that her sarcophagus was found in Ostia. The remains of the saint were brought to the church of St. Augustine in Rome in 1430, and in 1945 fragments of the lid of the sarcophagus were found at the church of St. Aurea in Ostia (*Rend. Pont.* 21 (1945-46), 15-16, and 27 (1952-54), 271-73. Of the excavated places in Ostia there is really only one which might fit St. Augustine's description of their hostel: the sill of the window facing the garden in Insula di Bacco Fanciullo or its neighbour Insula dei Dipinti might have been the stage. It is speculation, but it is not too far out of the way to look at this block, because the neighbouring house Insula di Giove e Ganimede, which shares the garden with Insula di Bacco Fanciullo, according to Calza may have been a hotel during the latter part of its life. (*Monumenti Antichi* 26, 1920, 374). In antiquity the operators of the same professions tended to cluster together (on hotels, see below pp. 151-52). This bold guess has been provoked by A.C. Deliperi's claim that St. Augustine and St. Monica were accommodated in rooms in the "Christian Basilica" of Ostia (*Pantheon* 5, 1951, 272-73); the garden which Deliperi believes them to have looked into is actually a room in the Baths which predates the "Basilica." On the other hand, Portus might be a more likely place to look for St. Augustine's hotel; in the late fourth century the sea traffic had concentrated at Portus, and St. Jerome records a hotel there (*Ep.* 66, 11; *Ep.* 77, 10). But the fact that the lid of her sarcophagus, and the sarcophagus itself, were found at Ostia Antica speaks in favour of Old Ostia. Moreover, St. Augustine's text reads, "Ostia Tiberina," not Portus.

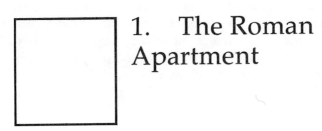

1. The Roman Apartment

New Discoveries

The Roman apartment, the *cenaculum*, has only been known since Ostia was uncovered. Less than a hundred years ago, when Marquardt published his *Das Privatleben der Römer*, he wrote about the *insulae*, saying that "we have no idea what they look like."[1] And it was not until after the latest mammoth excavations, executed between 1938 and 1942, that the later (post-Pompeian-Herculanean) phase of Roman domestic architecture became known to us. These excavations acquainted us with the later *domus*, so well described by the late Giovanni Becatti in his study *Case Ostiensi del tardo impero* (Rome, 1948), but more important to this study are the new finds of *insulae*.

The Roman *insula*, the apartment house, was well documented by such older finds as the houses in Via della Fontana,

Via dei Dipinti, and, unrecognized, in two small apartments in
Region II on the western border of the square of the four temples. What especially placed the Roman concept of the apartment before our eyes, however, were new finds like the group
of apartments in the Case a Giardino, and the wings that surround them, and also the Casette-tipo and a few others.

Besides giving us a world of information, the new finds
have posed a series of problems. Many scholars have been
engaged in sorting out the different types of houses and classi-
fying them in groups, and nobody has omitted to devise his
own system: Calza, Boethius, Meiggs, James Packer—systems
that may be useful guidelines in practical work. [2]

From the excavations emerged the new type of Roman
apartment: a series of rooms grouped on the three sides of a
long, narrow central room which faced the street. The two
rooms at the opposite sides of that central room were usually
bigger, and one of them in particular was more luxurious in
size as well as in decoration. The central room, which Meiggs
calls "the vestigial remnant of the *atrium*,"[3] is consistently
called *atrium*-hall by Packer,[4] who also calls the most important
room at the end of the central hall *tablinum* and the one at the
other end *triclinium*.[5]

In adopting these names one adopts the terminology
which was valid for the classical Pompeii-type houses. How
justified we are in using the same terminology on the apartments is worth some consideration.

The Rooms of the Apartment and Their Names

At the beginning of the period that interests us stand Vitruvius
and the Younger Pliny. Vitruvius informs us mostly about the
traditional Roman *atrium* house. He never goes into the
description of the kind of architecture which now to us is so
characteristic of Ostia. He acknowledges the existence of high-
rise *insulae* (II 8, 17), but only in one place does he use the word
in the meaning of apartment house (II 9, 16). He never men-

tions the *insula* in order to describe it in the same way as he describes the *domus*. Indirectly, he may (or may not) be thinking of an *insula* in VI 6, 7, where he speaks of the necessity of lighting the staircases because they carry a heavy traffic of many people, sometimes with burdens on their shoulders. Only in passing does he once use the word *cenaculum* (II 8, 17, in textually suspect surroundings), and he does not elaborate on it. The lowly *insulae* exist but are socially far below the levels where Vitruvius operates.

Tablinum to Vitruvius is the room by the *atrium*, the living-room of the *domus*. It is mentioned in connection with the *domus* (VI 3, 5; 5, 1). The *exedra* to Vitruvius is an open structure (definition in V 11, 2) in open air, containing a curved bench (philosophers speak and teach in *exedrae*). In VII 5, 2, he speaks of "patentibus locis uti exedris" ("open places like *exedrae*"); in VII 9, 2, "apertis conclavibus . . . id est peristyliis aut exedris" ("uncovered rooms . . . namely peristyles or *exedrae*"). But in Vitruvius we also see the development of the word toward the meaning of some kind of a room (VI 7, 3; 3, 8), toward the meaning of "Gesellschaftszimmer," to use Marquardt's expression.[6]

Oecus is a room; one could put one or more *triclinia* in an *oecus* (Vitruvius VI 7, 3 *in fine*). Vitruvius informs us about the Greek *oeci* and makes us think of Varro's remark about the fad of his day, to use Greek terms for Roman buildings: "nec putant se habere villam, si non multis uocabulis retineant Graecis, quom vocant particulatim loca procoetona, palaestram, apodyterion, peristylon, ornithona, peripteron, oporothecen" ("and they do not believe that they have a villa unless they use many Greek words in it, when they in particular call places procoeton, palaestra, apodyterion, peristylos, ornithon, peripteron, oporothece," *R.R.* 2, *praef.* 2). The word is used by Vitruvius and in the Older Pliny's *Natural History* but not elsewhere in Latin.[7] It seems to have been one Greek work which never became popular with the Romans.

Cubiculum is used by Vitruvius in such a way that it must be understood as the word for bedroom. In VI 5, 1, *cubicula* are mentioned as among the rooms where privacy is respected, as opposed to *vestibula, caua aedium, peristylia,* and similar rooms.

This seems to be the common use of the word in Latin.[8] The Older and Younger Pliny, Suetonius, and other still later texts also use the word for the general meaning of room, so the Younger Pliny feels compelled to use the expression "dormitorium cubiculum" (*Ep.* V 6, 21) or else "cubiculum noctis et somni" (II 17, 22) when he wants to stress that he speaks of a bedroom.[9]

To sum up: in the terminology which applies to the *domus* we meet *tablinum*, used about the living-room, and *cubiculum*, the favourite word for a bedroom. The word *cenaculum* is used once casually by Vitruvius and is missing completely in Pliny. The *insula* organization with the *cenacula* does not occupy these authors much. Speaking about an apartment, the Younger Pliny is more likely to use the word *diaeta*; he does not use the word *cenaculum* at all. Pliny uses the *diaeta* repeatedly to denote a unit of more rooms: "in hac diaeta dormitorium cubiculum" ("in this apartment there is a bedroom," *Ep.* V 6, 21, 31), but the word is also recorded as used about a single room (*Thes.*, under *diaeta*).[10] The word *exedra* to Vitruvius is the well-known apse with a bench in it—the ideal setting for philosophical disputations. In the Younger Pliny's work, *exedra* is mentioned once in the Vitruvian meaning (IX 70, 3).

There is not much material to determine the room names used by the *inquilini* of Roman apartments. However, one very clear example is in the *Digesta* 9, 3, 5, 2, the famous law about the responsibility of those who have caused material damage or bodily harm by pouring or throwing something from the windows. The text is from Ulpian's comment to the law as it was set forth in the *Edictum Perpetuum*. The character of this text makes it a witness of the highest order. The law says first that if several persons live in the same apartment, and damage is done by something thrown or poured down into the street from a window, they can all be sued for damage *in solidum*, because it is impossible to determine who did it (*Dig.* 9, 3, 1, 10-9, 3, 5 pr.). But if several persons share the apartment and inhabit separate parts, procedure can only be commenced against the one who inhabited that part of the apartment from where the object or liquid was thrown or poured down. The *Digesta* also inform us (9, 3, 5, 1-2) that if somebody rents an apartment to several persons and keeps a small part for himself, then all are collectively responsible: "Interdum tamen, quod sine captione actoris fiat, oportebit praetorem aequitate motum in eum potius dare actionem, ex cuius cubiculo vel exedra deiectum est, licet plures in eodem cenaculo habitent; quodsi ex mediano cenaculi quid deiectum sit, verius est omnes teneri" ("Sometimes, however, in the interest of justice, and without doing damage to the plaintiff, the praetor should rather start procedure against the person from whose bedroom or living-room the object has been thrown down, even though several persons live in the apartment. But if something is thrown down from the *medianum* of the apartment it is more right that everybody should be responsible").

As examples of usual room names, Ulpian mentions *cubiculum, exedra,* and *medianum.* These room names must necessarily have been plain and readily understood by everybody and must at the same time have been the correct technical terminology. The character of the three rooms is clear. The *cubiculum* undoubtedly is a bedroom, the *exedra* is a living-room, and the *medianum* is the central, hall-like room which, placed in the middle (*medianum*), gave access to all other rooms.

The word *medianum* is interesting. It is found in the *Florentinus*, which is the oldest of the two important manuscripts of the *Digesta* (sixth to seventh century), and that it is in the correct old tradition is testified by Leo VI's *Basilica* (60, 4, 5, 2), where *ex mediano* is translated *apo tu mesu.* Over the centuries, however, the concept of the city-Roman phenomenon *medianum* must have been forgotten and in the later manuscripts replaced by *menianum (maenianum),* a balcony, which was more readily understood by somebody who had never seen a Roman apartment. All that it took was to substitute a *n* for a *d.* The *menianum* was generally accepted in the text by later editors and caused scorn to be heaped on the Romans by modern classicists for their ridiculous legislation that everybody in a shared apartment should be responsible for what was hurled down from a balcony. If, on the other hand, the word is *medianum* and it means "the room in the middle," it makes sense from a legal point of view: the *medianum* was not the private domain of any individual *inquilinus,* it belonged to them all, since it was the only room through which everybody had to pass in order to get to their own room(s). That the word *medianum* was part of the language of the Romans of the time of the *Edictum Perpetuum* and also of Ulpian's time is shown by its use in two places in the *Itala*, the old Latin version of the New Testament, originating in Italy. In preparation for Passover, Jesus sent two of his disciples into the city where they would meet a man with a pitcher, who would show them a room where they could eat the Passover. Mark 14:15 reads, "ipse uobis ostendet locum medianum stratum in superioribus magnum"; Luke 22:12 says, "ille uobis ostendet maedianum stratum magnum."

Medianum is here a dining-room. The language of the translation of the New Testament is the unsophisticated language of the people and reflects the environment from which it originates and for which it is made. It brings us back into the middle of old Rome, where the humble people, the *humiliores*, had to share apartments, the kitchenless apartments. They could not light a brazier and prepare their food in their *cubiculum*, where they would be choked by the smoke, but they cooked in the *medianum* where the smoke could escape through the many windows, sitting on chairs at a table and eating in the same room—the *medianum*, the dining-room—no *triclinia* for the *humiliores*. Ostia has between forty and fifty apartments which were built around *mediana*.[11] The *exedra* of the apartment would correspond to the *tablinum* of the *domus*; the *medianum* would correspond to the *atrium* of the *domus*, although the functions of the two rooms show some differences.

Another room name may yet be added to the list, the *zotheca*. In two of the Ostian apartments that will be illustrated here (II iii 3 and V iii 3) there is an alcove at the end of the largest room (the *exedra*). In V iii 3 (fig. 4), the only entrance to the alcove is through the room in front of it, the *exedra*; there is also a door that could be closed between the *medianum* and the *exedra*, so that the privacy of those two rooms was secured. The *exedra* with the alcove constituted some kind of inner sanctum. In II iii 3 (fig. 7) and in the Insula delle Pareti Gialle III ix 12, where an *exedra-zotheca* combination is also found, there is a second door from the alcove, giving entrance to a side room, besides the door to the *exedra*. A remarkable detail: in V iii 3 the alcove is double or, rather, divided into two alcoves connected with each other by a wide door opening. The southern alcove is connected with the *exedra* in front of it through a door; the *cardo* hole testifies to that. The northern alcove connects with the *exedra* through a door, too, but there is no trace of *cardo* holes, so probably only a curtain covered the entrance; besides the door, there is a window opening between the *exedra* and the northern alcove. The pattern shown in the double alcove of V iii 3 corresponds to the standard pattern for the placement of beds: the two beds were placed along the wall, end to end.

This pattern may be studied in the bedroom of the *domus* of Amor and Psyche exactly in the room where the statue of Amor and Psyche is placed. The statue is not placed in the centre of the room but moved to the left in order to make space for the beds along the wall to the right. Having a statue in the bedroom cannot have been uncommon—compare the statue of Fortuna in Antoninus Pius's bedroom (SHA *Anton. Pius* 12, 5) and in Septimius Severus's bedroom (SHA *Sept. Severus* 23, 5-6). It was probably the same statue which was passed on from emperor to emperor (see *Sept. Severus* 23, 5); and the same statue had been in Marcus Aurelius's bedroom, too (SHA *Mar. Aurel.* 7, 3). The characteristic placement of the beds end to end is indicated by the pattern of the mosaic floor in the heated bedroom of the Domus della Fortuna Annonaria.

The name *zotheca* seems to be the correct name for this alcove. The word is not found in Greek literature. The Latins used it to denote a niche in which statues, for instance, were placed, "signis aereis n̄ iiii dispositis in zothecis" ("with four bronze statues placed in *zothecae*," *CIL* XIV 2793), but also in the sense of an alcove. The Younger Pliny uses it a few times, most clearly in his *Epistles* V 6, 38, where he speaks of his *zothecula*, which contained a bed, and in II 17, 21, which is the most detailed and elaborate example: "contra parietem medium zotheca perquam eleganter recedit, quae specularibus et uelis obductis reductisue modo adicitur cubiculo modo aufertur. lectum et duas cathedras capit" ("In the middle of the wall is a very refined *zotheca* in the form of a niche, which can be added to, or separated from, the bedroom by either closing the windows and curtains or opening them. In it is room for a bed and two chairs"). In the latter case it is very clear that behind the *cubiculum* is a smaller room which contains a bed and two chairs. It is very clear that between the two rooms are windows and openings, which may be covered or left open; if they are open the *zotheca* is added to the room before it, if closed the *zotheca* is separated from the *cubiculum*. This is an exact description of the alcove in Ostia V iii 3. It is then a fair assumption that the name in the early second century would be *zotheca*. This means that we have evidence of the alcove name from the same period from which the other room names are known. The room names in *Digesta* 9, 3, 5, 2 derive from the *Edictum Perpetuum*, first published about A.D. 130 by Salvius Julianus.

This lay-out of a room with an alcove behind it, so that the alcove received all its lighting from the room, is repeated in what is believed to be Tiberius's private quarters in the Villa Jovis on Capri. The inner room, which received the indirect light, must have been Tiberius's bedroom.[12]

We have, then, two different sets of names for two different Roman habitations. For all that we know at this time it is wrong to use the word *tablinum* to speak of apartments and it is equally wrong to speak of *atrium* in Roman apartments. The tradition supplies different names. *Exedra* is used in both types of dwellings but with different meanings. *Zotheca* may well have been used in both types of habitations. The widespread modern application of the word *oecus* is questionable. *Oecus* does not seem to have been much in use in Roman antiquity and certainly not in the imperial period which occupies us here. In Vitruvius's day it was a room that could also be used for a *triclinium* and not specifically a parlour or a living-room.[13]

Eight Ostian Apartments

The most widespread type of apartment in Ostia is the *medianum* apartment, which is characterized by the placement

3.
Apartment 1.
Scale 1:150.

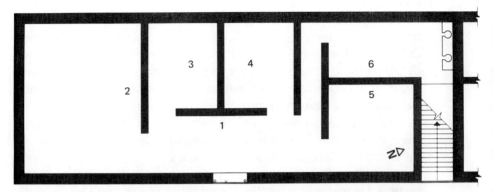

of rooms on the three sides of a central room, the fourth side of which faces the street or the courtyard. Ostia shows about forty or fifty of them in constructions dating from the early second to the fourth century A.D. The type, as a matter of fact, was so popular that it exerted a deep influence on the new *domus* of the Late Empire, to such an extent that it may be difficult to draw a dividing line between apartment houses and some *domus* in Ostia.

A few typical *medianum* apartments deserve a study:

1. The Casette-tipo. Region III xiii 2

In the so-called Casette-tipo we are confronted with some of the oldest apartments in Ostia. They are called Casette-tipo because they constitute a basic home, with the typical number of rooms to expect in a home. They are classed as Trajanic but so early that their date is believed to be at the end of the first century A.D.[14] On the outside, the walls are a reticulate divided into panels by upright bands in red brick. The inside walls are thrown up in a rather careless *opus incertum*.[15] The walls are not preserved high enough to show the location of windows. The walls are about 0,50 metre thick; together with the low height to which they have been preserved this is an indication that the buildings were rather low, hardly over two storeys in all.

Out of the two wings, Region I xii and xiii, which each contain two nearly identical apartments, the southern apartment of I xiii has been chosen for study here (fig. 3). It is a long, narrow structure, 6,39 by 18,36 metres (inside measure); after deduction of space for the staircase, its area is 112 square metres. The only entrance to the apartment is from the east, where a wide door opening (1,46 metres) leads into a long, narrow room (room 1, about 2,33 by 7,82 metres), the longest extention of which is parallel with the street. From this room, the *medianum*, there is access to the other rooms of the apartment. It is characteristic of Roman apartments that the individual rooms are not interconnected. At the southern end of the *medianum* is the entrance to the largest room of the apartment, the *exedra* (room 2, 5,05 by 6,34 metres). Along the west side of the *medianum* are doors into two *cubicula* (rooms 3 and 4, both about 3,60 by 2,98 metres), at the northern end the door to the second largest room of the apartment (room 5, 3,67 by 3,41 metres). Between this room and the last *cubiculum* is a corridor, which leads to a room in the northwest corner of the apartment. This room (6) measures 5,36 by 2,32 metres. At its north wall is the deep gutter of a latrine; the wooden(?) seat has been reconstructed in cement. At the northeast corner of the apartment is an entrance, with the travertine threshold still *in situ*. This was the staircase leading to the upper floor. The wooden stair has of course disappeared, but holes for the supporting beams may still be seen in the walls on either side of the entrance hall. The *subscalare* belonged to the apartment.

The *medianum* and the four rooms around it had white and black mosaic floors, which, however, have left only minor traces, except in room 5 where a few square feet of mosaic may be seen, although their decay is far advanced. No trace of mosaic may be seen in the latrine. There are patches of stucco left on the north wall of the *exedra* (2), nothing in the *medianum* (1), stucco in three places of room 3, and big patches on the north, south, and west walls of room 4; room 5 shows remains of stucco on the north, south, and west walls, with traces of red paint in the northwest corner. The latrine has much stucco on the north, west, and east walls. There is nothing in the staircase.

The picture we get is that of a comfortably large apartment, with stuccoed and painted walls and mosaic floors, all arranged around the *medianum*. The walls toward the east and the south must have had several openings for windows: in the east wall are two windows in room 5, about four in the *medianum*, and three in the *exedra*; in the south wall there are possibly four for the *exedra*. Windows in the west wall are unlikely, except possibly a couple of loopholes in the kitchen-latrine. There is no evidence of water having been piped into the apartment.

2. An Apartment called a domus. Region V iii 3

The complex Region V iii 3, 4, and 5 contains two *medianum*-type apartments and is of special interest to this study because of the elements which go into it. There is general agreement that it is a structure of the age of Hadrian,[16] with changes and remodelling of V iii 3 made in the second half of the third century A.D.[17] V iii 3 and 4 are listed as *insulae* in *Scavi di Ostia* I (236), while iii 5 is called a *caseggiato*. After the remodelling has been done to iii 3, Becatti has treated it as a *domus* and given it a place in his book on *Case Ostiensi del tardo impero*.[18] James Packer considers them three different buildings and believes that V iii 5 was three floors high, while iii 3 and 4 had only one floor.[19]

The building is constructed in such a way that the façade and the inside of V iii 5 is in red brick; the south and east façades of iii 4, the whole façade of iii 3 and 4 on Via della Casa del Pozzo, and the inside of room 1 in iii 3 are similarly in red brick; and the whole inside of iii 3 (except room 1) and 4 is *opus mixtum*, so that the partition wall between 3 and 5 has brick on the side toward 5 and *opus mixtum* toward 3. How casual the distribution of brick and *opus mixtum* may be is shown in the wall between the corridor and room 3 in iii 4: the wall was started in brick, then about 0,45 metre off the ground a long, 0,28-metre-high panel, consisting in three runs of *tufelli*, is put in, which then again is abandoned, and the wall is finished in brick as high as it is preserved, 1,83 metres. The *opus mixtum* walls in antiquity were covered with stucco, while the brick walls were left untreated.

Despite the apparent division into three different houses,

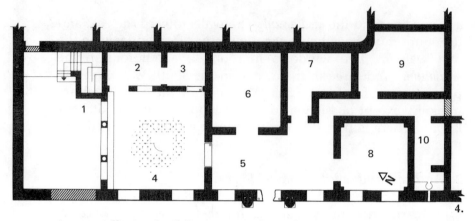

4.

it was all one building erected at the same time and in one operation. The wall that faces the Via della Casa del Pozzo and that covers iii 3 and 4 is one uninterrupted sheet of red brick. The north wall that covers and combines the north ends of iii 3 and 5 is one continuous construction, erected after the wall of the neighbouring *caseggiato* V iii 2. The door which connects rooms 1 of iii 3 and the corresponding room of iii 5 is part of the original wall and was put in as part of the first construction work. It is constructed in the same way as an arch in the wall between the two northern rooms 6 and 7 of iii 5 and integrated into the north wall in the same way as the latter is embedded in the partition wall. The inside surfaces of the walls of room 1 in iii 3 and of the walls in iii 5 are of the same solid brick, as opposed to the *opus mixtum* of iii 3 and 4—a strange coincidence if iii 3 and 5 were not one and the same house. The uniform plan of the two latrines points to their common origin: not only do they follow the same plan and dimensions but they have a common gutter and had the water piped into them in the same way, presumably in lead pipes, through the holes in the west wall (see figure 4 and, for the plan of the whole block, figure 44).

The outside walls and the main partition wall running through the length of the building are all 0,60 metre thick, an indication that the whole building may have been three storeys high. There is no evidence that iii 3 and 4 were only one storey high. On the contrary, in room 1 of iii 3 is ample evidence that there was at least one storey more: in the southeast corner

4.
Apartment 2.
Scale 1:150.

5.
Apartment 2. East and
south walls of room
1 show clear marks of
stairs to upper floor(s).
Photo: Bill Barazzuol.

there are marks of a stairway on the south and east walls. A
flight of stairs was embedded in the brick wall (fig. 5); it was
later removed when room 1 was added to apartment iii 3, if it
was added later. Becatti assumes that there was a door, which
was widened to the present size when the two columns were
put in.[20] The marks of the missing steps now give the complete
outline of the stair, step by step; the wall was later covered with
stucco when the steps were removed. If that stairway did not
serve an upper floor, what function could it have had? Furthermore, it is not conceivable that only room 1 was part of an original building iii 5 and had three floors, because the wall between
rooms 1 and 4 would then have been an outside wall, a wall
which carried a full load, and would have had to be 0,60 metre
thick to support the weight instead of measuring its present
0,45 metre, which is the measurement of the partition walls of
the building.

The thickness of all the outer walls would then indicate
that the three parts of the house all had the same height of at
least two storeys. Only the stairway in the south end of iii 5 has
served the second floor after the stairs in room 1 of iii 3 were
taken down; the upstairs apartments would not necessarily
have to follow the pattern of the ground floor, for it all
depended on the type of partition walls. One stairway serving
the entire upstairs is certainly not unparalleled in Ostia (compare, for example, Caseggiato del Larario and Caseggiato del
Temistocle).

The development of the house, in broad lines, is the following: in the city block V iii, south of a late first-century Trajanic structure (iii 2), was built the house iii 3, 4, and 5. The ground level, prior to the construction but after the completion of iii 2, had been raised by about one metre. Today there is a considerable difference between the floor levels, especially of rooms 1 and 4 of iii 3; the reason is that the floors of iii 3 were raised during the remodelling of the apartment. The floor of room 1, the former *taberna*, is now about 0,65 metre above the top of the threshold on Via della Casa del Pozzo; the door in the opposite wall, opening into the northernmost room of iii 5, was placed on the same original level. The stair in the southeast corner of iii 3, room 1, started from the same lower floor level. In the same corner there are also steps leading down to a low, vaulted basement room under part of room 2 and room 4. Becatti calls it a cistern.[21] The stone table or stone shelf at the far end of this small room reminds one, however, of similar basements in Caseggiato del Termopolio and in Domus del Protiro; it was probably a pantry.

There seems to have been close connections between the three units iii 3, 4, and 5: an original door existed between rooms 1 in iii 3 and room 7 in iii 5; the *angiportus* room 2 in iii 5 connected with room 9 in iii 3, where the rounded corner was made to remove an obstacle to a hurried passage from iii 3 to iii 5; and it should also be noted that there is a door from the *tabernae* into the *angiportus* (from room 2 to room 3). It is interesting that the wall between the *angiportus* plus staircase in iii 5 (rooms 1 and 2) and room 9 in iii 3 does not follow the property line which would have existed if iii 3 and iii 5 had been independent properties.

It is impossible to say today what kind of activity took place in this whole complex, with its five *tabernae* on Via delle Ermette. The average size of the *tabernae* is 6,68 by 3,50 metres, and they are interconnected so that one could walk from *taberna* to *taberna* and into the apartment behind them at the north end as well as the south end. Elsewhere it will be argued that it all was guild property (see p. 113).

This complex was broken up when the apartment was remodelled in the second half of the third century. The *taberna* door on Via della Casa del Pozzo was bricked over, and so was the door to room 7 in neighbouring iii 5; the floors were repaved and some of them were raised considerably (rooms 1, 2, 3, and 4, fig. 5).

Before room 1 was added, the apartment was very ortho dox, reminiscent of the Casetta-tipo, which was described above (p. 25). From the *medianum* (5) there was entrance into the *exedra* (4), and the other rooms (6, 7, 8) are arranged traditionally around the *medianum*. What is different is room 7, which suffers an indentation to make space for a passageway to rooms 9 and 10. The position of these two rooms is like the position of the corresponding rooms in the Casetta-tipo, where latrine and *culina* are placed to the right of somebody entering, behind the second most important room of the apartment.

The addition of room 1 gave a touch of elegance to the apartment, since at the same time marble was brought in for two columns in the doorway between rooms 1 and 4, and for *opus sectile* floors in rooms 1, 2, 3, and 4. The pavement in the *exedra* shows that in the middle of the floor there was a circular space for a statue or some other decoration, a phenomenon which was mentioned above (p. 23). The role of the double alcove (rooms 2 and 3) was also discussed above (p. 23).

Rooms 1, 2, 3, and 4 undoubtedly constituted the most private quarters of the family. Between rooms 4 and 5 was a door which could be closed—the threshold shows the mark of a *cardo* hole.

The apartment belongs to the last phase of the building's history; what it was like when it was in the beginning phase and serving a guild is unknown.

3. An Apartment for a Guild Official? Region V iii 4

This apartment is the southern end of the complex V iii 1-5 which is discussed pp. 27-31, 76-77, 113-15. It is placed so that the width of the building is the longest extension of the apartment (fig. 6). It measures (inside measure) about 14,90 by 7,10 metres, covering about 105 square metres. It is somewhat smaller than the 115 square metres of the Casetta-tipo, which was described above. Although it contains exactly the same elements (the same number of rooms and the same facilities),

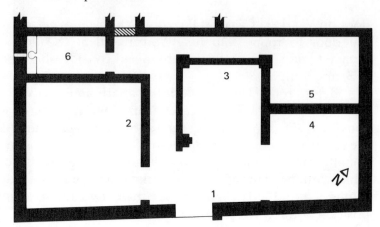

6.
Apartment 3.
Scale 1:150.

they are arranged in a more compact way. One enters the *medianum* (room 1, 5,25 by 2,40 metres) from the south, to the left is the main room of the apartment, the *exedra* (room 2, 5,48 by 5,16 metres), at the opposite end of the *medianum* is the second largest room (4), measuring 3,65 by 3,70 metres, and between these two rooms and facing the *medianum* is a *cubiculum* (room 3, about 3,15 by 3,50 metres). The innovation of the floor plan, as compared with the Casetta-tipo, is that the apartment is divided, as it were, into two halves: behind the front part, which is formed by the *medianum* (room 1) and the three surrounding rooms (2 to 4), there is an equally long but much narrower part, which is made up, west to east, of a latrine (room 6, 1,62 by 3,66 metres), a 0,91-metre-wide corridor, and a room (5, about 3,65 by 2,90 metres). A 1,15-metre-wide corridor leads from the *medianum* to this segregated part of the house.

The walls, especially in the eastern part, have suffered much and are preserved only to a low level. The partition wall between rooms 4 and 5 has, practically speaking, disappeared. The entrance from the outside in the south wall was flanked by brick pilasters, of which the western one has disappeared—so much so that it is impossible to measure the width of the doorway. There is no flooring left and no stucco on the walls.

4. An Apartment for a Civil Servant? Region II iii 3
A more developed, more prestigious apartment, originating in

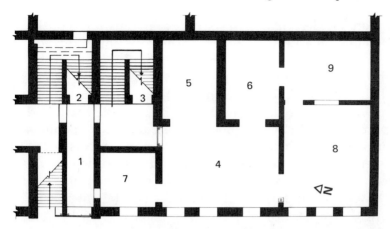

7.
Apartment 4.
Scale 1:150.

the last years of Hadrian,[22] is situated in Via dei Vigili across from the Baths of Neptune. It is part of a building which, perhaps, was designed to contain *horrea* and which certainly is built in the grand, aristocractic style of Hadrian. The apartment did not have more rooms than the Casetta-tipo, which has just been described, but while that apartment contained an area of about 112 square metres this apartment covers about 150 square metres. In several places the walls are preserved to the full height of the ground floor, and the ceiling mouldings in the east wall of room 7 and the north and south walls of rooms 5 and 6 show that the ceiling was about 3,90 metres high.

Right at the entrance to the house is the first problem (fig. 7): where does the apartment begin? It begins where there is a door that can be closed and locked. One enters the hall (1), and after having arrived in the middle of the house one may walk through a doorway to the left into apartment II iii 4 or to the right into the apartment which is under study here. Once inside the hall in apartment iii 3 (or the corresponding hall in iii 4) one may proceed straight ahead into the apartment or take a flight of stairs (2 or 3) on the east side to an upper floor. The travertine threshold with a *cardo* hole shows that there was a door between rooms 3 and 4, which could be locked. On the other hand there is no trace of a door between rooms 1 and 3. The stairway 2 must have been a public one, and the apartment begins at the door between rooms 3 and 4. The *medianum* (room 4, measuring 5,15 by 7,63 metres), which is lighted by three

windows on Via dei Vigili, gives access to the main room, the
exedra (room 8, measuring 5,78 by 6,36 metres). This room also
has three windows on the street, and behind it is a second
room, the *zotheca* (room 9, about 3,81 by 5,70 metres), which
gets its light from a window (1,61 metres), opening into room 8
and entered through a doorway (1,18 metres) at the north end
of the partition wall.[23] From the *medianum* are door openings
into rooms 5 and 6. The rooms 5, 6, and 9 cannot be inspected
closely, because they are filled in with earth after the excavation (presumably to counter pressure on the east wall from
without). Rooms 5 and 6 are both the same size (about 5,04 by
3,54 metres). The last room (7) is the smallest (3,56 by 2,42
metres), with a window on the street. A doorway, crudely cut
out in the wall between the vestibule (room 1) and this room,
was not part of the original plan but is a later phenomenon.
Considerable patches of a black and white mosaic floor are left
in room 8, and a few scattered *tesserae* are left in room 4. There
are areas of stucco on all walls; in room 8 the south wall and to
a lesser degree, the north wall have remains of painting in a
pattern of red and yellow panels.

Right outside the apartment are three stairways. One is to
be entered directly from the street, immediately to the left of
the main entrance. In the centre of the house are the two stairs
that have been mentioned before, each of them opening into
the hallways in front of apartments iii 3 and 4. They both are
the same type, a scissor-type of stairs; one flight takes the
walker to a landing half-way between the ground floor and the
next, and here the walker turns to the right into the second
flight, which goes to the second floor, the floor above the
ground floor. The room under the stairway (3) is entered from
the same hall, with a travertine threshold across the entrance.
The stucco of the room still covers most of the walls and the
vault. A loophole-type window opens in the east wall, opposite the entrance. From the hall of the main entrance one enters
the understairs, the *subscalare* of the other staircase (2). In the
east wall opposite the entrance is a rectangular window opening. There are remains of stucco on the walls. A gutter is constructed along the east wall, going through the whole *subscalare*, evidently the gutter of a latrine. At the south end of the

8.
Apartment 5.
Scale 1:150.

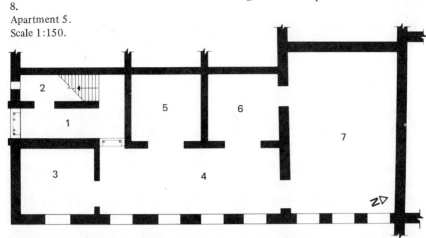

gutter there is a support for the seat; a similar construction is
missing at the north end, but marks in the wall indicate that
there was one. In the northeast corner is space in the wall, from
ceiling to floor, for a drain pipe, which connected the upper
floors with a sewer system. The latrine may have served several apartments.

The three stairways gave access to the upper floors, but it
is impossible to even guess about their course through the
building.

5. *Insula del Graffito. Region III ix 21*

For sheer collective elegance, the building complex called the
Case a Giardino ranks above all others in Ostia. The complex
was built about A.D. 128.[24] A frame of four wings surrounds
two parallel blocks in the middle and isolates them from the
rest of the city. Inside the frame those two parallel blocks were
set in a garden with six big water basins. In the four wings and
the two central blocks are at least thirteen *medianum* apartments, and in size, concentration, and rational planning they
surpass similar constructions in Ostia.

The Insula del Graffito gave about 180 square metres of
living space on the ground floor, calculated from inside measurements (fig. 8), to which area must be added a first floor.[25]
Nothing is known about the upstairs. The height of the ceiling,
which can be measured in three corners of room 7, is about 3,95
metres. One enters the apartment from the south, through a

doorway which is flanked by pilasters in brick. One passes over a threshold with four *cardo* holes; the dimensions of the door have apparently varied during the life of the building. Inside the door is the vestibule, which was paved with a black and white mosaic floor. There is an opening to the *subscalare* immediately to the left, and at the bottom of the vestibule one may turn to the left and enter the staircase or go to the right and enter the *medianum* (room 4). The *medianum* measures about 10,50 by 3,70 metres and has four big (1,33 metres) windows facing east to the street. It was presumably paved with black and white mosaic, but nothing can be seen now. At the north end of the *medianum* is the main room (7), the *exedra,* with three windows to the street and rather impressive dimensions (10,25 by 6,45 metres). There are patches of a black and white mosaic floor and big stuccoed areas with red and yellow paint on the south and west walls (and on the south wall the graffito of a vessel, which gave the name to the house). Opposite the *exedra,* at the other end of the *medianum* in the orthodox pattern, is another room, the smallest of the apartment (room 3). It measures 3,37 by 4,34 metres, with one window (1,48 metres) facing the street and one wide door opening (1,48 metres) from the *medianum.* Of flooring and stucco nothing is to be seen. No flooring is discernable in the remaining two rooms (5 and 6). They are the same size (3,82 by 4 metres), with a wide door opening from the *medianum* (both 2,08 metres). For light they both had to depend on what light came in through the *medianum.* Moreover, room 6 has a smaller door (1,17 metres) connecting with room 7, the *exedra.* There are small areas of stucco in these rooms. Room 5 has a narrow stripe of yellow paint in the southwest corner, and room 6 has bigger areas of stucco with yellow paint on the south wall and in the southwest, northwest, and northeast corners.

It is a harmonious, well-lit, and airy apartment. But what constituted the apartment? The five rooms downstairs, 3 to 7, may have been the whole apartment. Apart from the door of the main entrance there is also, between rooms 1 and 4, a solid threshold with *cardo* holes for a door which secured the privacy of the apartment. The situation is then the same as that of the previous apartment II iii 3. The upper floor may very well have been independent of the ground floor, and the staircase (2)

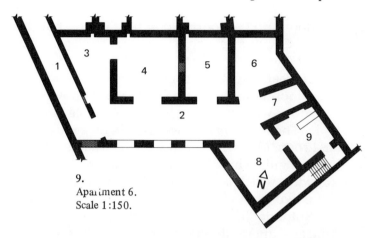

9.
Apaιιment 6.
Scale 1:150.

may indeed have served more than one upper floor. The outer walls measure 0,60 metre, which would allow for three floors.

6. An Apartment with Odd Angles. Region IV iv 6

An example of the great adaptability of the *medianum* apartment is given by the apartment IV iv 6. On a trapeze-shaped building lot, where the Via del Tempio Rotondo meets the lower Cardo Maximus immediately south of the Forum, a house was built (a *caseggiato*) in the time of Alexander Severus.[26] The house was built in two wings which met at an obtuse angle around a street corner, in such a way that the outside halves of the *caseggiato*, the halves which face the streets, are occupied by six *tabernae* and five entrances to stairs and *angiportus*. The inside angle, facing south and west, is occupied by an apartment on the whole ground floor, with the exception of a staircase in the southeast corner, leading to the upper floors. The walls are about 0,60 metre thick, and it is likely that the house was three floors high.[27]

Completely isolated from the rest of the house, this apartment was built with a very unorthodox floor plan, forced upon the architect by the unorthodox shape of the building lot (fig. 9). The entrance (room 1) is a long but narrow (1,86 metres) corridor, which leads directly into the *medianum* (room 2). The *medianum* faced the inner courtyard, which was created by the house itself on the north and east sides, the Domus di Giove Fulminatore on the south, and a big bath on the west side. Originally the corridor from the street, Via del Tempio

Rotondo, had a door into the courtyard at the far end, but this door was later closed with masonry. There is no evidence of an inside connection between the apartment and the courtyard. A wide door opening leads from the corridor into the *medianum*, which has three windows in the south façade on the courtyard, of which the middle window—the only measurable one—is 1,50 metres wide. The *medianum* measures 2,96 by about 11,50 metres. The first room (3) to the left in the *medianum* is a triangular room; the triangular shape is there to create the transition between the corridor, which is parallel with the Cardo, and the *medianum* and the two main rooms, which are parallel with the Via del Tempio Rotondo. The following room (4) must be the main room of the apartment, the *exedra*, the largest in extension (5,09 by 4,87 metres), with a wide door opening (2,36 metres) to the *medianum* and also a smaller door opening (1,20 metres) connecting with room 3. The next room (5) measures 3,26 by 4,87 metres and opens to the *medianum* with a door of 1,70 metres in width; the last room in this line (6) is entered from the *medianum* through a door which is 1,79 metres wide; the room measures 4,87 metres and 3,39 metres along the west and the north walls, respectively, while the east and south walls are square with the Cardo and force irregular lines on the room. Room 7 is a dead-end room, wider at the front than at the bottom (2,01 metres versus 1,60 metres), and from this room there is a door into room 9, which appears to have been a latrine, with a door opening to the *subscalare*. Finally, there is room 8 with a large window (2,06 metres) to the courtyard. This last room measures 5,56 by 4,26 metres; it gave light to the room behind it (9) through a very wide window, which later had its width reduced.

The long entrance corridor runs parallel with the entrance to the neighbouring baths. It is not part of the apartment—the apartment begins at the door between rooms 1 and 2—but originally it led to the courtyard as well as to the apartment. Presumably, after the construction of the baths, the exit from the corridor to the courtyard was blocked, because the yard lost its private character, and now the corridor served only the apartment. How the problem of lighting the corridor was solved is not indicated. This apartment gives an example of a lopsided apartment plan. The second most important room (8) has no counterpart at the opposite end of the *medianum*; the most important room (4) is at the proper distance from room 8, but the symmetry has been broken.

The building was constructed in red brick and mortar in the time of Alexander Severus;[28] the neighbouring baths were built at a much later time.[29] In the *insula* there is a line of red *bipedales* running through all the walls about 1,12 metres above the floor. Gismondi explains that these are not true *bipedales* but simple bands, *bipedales* in length but only 18 to 22 centimetres wide.[30] There are traces of stucco on the north and east walls of room 4 and scattered traces of stucco all over in room 5; a red line in the northeast corner is what remains of wall paint in the southeast and northwest corners. In the south corner of room 9 there is a narrow strip of stucco with some red paint. There is no mosaic floor left, only a certain number of black and white *tesserae* scattered over these three floors. There is no discernable evidence of mosaic floor in the *medianum* (2) or in rooms 3, 7, 8, and 9.

7. *An Apartment for an Aristocrat or an Institution. Region III ix 3*

In the southern wing of the four which close in the Case a Giardino is one of the most artistocratic apartments of old Ostia. Not only is the number of rooms greater, but the apartment is spread over two storeys. Exactly how many rooms on the second floor belonged to the apartment we shall never know. The 0,60-metre outer wall would support three floors, anyway, and to the west outside the apartment two staircases lead to the upper floors.

One enters the apartment through a doorway in the north wall (fig. 10). The entrance is not particularly noticeable, 1,48 metres wide, and it lacks the low-profile pilasters which are the standard decoration of other entrances in this complex. Once inside the vestibule (room 1) the *inquilini* could walk through a door immediately to the left and take an inner staircase to the next floor. Contrary to what was observed in the Insula del Graffito there is no inner door that might isolate the staircase and the upper floor from the apartment. This is a clear indication that the next floor was part of the apartment. The apart-

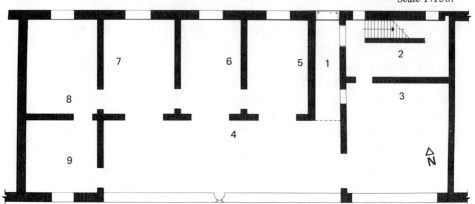

ment follows the pattern of the main blocks of the whole complex III ix 13-20: each of the ground-floor apartments has an interior staircase while, unconnected with the ground floor, there are two staircases in each wing leading to the upper floors.

The vestibule (room 1) leads directly into the spacious *medianum* (room 4, 14,88 by 4,18 metres), which in the south wall, facing the street, must have had a series of windows (six?), but that wall is not preserved high enough to show windows. In the centre of the south wall is the niche of a wall fountain (0,66 metre wide, 0.95 metre high), similar to the ones in the *exedra* of the so-called Domus del Ninfeo, in the courtyard of the Tempio Collegiale (V xi 1), in I xiv 9, and others. The *medianum* is paved with marble slabs, and so is room 6, which faces the fountain across the *medianum*. By this paving the two rooms (6 and 4, the *medianum*) are distinguished from the other rooms of the apartment, which are paved with black and white mosaic, and they seem to constitute an elegant unit. The *exedra* (room 3) at the east end of the *medianum* measures 6,74 by 6,42 metres. The room at the opposite end (room 9, 4,53 by 5,14 metres) has one window in the south wall (1,40 metres); besides the door from the *medianum* (1,35 metres) there is in the north wall a door into the next room (8). It is characteristic that rooms 5, 6, 7, 8, and 9 all are internally connected, so that every room may be entered from the *medianum* as well as from the neighbouring rooms. The door openings which interconnect the individual rooms are narrow (1,18 to 1,20 metres), narrower than the ones which give access to the *medianum* (about 2,35 metres). All the rooms 5, 6, 7, and 8 have windows in the north wall (about 1,48 metres wide). All rooms, except the *medianum*, have areas of stucco with remains of various sizes of yellow and red paint. This and a few similar apartments are interesting in that in size and plan they are little different from the later *domus* of Ostia (see p. 44-45).

A matter which could be debated is whether III ix 3 is a private residence or the seat of some organization. The internally connected rooms do not belong in private houses. They seem to be a characteristic feature of guild-owned *tabernae*.

8. An Unorthodox Apartment. Region V xi 2

In the east wing of the collegiate property behind Divus Pertinax's temple there was a row of rooms in the original Hadrianic building, each with its own entrance from the *angiportus*. To judge from the original door openings in the part of the wing that is still open for examination, there must have been ten rooms, and to these must be added one room, now buried under the *insula* on the Decumanus.

At a later time, not later than Gallienus,[31] the whole wing was remodelled and the ten rooms distributed in four apartments. The remodelling could have been done when the *insula* on the Decumanus was built, but it must have been done at, or before, the time of Gallienus: one door in the northernmost apartment supplies backing for a partition wall which has been decorated in a style characteristic of Gallienus's time.

As an example of these apartments the second apartment from the north will serve (fig. 11). One enters the *medianum* (3) from the *angiportus*. The *medianum* is paved with brick in the herringbone pattern and right inside the door is a drain-hole with a pierced travertine cover, all of which shows that there was a skylight in the roof. On the north wall there is plaster with stylized architectural framework and there are garlands and rosette in red paint on a white background. Counting from the bottom, the second course of brick in the platband of the *opus mixtum* on the east wall shows traces of red paint, which is discussed on pp. 106-7.

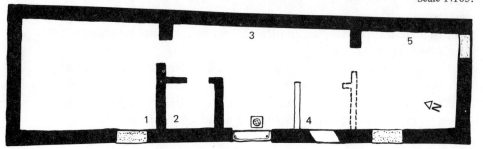

The northern room (1) is the *exedra,* the biggest room of the apartment (4,95 by 6,43 metres), paved in white mosaic with a black border following the walls. Most of the north wall, which is preserved to the height of over three metres, is plastered and has red decorations (masks and the like) on a white background; there are small patches of plaster on the east and west walls, with traces of red paint. Room 2 is a *cubiculum* with a white mosaic floor and black borders along the walls. The south wall has a spare, schematic architectural framework with stylized floral motifs on a central panel and a mask in red on a white background on the centre of the side panels. Room 4 is the smallest of all rooms (4,17 by 2 metres); all three partition walls have disappeared but have left their imprints on the floor. The room has a 1,19-metre window opening in the west wall; the window is twisted toward the south so as to collect more sunlight. There is no floor covering left in this room. Room 5 the other major room, opposite the *exedra* (1), occupies the narrow end of the wedge-shaped apartment. The north wall of room 1 is 4,95 metres as opposed to the 4,17 metres of the south wall of room 5. The width of the room, the north-south extension, is 4,75 metres. It has the white mosaic floor with a black border that was seen in rooms 1 and 2. On the south and west walls is some plaster with traces of red lines.

The remodelling of the east wing presumably happened in the third century, most likely when the decorating was done. There is no trace of any previous decorating underneath the

Gallienian or in any other place of Themistocles's house. The remodelling was done at a time when Ostia was in full decline, and, as the decreasing population moved to Portus or elsewhere, it handed over more space to those who stayed behind. One observes the same trend that is so obvious in the new *domus: insulae* were acquired and with the magic of marble and fountains transformed into luxurious single-family homes. If it is correct that the Caseggiato del Temistocle was the property of the *fabri tignuarii,* it is clear that the few builders who were left in a decaying city must have made the best of it.

Apartment Living and Its Influence on the Late *Domus* Architecture

The new architectural element which appears in the apartments is the central room, which undoubtedly must be called the *medianum*. It is not central in the same sense as the *atrium* in the *domus* because the *medianum*, placed on the one side of the house, looks out on to the street or the inner courtyard of the *insula*, while the *atrium* is introspective and turns its back on the world. Its function is also different from that of the *atrium*. It is characteristic of the apartments of Ostia that, with two exceptions, they completely lack kitchens. Of those two exceptions one is the kitchens on the first and second floors in Casa delle Volte Dipinte, which more likely was a hotel than an ordinary residential building, and the other is behind the Casa degli Aurighi and must have served an association or organized group of people. The lack of kitchens—or of rooms which by the presence of a fireplace have been formally appointed as kitchens—led for some time to the belief that *inquilini* in Ostia must have eaten out in bars and restaurants.[32] But the truth is that most common people in Ostia as well as in Rome must have eaten at home in their *medianum*. The smoke, which the Romans found so disturbing, came from the braziers behind the windows of the *mediana* of the lower floors. Here is the perennial Roman fire hazard, which forced the Roman *inquilini* to keep water in their apartments at all times (*Dig.* 1, 15, 3, 4).

A look at some of the *mediana* should show how well they served the purpose. The sizes of the ones which have been described above vary from 15 by 4,5 metres to 6,50 by 3 metres. The Romans did not necessarily have to lie down at table—a *triclinium, stibadium,* or *sigma* were not necessary; the *triclinium* was more aristocratic and festive, but many illustrations show common Romans sitting at tables to have their meals.[33] The space in a *medianum* was also more suited to a long narrow table with chairs or benches than to a *triclinium* or *biclinium*.

The *mediana* were large, pleasant rooms with lots of air and light in comparison with the darkened rooms behind them, and it is natural to expect that much of the family's activity took place in the *medianum*. The new house plan apparent in the apartments influenced the design of other structures. The long, narrow dining-room was adopted in places where there was no need to introduce it. Some of the meeting places of the guilds have an aisle of their peristyles equipped as banquet rooms. This was done in the so-called Tempio Collegiale (I x 4, fig. 47) and, much more obviously, in the centre of the Augustales (V vii 2, fig. 21). In the latter case the eastern aisle of the peristyle is about twice as wide as the western aisle, and, to demonstrate the purpose of the room further, many fragments of terracotta and vases were found here during excavation.[34]

But the influence of the *medianum* goes further and makes itself felt in the new type of *domus*, which became fashionable from about A.D. 300. In the Domus di Amore e Psiche (I xiv 5) there is a *medianum* stretched in front of three rooms; at the far end of the *medianum* is the stateroom of the house (*exedra*), and outside the *medianum*, corresponding to the street in the ordinary *insula* apartment, is the *nymphaeum* garden. All ideas of the old-fashioned *atrium domus* have been abandoned. A similar plan is seen in the Domus del Ninfeo.

Even where a *domus* is built in accordance with the orthodox *atrium* plan, of which there are examples in Ostia, there is influence from the *medianum* apartment. The Domus del Tempio Rotondo (I xi 2) is dated to the time of Alexander Severus (*ScO* I 237). It is classed as a *domus*; it is built with an *atrium* with a water basin in the middle, with a *tablinum*(?) against the north wall, and with a peristyle surrounding the other three sides of the centre (*atrium*). The west wing, with four rooms and a *hypocausis* room in a row and with entrances to four of the rooms from the peristyle, must be classed as the living quarters: the rooms could be heated and the marble pavement is luxurious. And the aisle of the peristyle on this side is twice as wide as the peristyle on the east side, 3,20 metres versus 1,76 metres, so that the builder in this western unit has created a *medianum* apartment within the *domus*. The lopsided peristyle with a wide aisle combined with the living quarters is a new concept of living.[35]

The study of these apartments already indicates a pattern of life: in the daytime the centre of activity of the apartment in most cases was the *medianum*. At night the family would retire to the inner rooms, the *exedra* with the *zotheca*, if any, behind it, or else to a different room off the *medianum*, which had been appointed as bedroom, as seen in the first room of the Insula del Soffitto Dipinto where the pavement indicates the placement of a bed. Here, of course, we are considering the middle-to-upper-middle-class people who lived in Ostia. The people who lived in the *taberna* had only the *cenaculum* above or behind the *taberna* for privacy.

About apartment living and the hardships of the apartment dweller we have the well-known testimonies from Martial and, especially, Juvenal. There is also a vivid description of the experience of the apartment dweller by Seneca, who lived above a bath in Rome (*Ep.* 56). A variety of sounds came up to him from that bath on the ground floor: the grunts of the exercising bathers in the palaestra and the cries of the hawkers and of the ball players must all have come up from the outdoors, as well as the splashes of those who jumped into the pool. But the noise generated by the masseurs and by those who sang in the bath or had their armpits plucked must have penetrated the *concameratio*, which possibly separated Seneca's apartment from the *balneum*, if *concamerationes* already were the usual thing.[36] The noise could have come out through the doors and in through the windows. Seneca shows the true adaptability of the happy apartment dweller: he does not mind a constant, continuous noise, but one which repeats itself at intervals disturbs him (*Ep.* 56, 4). What more could be asked of a Stoic philosopher?

Another letter of Seneca's (*Ep.* 122) depicts a similar city-Roman environment. It is about people who turn night into day, the *lychnobii.* Pedo Albinovanus lived above Sp. Papinius[37] and tells us that Papinius was awake and around at night and that through the night Albinovanus had to listen to the noises of Papinius's domestic activities: how he received the household accounts; at midnight he did his voice practices; in the small hours he went out for a carriage ride; and at daybreak he had his supper.

One tends to overlook the fact that apartment living in Rome was not just for humble people. The Roman apartment is best known to us through the Roman legislation that governed the conflicts arising among apartment dwellers who shared apartments or who violated the by-laws of the city. Indirectly, the provisions of the law describe the apartments to us. But somebody in Seneca's circumstances was not a humble person, and an apartment like that which is described above (III ix 3, see p. 39-41) would be adequate for Seneca. With all his appreciation of animal comfort he would not be without his *coquus* or *pistor* or *atriensis* or what other slaves he must have had around him (*Ep.* 123, 1). Seneca would have had plenty of accommodation for a numerous *familia* even though his attitude toward slaves was more humane than that of some of his fellow-Romans (compare *Ep.* 47).

The other, less humanely treated slaves? Their quarters are not clearly defined; a person does not need much space to sleep. Columella tells of how slaves should use the kitchen for a living-room.[38] Columella's words about the treatment of *servi soluti* and *vincti* do not contain much concern about their comfort.[39] The many freedmen of the *mausolea* of Ostia and Isola Sacra point to a rather numerous slave population. The industrial slaves were accommodated informally somehow on or near the job, and some of the sites of the professional guilds have space for many slaves—the House of Themistocles and the so-called Basilica are examples of this. The domestic slaves were accommodated equally informally somewhere in the house. Lucius's two slaves in Apuleius's *Metamorphoses* are laid to sleep in Milo's peristyle; the *ianitor* sleeps on the ground

near the door of the hotel (*stabulum*). [40] A slave in a small apartment, if the *inquilinus* owned one, could lie down to sleep in
any corner near the door, together with his small bundle of
belongings, while his master and mistress had barricaded
themselves behind the bedroom door or the *exedra* door. The
subscalaria saw heavy use in antiquity and show it in Ostia;
there is most likely an old tradition behind the legend of St.
Alexius, who slept under the stairs in his father's house when
he returned without being recognized. [41]

A Survey of *Medianum* Apartments in Ostia

If a *medianum* apartment is defined as an apartment with a central hall from which one gains access to the various rooms, and
if the *medianum* has to be located in such a way that its windows
open on to the street or the courtyard, a list of *medianum* apartments in Ostia would include the following, listed by region,
isolato, and house number:

1. I iii 3 and 4 Casa di Diana (time of Antoninus Pius, *ScO*
I 216, 237). Calza (*NSc*, 1917, 312-26) finds indications of three
apartments on the ground floor and two on the third floor.

2. I iv 3 Insula di Bacco Fanciullo, and

3. I iv 4 Insula dei Dipinti
are both built A.D. 128-138 (*ScO* I 216, 235).

Insula di Bacco and Insula dei Dipinti both have the classical arrangement with a major room at each end of the
medianum; they both have *zothecae* behind one of the smaller
rooms at the end of their *mediana*, and the *zothecae* are connected with the room in front of them through a door and a
window, their source of light. There is a passageway from the
zotheca through the neighbouring *cubiculum*, so that the *zotheca*
is connected with the main entrance to the apartment. This is a
special feature of the Insula di Bacco Fanciullo and the Insula
dei Dipinti.

4. I viii 3 Horrea Epagathiana (about A.D. 145-150, *ScO* I
217, 237). An upstairs apartment with seven rooms of rather
small dimensions. The biggest room, placed at the east end of

the *medianum*, in the location of the *exedra*, measures only about 4,50 by 2,50 metres. The whole character of the apartment suggests a dormitory. The south wall is not preserved to a height that is sufficient to indicate the placement of windows.

5. I xiv 4 (fourth to fifth century, *ScO* I 238) consists of three rooms and a *medianum*, arranged in an atypical pattern.

6 and 7. II iii 3 and 4 (Hadrianic, *ScO* I 236), both examples of the fine Hadrianic architecture. II iii 3 has been described on page 32. II iii 4 is slightly longer, and, by utilizing the space which is taken up by a staircase in II iii 3 and by reducing the size of the rooms behind the *medianum*, as compared to the four rooms plus *medianum* and *zotheca* in II iii 3.

8 and 9. II vi 3 and 6 (last years of Hadrian, *ScO* I 220, 236). II vi 3 is an orthodox apartment, consisting of four rooms and a *medianum* and inside stairs leading to an upper floor. II vi 6 follows the same pattern; the first room off the *medianum* has the place of the bed marked in the mosaic floor. Here, too, are inside stairs to the upper floor. The *exedra* has been bricked off at a later time and is not part of the apartment in its present state.

10. II viii 8 (Hadrianic, *ScO* I 235) is a building with two small apartments, both self-contained and each with two rooms. The one consists of two rooms plus a connecting *medianum*.

11 to 14. III i 12 and 13 (Trajanic, *ScO* I 235, compare 126), four apartments, of slightly varying floor plans, each consisting of four rooms grouped around a small *medianum*. Modest apartments in a parsimonious atmosphere, a long way from Hadrianic elegance.

15. III ii 9 (Hadrianic, *ScO* I 235). The exact number of rooms cannot be established; the two rooms at the ends of the *medianum* are quite clear.

16. III vii 5 (second half of the first century A.D., *ScO* I 234). The *medianum* has the form of a long corridor—three rooms in a row, with stairs in the middle leading to an upper floor and a second corridor leading to the back of the house. There is no wall between the *medianum* and the first room, the largest of them all. The corridor gives access to a room at the

one end and a latrine and still another room at the opposite end. The floor plan is interesting in that it repeats a pattern which also appears in V iii 4 and II viii 8, containing two corridors, one following each of the long walls. In II viii 8 the two corridors have the function of dividing the house into two apartments.

17 to 29. III ix 3, 6, 8, 12-21 (about A.D. 128, *ScO* I 223, 236), all standard *medianum* apartments. For planning and design, this is the most attractive group of residences—Hadrianic elegance set in a green garden. Conspicuous are the two central wings (III ix 13-20) with eight apartments of five rooms each around a *medianum* and with negligible variations in the individual floor plans. In three of the surrounding wings there are apartments of greater variations; no two apartments here are alike. In III ix 6 the *exedra* is not placed at the end of the *medianum* but in the centre, with two columns and no wall between *medianum* and *exedra*; the two rooms at each end of the *medianum* and the room beside the *exedra* have all been divided into a front room and a back room. III ix 8 is not fully excavated but seems to have been a mirror image of III ix 6. Insula delle Pareti Gialle, III ix 12, has four rooms, one with a *zotheca*, and an entrance hall around a *medianum*, to all of which is added an upstairs. III ix 3 and 21 have already been described (p. 39 and 35).

30 to 33. III xii 1 and 2; III xiii 1 and 2 (Trajanic, *ScO* I 235), four apartments with insignificant variations in the floor plans. III xiii 2 has been described on page 29.

34 and 35. III xvi 2 (Hadrianic, *ScO* I 236), two apartments, each with three rooms and a *medianum*.

36. IV iv 6 (time of Alexander Severus, *ScO* I 236), six rooms around a *medianum*, described on page 37.

37 and 38. V iii 3 and 4 (Hadrianic, *ScO* I 236) have both been described on pages 27 and 31.

39 to 41. V xi 2 (Hadrianic, *ScO* I 236), Caseggiato del Temistocle, three *medianum* apartments in the east wing, one of which has been described on page 41.

Notes

1. ". . . über deren Einrichtung wir ganz im Unklaren sind," 2d edition (1885), I, 221.

2. Systems; See James E. Packer, "The Insulae of Imperial Ostia," *Memoirs of the American Academy in Rome* 31 (Rome, 1971) 5-19; a remark about the combination of types in Caseggiatto del Trifore is on page 19, column 1. On legalities, see B. W. Frier in *JRS* 67 (1977) 27-37.

3. Meiggs, 247.

4. o. l. 140, no. 5; 173, no. 9.

5. o. l. 140, no. 7; 173, no. 10.

6. Joachim Marquardt, *Privatleben der Römer*, 2d ed. (Leipzig, 1886), 249 with n. 6.

7. N.H. 36, 184, about Sosus's *asaroton oecon* in a completely Greek atmosphere.

8. *Thes.* IV, 1266-68.

9. *Thes.* IV, 1268; compare A.N. Sherwin-White, *The Letters of Pliny* (Oxford, 1966), 191 under *cubiculum*.

10. Pliny may also have used the word *cubiculum* about niches like those in Domus Aurea (Nash, fig. 409) and in the ten bedrooms of Villa Adriana's Hospitalia. See S. Aurigemma, *La Villa Adriana*, 6th ed. (1969), 59-61 with fig. 13 and tavola II; also Heinz Kähler, *Hadrian and seine Villa bei Tivoli* (Berlin, 1950), 36-37.

11. For references and more material on the *medianum*, see *Phoenix* 24 (1970), 342-347. More about the function of the *medianum* on pp. 43-45. A list of Ostian apartments follows at the end of this chapter. When *medianum* is used in Greek form in connection with a mausoleum, it may simply be a reference to an eating place for celebrating anniversaries, like the *biclinium* built in front of a mausoleum in Isola Sacra; compare Calza, *Isola Sacra*, 58, fig. 16.

12. See A. Maiuri, *Capri, Storia e Monumenti* (Rome, 1957), fig. 14. A third example, the Insula delle par. Gialle, was mentioned above. The northern rooms of II iii 4 of the Insula dei Dipinti and of Insula di Bacco Fanciullo I iv 3 and 4 are further examples. Compare a similar arrangement in two bedrooms with alcoves in Domus Aurea; see room 3 and the second room west of it on the plan in Nash I, 339, fig. 407, and picture, 341, fig. 409.

13. Vitruvius VI 7, 3 *in fine*: "ad meridiem vero spectantes oecos quadratos ita ampla magnitudine uti faciliter in eo quattuor tricliniis stratis ministrationum ludorumque operis locus possit esse spatiosus."

14. Becatti, *ScO* I, 125.

15. *ScO* I, tavola 52, 1 and 2; see also Gismondi's critical words, ibid, 199 col. 1.

16. *ScO* I, 236.

17. *ScO* I, 238.

18. pp. 25-26.

19. Packer, 86 and 90. On page 11, column 1, he states specifically that the formal rooms of these two houses were not over one storey high, "and in fact, lacking internal stairways, the buildings themselves were no higher" (11, col. 1). He was probably misinformed by Meiggs (257).

20. G. Becatti, *Case ostiensi del tardo impero* (Rome, 1949), 25: "La porta primitiva di comunicazione è stata infatti allargata."

21. *Ibid.*, 26.

22. *ScO* I, 133.

23. Section four of the big plan in *ScO* I erroneously gives the impression that there were two windows and a door in this wall.

24. *ScO* I 236; general remarks, 136-37.

25. One floor upstairs; Packer, 89.

26. *ScO* I, 237.

27. Packer says five floors on page 90; on page 85 he says four floors. The thickness of walls is often evaluated differently. Observations in Ostia give the following guidelines: Casette-tipo have a wall thickness of 0,50 metre, and evidence of stairs indicates that there was an upper storey. Caseggiato del Serapide measures 0,80 metre on the ground floor, about 0,64 metre on the second floor, and 0,52 metre on what is left of the third floor. The 0,52 metre on the third floor could support an upper floor, for a total of four floors. The Casa delle Volte Dipinte measures 0,55 to 0,60 metre on the ground floor and 0,40 to 0,46 metre on the second floor. The lower figures apply to the southeast wall, which is up to five centimetres thinner than the others. The beginning of a flight of stairs on the second floor proves the existence of a third floor. The height to which the outer walls of this *insula* are saved would by itself indicate a building higher than two storeys. Moreover, the walls of the ground floor are reinforced by twelve pilasters. This would go against the reserves expressed by Bianca Maria Felletti Maj in an interesting discussion in *Bollettino d'Arte* 45 (1960) 51-52 (with n. 6): she is uncertain about the number of upper floors since the vaults of the ground floor are very low and exert a great side pressure that could not be supported on an upper floor because of the weak walls. But it is very unlikely that the upper floors had other than the usual plank floor/ceiling with plaster and mosaic flooring. Occasionally, 0,15 to 0,30 metre walls occur (for example, in Caseggiato del Temistocle), but those walls are exclusively partition walls and are not designed to carry a load. A rule of thumb would be: 0,50 metre equals two storeys; 0,60 to 0,65 metre equals three storeys; 0,80 metre equals four storeys; 0,90 metre equals five storeys; and one metre equals six storeys. On the other hand one should not overlook the fact that sometimes walls were built thicker than necessary, so that heavy walls are built in places where the buildings could not possibly have the proportionate height. Neither should it be forgotten that a builder

could add an extra top floor in light *opus craticium* or lumber, so that the standard 0,60 to 0,65 metre wall might be enough for four storeys.

28. *ScO* I, 237, col. 2.

29. *ScO* I, 238, col. 2.

30. *ScO* I, 205 and 206.

31. C.C. van Essen in *Bullettino Comunale* 76 (1956-58), 178. The building history of the House of Themistocles is discussed on pp. 96-111.

32. See *Polis and Imperium: Studies in Honour of Edward Togo Salmon,* Toronto (1974), 171-73.

33. For example, Kleberg, *Hôtels,* figs. 13 (equals fig. 16 reconstructed), 14, and 15. See also the third-century caricature in M.J. Vermaseren and C.C. van Essen, *The Excavations in the Mithraeum of the Church of S. Prisca in Rome* (1965), plate 52, 1.

34. Guido Calza in *NSc* VII, 2 (1941), 198.

35. There are elements of the same in Domus dei Pesci and Domus delle Colonne. J.B. Ward-Perkins, in commenting on *domus* from the Antiochia area with a floor plan similar to those in Ostia, has hinted that the Orient may have supplied the pattern for the late Ostian *domus*. See Boethius and Ward-Perkins, *Etruscan and Roman Architecture* (1970), 427 with fig. 160. This seems less likely when one considers that neither the *medianum* apartment nor the late *domus* is a natural development of the *atrium domus* while, on the other hand, the *medianum* apartment and the *domus* have lived side by side since the end of the first century A.D. The plan of the *medianum* apartment is dictated by the narrow, rectangular shape of the *insula*. In Ostia one can observe how this new, practical concept of living, created by the *medianum* apartments, is imposed on guild seats and *domus*. If there is a connection between Ostia and Antiochia, the influence might rather come from Ostia-Rome.

36. Compare *Codex Justinianus* VIII 10, 1.

37. "Pendonem Albinovanum narratem audieramus . . . habitasse se supra domum Sp. Papini" (*domum* equals residence). ("We heard Pedo Albinovanus tell that he lived above Sp. Papinius's residence," *Ep.* 122, 15).

38. "At in rustica parte magna et alta culina ponetur, ut et contignatio careat incendii periculo et in ea familiares omni tempore anni morari queant." ("In the farm quarters there should be a large kitchen with a high ceiling, so that the roof is in no danger of catching fire, and the slaves can stay there the year around," Columella I vi, 3).

39. *Ibid.:* "Optime solutis servis cellae meridiem aequinoctalem spectantes fient; vinctis quam saluberrimum subterraneum ergastulum plurimis, sitque id angustis inlustratum fenestris atque a terra sic editis, ne manu contingi possint." ("For free slaves it is best to build cells facing south; for most chained slaves an underground compound is most healthy, and this should

be lighted by narrow windows that are placed so high off the ground that nobody can reach them with his hand.")

40. Apuleius *Met.* II 15; I 15.

41. *Acta Sanctorum* 31, 242.

2.   The Guilds of Ostia

If the scavengers of marble slabs and the operators of the lime kilns had worked with higher efficiency in Ostia toward the end of antiquity and in the Dark Centuries, we would have had no information at all about the guilds of Ostia. But the lime kiln operators left a great number of inscriptions and fragments of inscriptions behind, and it is now these inscriptions that have identified the few guild sites that are known to us. It is also these inscriptions which paint a colourful picture of the activities that were carried out in Ostia and her harbour. Being the only source they are priceless, but despite everything they offer they are far from giving a precise, or even a rounded, picture.

We have information on close to forty Ostian guilds out of a potentially much higher number (Waltzing II, 144 ff.). What dominates the picture are all the activities connected with the import of goods to the City of Rome from all parts of the world and with the general traffic of people travelling by boat to and from Rome. To this must be added all the services needed by the population of Ostia.

A Survey of Guilds

In order to be specific about these activities a short survey of the guilds will show what we have to work with. The guilds of Ostia can be divided into six groups: the guilds for grain shipping and related services, commerce, transport, trades, civil service, and cults.*

1. Grain shipping and related services
   naviculari Ostienses 3603, S4648, Bloch 32
   domini navium 99, 4142 refer to shipowners from Carthage and Africa, respectively. Their organizations may have been guilds but not Ostian guilds. Many guilds in this category have offices and representatives in the Piazzale delle Corporazioni.
   sacomarii 51, 309, 409 (cf. group 5, Civil Service)
   corpus me(n)sorum frumentariorum Ost. 172
   mensores frumentarii Cereris Augustae 409
   corpus mensorum frumentariorum adiutorum et acceptorum Ost. 154
   QQ. corporis mensorum (frumenta)riorum nauticariorum Ost. 289
   corpus mensorum frumentariorum adiutorum Ost. 4140

---

* In cases of uncertainty whether a source refers to a non-Ostian or an Ostian guild, that source will be disregarded. The list is not a complete enumeration of inscriptions about guilds; only representative or more significant inscriptions will be quoted. Simple numbers refer to *CIL* XIV; S = Supplementum of XIV. For an English translation of the guild list, see pp. 239-41.

corpus m(ensorum) adiutorum 2
QQ. nauticariorum 2
QQ. II acceptorum 2 (album 150?)
susceptorum Ostiensium sive Portuensium antiquissimum corpus
    CIL VI 1741

The grain measurers' guild, which demonstrates a natural connection with Ceres (409), was sometimes listed under names of smaller groups inside the guild. One observes the *mens. frum. adiutores et acceptores* (154), the *mens. frum. nauticarii* (289), or *corp. mens. frum. adiutorum* (4140), or expressed briefly: *corp. mens. adiutorum*, or *nauticarii*, or *acceptores* (2). These three subdivisions seem to have been governed independently: the *adiutores* have their own *patronus* and *quinquennalis perpetuus* C. Caecilius Onesimus, the *acceptores* and *nauticarii* each their own *quinquennalis* (all in 2). It is apparently the question of three *decuriae* of the same guild. The functions of the different *decuriae* are not known; *acceptores* may not have been different from the *susceptores*. *Susceptor* is used to denominate the official who received and gave receipt for grain, when *frumenta fiscalia* went into the fiscal *horrea*, and at various stages of the shipping of the grain and wine (Waltzing II, 98).[1]

2. Commerce

    argentarii 409
    num(m)ularius, Rendiconti dei Lincei, Scienze morali, series VIII, vol. XXIX, 1974, 313-23.[2] *Nummularii* are to be distinguished from *argentarii,* as pointed out by Waltzing (II, 114).
    mercatores frumentarii 161, 303, 4142, 4234
    olearii 409
    negotiantes fori vinarii 403
    corpus splendidissimum inportantium et negotiantium vinariorum Bloch 2
    piscatores propolae 409. Waltzing suggests reading *piscatores (et?) propolae,* referring to CIL II 5929 *piscatores et propolae* (II, 110, footnote 6). However, the combinations *piscatores et urinatores* and *piscatores urinatores* are found (Waltzing II, 77). The Ostia inscription may refer to fishermen who peddled their own catch.

3. Transport
   cisiarii 409
   codicarii 4144, 170, 309, 4234, S4549, 43
   quinque corpora lenunculariorum Ostiensium 352, 4144
   ordo corporatorum lenunculariorum tabulariorum auxiliariorum Ostiensium 250 (album), 251
   ordo corporatorum lenunculariorum pleromariorum auxiliariorum Ostiensium 252 (album), with note p. 614
   corpus scaphariorum et lenunculariorum traiectus Luculli 409
   corpus traiectus togatensium 403, S4613, 4616
   corpus traiectus Marmorariorum 425
   corp(us) tr(aiectus) Lucul(li) unpublished inscription, Ostia inv. no. 7906.[3] The *corpus* may be the same as the *corp. scaph. et lenunc. tr. Luculli* above.
   corpus scaphariorum traiectus Rusticeli S5327-28; S4553-56 omit *scaphariorum.*[4]
   curatores navium marinarum 363, 364 (which adds *et navium amnalium*), 409, 4142
   lyntr(arii) S4459

4. Trades
   calcarii S4550
   fabri navales 168, 169, 256 (album)
   fabri tignuari S4569 (album)
   fullones 409, S4573 (album)
   pelliones 10, S4549,2 (=277)
   pictores, collegae pingentes S4699
   pistores 101, 374, Ostia alone? 4234
   restiones S4549,1
   stuppatores Bloch 9, S4549,1
   urinatores 303

5. Civil service
   scribae cerarii, scribae librarii 346, 347, 353, 376, 409
   lictores et viatores 409
   praecones 409
   familia publica libertorum et servorum 32, 255 (album), 409
   . . . *lictorum et servorum publicorum qui in corpore sunt AE,* 1948, 26

lictores et viatores et honore usi et liberti Coloniae et servi publici corpor. AE, 1948, 27

togati a foro et de sacomario 409. *Togati* must refer to civil servants (cf. *Cod. Theod.* 6,2,26(=21) and 7,8,10, resp. A.D. 428 and 410); *sacomarium* ("standard weight chamber") suggests a comparison with 376, 23-24: *idem pondera ad macellum et mensuras ad forum vinarium s. p. fecit.*

6. Cults

hastiferi AE, 1948, 28-29

cannophori 34-37, 40, 118, 119, 284 (album), 285, S4301

dendrophori 33, 45, 53, 280, 281 (album), S4301

augustales S4563, *fasti:* S4561, 4562

cultores Iovis Tutoris 25

cultores Larum et imaginum dominorum nostrorum Augustorum praediorum Rusticelianorum S4570

sacerdotes Volcani 341, 373, 375, 376

sacerdotes Solis Invicti Mithrae 403

sodales Arulenses 341, 373

sodales Herculani Bloch 49, Bloch 54

sodales corp. V region. Col. Ost. 352(?)

ordo corporatorum qui pecuniam ad ampliandum templum contulerunt 246, S5374, S5356

Nearly half of these guilds have to do with navigation and the grain trade. It is characteristic that so many guilds of the smaller craftsmen (like cobblers, butchers, and barbers) are missing in the list and that the old important guild of the *centonarii* is missing in Ostia—*centonarii, fabri,* and *dendrophori* constituting *tria collegia principalia* (Waltzing II, 198). There are no *horrearii* or *apothecarii* in a city full of *horrea.* Also surprising is the absence of *saccarii* in our tradition, although the existence of their powerful guild is quite obvious (cf. *Cod. Theod.* XIV 22); one *saccarius* is depicted in a mosaic in the Piazzale delle Corporazioni (Meiggs, plate XXVa). These lacunae are probably due to the accidents of the tradition.

It should be added that the unpublished inscriptions of Ostia only bring evidence of one guild whose presence was not known before: the guild of the *nummularii,* if the *nummularius* listed above in group 2 may be taken as evidence of a guild in Ostia. The new inscriptions, however, give additional information about the guilds that were already known.[5]

All these guilds had to meet regularly, and they would need a meeting place. It was not uncommon for guilds to have their meeting and also their banquet and distribution of *sportulae* in a public temple (Waltzing I, 210-11), the temple of the god who was the protector of their association. After all, guilds were religious associations, and some guild brothers, mostly of *collegia funeraticia*, called themselves *cultores* (Waltzing I, 260 ff.). In inscriptions from all over one finds evidence of guild meetings in temples, and Ostia is no different in this respect; an inscription describes *corporatus in templo fori vinari inportatorum negotiantium* ("Guild brother of the importers and merchants in the temple in the wine forum," *AE*, 1940, 54). However, unless new evidence is dug up in Ostia we shall never know which, or how many, guilds would have met regularly in the temples of Ostia. On the other hand, there were wealthy guilds who could build their own sanctuaries, and we are sufficiently well informed to identify a fair number of guild seats in Ostia. But we are far from being able to identify a number of guild seats that is equal to the number of known guilds. A study of identified guild seats may teach us what to look for when searching for unidentified ones.

The official functions of the guilds that will be of interest to this study were worship, banquets, and assemblies (*conventus*). The guilds held many religious ceremonies during the year, and in connection with those or with anniversaries for defunct brothers who had given legacies they held their banquets or distributions of *sportulae*, or both.[6] We have elaborate records of the rich and numerous ornaments and furniture which were brought into the banquet hall after the hall had been cleaned, and there are prescriptions for the celebrations of banquets, down to the regulations for the supply of the brothers' bath oil.[7]

To find a guild, then, one must look for the sanctuary and for the facilities for meeting and banquets; a good water supply in the immediate neighbourhood is also necessary, both for ritual purposes and for consumption.

Seats of Identified Guilds

Guild of the stuppatores. A guild seat with its own sanctuary and all the necessary facilities is the guild of the *stuppatores* (I x 4), on the corner of Via del Pomerio and Via del Tempio Rotondo (fig. 47). It is a building from the time of Alexander Severus (*ScO* I 237). One enters a courtyard from the west, opposite the entrance is the temple, and on the other three sides the courtyard is surrounded by a portico. The northern portico is one undivided room as long as the courtyard (14,30 by 3,98 metres, 16 centimetres wider than the southern portico). The west end of it is an antechamber with a well in it, and at the east end there is an entrance to the sanctuary. The sanctuary was planned as a traditional prostyle temple on a high podium with a frontal approach, and the outer walls for the podium had been erected with space left open for the heavy groin vault that should have supported the temple walls and the columns. However, the construction was halted abruptly and the temple was never completed. What happened was most likely that the guild lost all its funds because Alexander Severus's successor Maximinus confiscated them (see Herodian VII 3, 5-6).[8] After a long interval in the second half of the century (*ScO* I 153), one Fructosus converted the void basement into a Mithraeum. An inscription in two fragments was found in the street right outside the temple: "[. . .]rius Fructosus patron. corp. s[. . ./. . .te]mpl. et spel. Mt. a solo sua pec. feci" ("[. . .]rius Fructosus, patron of the guild of the s[. . .] have built the temple and cave for Mithras from the ground up with my own money").[9] It was a Mithraeum, as the many finds inside the sanctuary indicate, and that it was the seat of the caulkers is made very likely by two other inscriptions: an *album* of the st[*uppatores*] lists a *Fructosus se*[*nior*], and a different inscription lists a *Fructosus* in large letters, consequently a *patronus*.[10] It is

hard to reject the suggestion that it all is the same Fructosus
and that the inscription from the sanctuary of this guild should
read: *corp. s*[*tuppatorum*].

Here we see a sanctuary, a *cenatorium*, in the northern
wing of the peristyle, and a well which could supply the water
needed in the sanctuary and for the *calda* of the banquets. At
the east end there is a latrine in the *subscalare*. Near the northeast corner there is a side entrance from a large room which
may have served as kitchen or banquet hall; the room is cut into
the block of *tabernae* straight north of the temple. This could
indicate that the block belonged to the *stuppatores*. A solid wall
between the *taberna* block and the kitchen keeps the religious-
collegial activities separated from the professional business
activities. This and related problems will be discussed elsewhere (p. 119). The shops seem to contain the facilities so necessary for the production of *stuppa* from flax.

The seat of the Augustales (V vii 2) has been identified beyond all
doubt by four inscriptions, one of which is the dedication of a
statue of the *sevir augustalis A. Livius Chryseros,* and by statues
of members of the imperial family from the second century.[11] It
was built at the same time of Marcus Aurelius, and an apse was
added to the sanctuary in the second half of the third century
(*ScO* I 237, 238). One enters from the Decumanus into an ante-
chamber, from which one can walk to the right or straight
ahead. To the right one enters the north wing of the *porticus*
which surrounds the courtyard; straight ahead one enters the
east wing, which is twice as wide as the west wing (6 metres as
against 3,25 metres) and must have been the *cenatorium* of the
guild. In the middle of the courtyard is a water basin; there was
also a well in the southwest corner of the courtyard. The sanctuary is in the south wing, a *tablinum*-type room, extended by
an apse (fig. 43).

The Caseggiato dei Triclini, The House of the Triclinia (I xii 1) is
solidly identified as the meeting place of the *fabri tignuari* by the
inscription S4569 on the empty base for a statue of Septimius
Severus, dedicated by the *fabri tignuari* and found *in situ*
(fig. 12). The inscription also gives the *album* of the guild. The

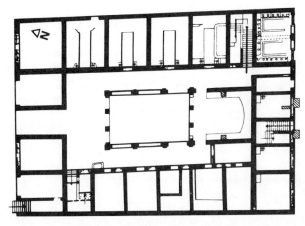

12.
Seat of the house
builders' guild.
Scale 1:550.

entrance from the Decumanus leads into a courtyard. Opposite
the entrance is a *tablinum*-type sanctuary. In the eastern wing
are four *triclinia* off the *porticus*. A room in the southwest corner
has been designated as kitchen. Water is piped into a basin in
the northwest corner of the *porticus*.

Tempio dei Fabri Navali, The Shipwrights' Temple (III ii 1 and 2).
The entrance from the Western Decumanus leads into a courtyard; facing the entrance is a traditional temple on a high
podium with marble steps leading up to it (fig. 13). The courtyard is surrounded by a *porticus* on all sides except the side of
the temple. On the side of the entrance the *porticus* is twice as
wide as on the other two sides, and the ceiling is supported by
two extra pillars in the middle of the room to form an entrance
hall. Behind the temple is another courtyard, a little over half
the size of the front court. It has a *porticus* on the two long
sides; in the rear wall is what may have been a drinking fountain. The rear *porticus* was undoubtedly the theatre for the celebrations of the guild's banquets and *conventus*. That the guild is
that of the *fabri navales* is suggested by the statue base found *in
situ* in front of the temple. Its inscription says that the "plebes
corporis fabrum navalium Ostiensium" ("members of the
shipwrights' guild in Ostia") erected the statue for their patron
(Bloch 31). An *album* without the name of the guild was found
in front of the temple (Bloch 43). Finally, a mosaic of a ship in
the entry hall confirms the inscriptions (Becatti in *ScO* IV 94).

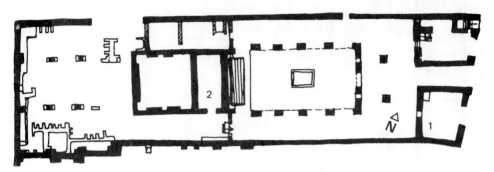

Tempio Collegiale, guild temple (V xi 1). The entrance from the eastern Decumanus leads directly into a porticoed courtyard, with an altar in its middle and with a high podium with steps in front, which is across from the entrance. There is a hall on either side of the temple, which is the full length of the temple. In the west wall of the courtyard is a traditional drinking fountain (fig. 33).

Fausto Zevi has argued that the inscription which is now placed on the Decumanus in front of the entrance to the guild seat, and which contains the phrase "Divo Pio [P]ertinaci Au[gusto] collegium fabrum [tignu]ariorum O[stiensium]" ("To the deified, pious Pertinax Augustus, the guild of the carpenters of Ostia"), indicates that the builders' guild had erected the temple.[12] Half of the inscription was found outside the temple, the other half had been used in construction in the space between the Decumanus and the Via della Foce. It could be asked, Which one of the two places is closer to the provenance of the fragments? The proximity of one-half of the inscription and the anonymous temple has some weight, and Zevi's explanation is the only one offered so far. This identification is not in conflict with the fact that the *fabri tignuari* had a guild centre further west on the Decumanus. The Caseggiato dei Triclini is their forum for guild affairs while the temple for *divus* Pertinax is an expression of their loyalty. It would be a small effort for builders to build a temple, especially since it can be shown that the temple was built on the guild's own land.

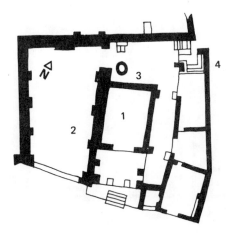

14.
Seat of the grain mea-
surers' guild. 1. Temple
of Ceres Augusta.
2. *Schola* of the guild.
3. Yard with well.
4. Latrine.
Scale 1 :500.

La così detta basilica, The so-called Basilica (I ii 3). No other guild site is like it. The building could be entered from the Decumanus as well as from the Square of the Lares. Its main hall had dimensions of about sixteen by eight metres, including a vestibule in front on the Decumanus. An apse in it seems made for a sanctuary. A water basin was built in the middle of the hall in the fourth century. Along the east side is a long hall (3,75 by 7,10 metres, excluding the vestibule, which in front of the hall is 3,75 by 3,30 metres), reminiscent of the *cenatorium* of the *stuppatores* (3,98 by 14,30 metres). There are doors to the north, to a smaller room and a latrine, and to the west. The whole building—the basilica and the House of the Thermopolium—seems to be an integrated unit, and it will elsewhere be argued that it was all under one ownership (see pp. 117-19, fig. 46). An unpublished inscription (inv. no. 7906) found at the site connects the building with the *lenunculari traiectus Luculli* (*ScO* I 132; for the full text, see p. 115). It seems to have been the guild seat of the guild of the ferrymen at one of the four known ferry crossings; it can hardly have been a big guild.

The Guild of the Mensores Frumentarii (I xix 1-3). A temple on Via della Foce, with entrance from Via della Foce, is surrounded by an *aula* to the left, also with access from Via della Foce, and by a narrow building to the right. At the north end of the building is a latrine, behind which is a courtyard with, among other

15.
The Serapeum.
Scale 1:650.

things, a well (fig. 14). These constitute the basic necessities of a guild. The mosaic floor of the *aula* shows a grain measurer at work, with helpers and controllers, dated to the middle of the third century.[13] An empty statue base, still *in situ,* has an inscription in front, stating that the statue was erected by the grain measurers to honour their patron.[14] That is proof that the whole complex was the seat of the grain measurers' guild.

A clue to the identification of the divinity which is worshipped in the temple might be found in the inscription 409, where Cn. Sentius is called "patronus . . . mensorum frumentariorum Cereris Augustae." Ceres Augusta is the goddess of the grain measurers and the mistress of their temple.

The Serapeum (III xvii 4) is part of an interesting building complex. From the Via del Serapide one enters a courtyard with a colonnade on either side; the wall opposite the entrance is covered by a temple with halls on either side, the halls being extensions of the colonnades (fig. 15). That the temple was dedicated to Serapis is proven by the inscription "Iovi Serapi(di)" on a marble slab, which was part of the pediment (Herbert Bloch in *AJA,* 1959, 226), and by the mosaic picture of the Apis bull in the entrance and the many Egyptian motifs of the mosaic floor of the courtyard.[15] An empty statue base carries the inscription that the statue was dedicated by "Publius Calpurnius/princeps equo publ./omnibus honoribus functus/educator." An *educator* is so far an unknown title; he was presumably a high official in the Serapis cult and comparable to Apuleius's *grammateus* (*Met.* XI 17). The Serapeum was built after A.D. 123 and dedicated 24 January 127 (Degrassi, *Inscr. Italiae* XIII i, 205 and 234).

From the northern colonnade one could walk into the courtyard of Caseggiato di Bacco e Arianna. This courtyard has a basin in the middle. On the north side of the courtyard is a colonnade, from which there are entrances to four rooms. Only two rooms have been excavated. One is a larger hall with a fine mosaic featuring Bacchus and Ariadne, which was probably a meeting hall. Next to it to the east is a somewhat smaller room, and here also is a good mosaic, which is interesting in that the pattern of the floor mosaic shows where a *biclinium* was placed. At the entrance to the Caseggiato di Bacco e Arianna is built a large, conventional drinking fountain of the type that is seen in baths, guilds, and bars where many people meet. This was built after the opening between the two courtyards had been closed.

It is beyond the scope of this survey to describe the "Public Building" and the Mithraeum which join the Serapeum on the opposite side from the Caseggiato di Bacco e Arianna.[16] Anyway, it is clear that the complex north of the Serapeum is a guild site connected with the Serapeum. There is nothing to indicate that it is a professional guild. Indeed, it would be natural to consider it a religious guild in charge of the Serapis cult. A guild of *cultores Serapis*, who built and dedicated a *schola* for Isis and Magna Mater, existed at Portus, if Lanciani's emendation is correct (*CIL* XIV, 123). The closing of the door between the Serapeum and the guild site does not necessarily mean that relations were severed and that it passed into other hands[17] (cf. above the *stuppatores'* guild and V xi 1 and V iii 1 in the following).

The Sanctuaries of Magna Mater Idaea, Attis, and Bellona (IV i 1-10) are on the west side of the Cardo Maximus, right inside the Porta Laurentina and in the so-called Campo della Magna Mater. The Campo della Magna Mater is a triangular square with the Sullan Wall and the Cardo Maximus as the two sides (fig. 16). It was originally excavated by Visconti, but the exca-

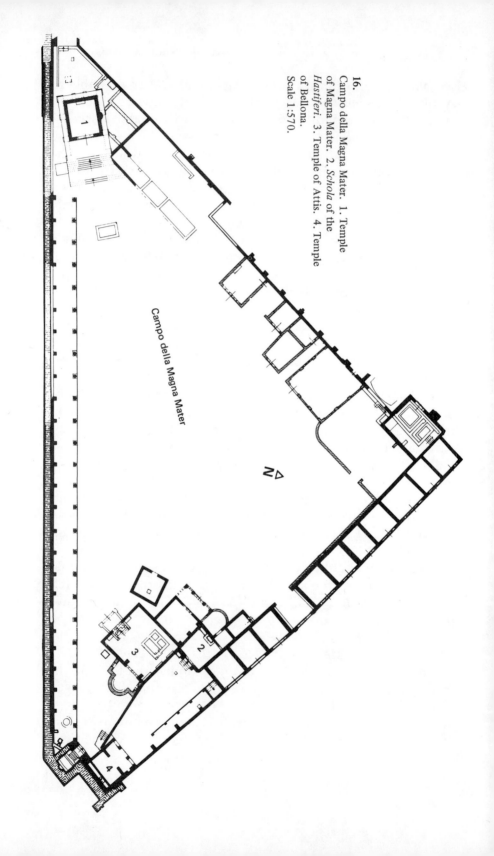

16.
Campo della Magna Mater. 1. Temple of Magna Mater. 2. *Schola* of the *Hastiferi*. 3. Temple of Attis. 4. Temple of Bellona.
Scale 1:570.

Campo della Magna Mater

vation stopped abruptly with the Risorgimento, so that 1869 was the last year of excavation. In 1940-41 Guido and Raissa Calza continued the work, but at that time much that could be observed by Visconti had completely disappeared.[18]

At the western corner of the triangle is the temple of Cybele, the Great Mother. The podium and the wall up to the height of 0,70 metre have been preserved. A great number of inscriptions have been found and have identified the sanctuary beyond all doubt—close by was found the inscription (45), "Numini Domus Aug. D[endrophori Ostien] ses Sco-lam/Quam Sua Pecunia Constit[uerant novis sum]ptibus/A Solo [restituerunt]" ("For the spirit of the house of the Augustus, the *dendrophors* of Ostia have rebuilt, from the ground up and with new expenditures, the *schola* which they originally had built with their own money"). Visconti read and amended the inscription. Here is evidence that there was a guild's *schola* inside the Campo. *CIL* XIV 281 gives a fragment of the *album*, which demonstrates that the *dendrophori* were numerous, and this, of course, is to be expected in one of the three most important guilds ("principalia," Waltzing II, 198). In Ostia, moreover, the guild of the *dendrophori* "included men of great distinction" (Meiggs 361). However, the location of the premises of this guild cannot be pin-pointed now. One should look for it among the ruins adjacent to the temple.

At the eastern corner of the triangle are other temples, including one for Attis, but there is no identifiable *schola* of the *cannophori*, whose presence is documented by many inscriptions.[19] If they had had a separate *schola*, it must have been the so-called *sacello* west of the *schola* of the *hastiferi*.

In the farthest eastern corner of the triangle, fenced in by a wall and facing each other, are the temple of Bellona, who was closely associated with Cybele, and the *schola* of the *hastiferi*.[20] This guild had a separate temple and *schola*, and the *schola* may have been the only place where they held their *conventus* and banquets.[21] The temple is small (fig. 17), built in red and yellow brick, and measures internally some 7,00 by 5,75 metres in all, *cella* and pronaos (fig. 18). It has two brick columns *in antis* in front, and the whole bottom wall of the *cella* is covered by a low podium, 0,79 metre wide and 0,70 metre high, from

17.
Bellona's temple. One slab of the marble doorstep remains. The marble doorstep on the *cella* has bolt holes and scratch marks of the bolts. The well-head outside the temple is near the northwest corner.
Scale 1:140.

18.
Bellona's temple.

19.
A close-up view of Bellona's temple showing the low podium.

20.
The *schola* of the *hastiferi*.
Scale 1:120.

21.
The *schola* of the *hastiferi*, with inscription in front.

22.
The *schola* of the *hastiferi*, entrance.

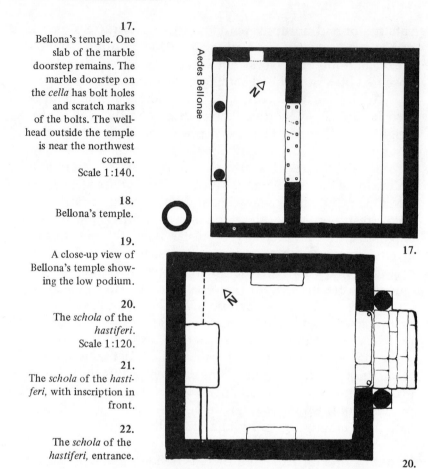

Aedes Bellonae

17.

20.

side to side (fig. 19). In the corner between the temple and the west wall is a well with a 1,03-metre-wide well-head. The *schola* is even smaller than the temple (fig. 20), some 5,32 to 5,67 by 5,46 to 5,66 metres; the walls are not parallel (fig. 21). One climbs five marble steps and enters between two columns. Against the wall is an altar (fig. 22). The temple, courtyard, and *schola* of the *hastiferi* are surrounded by walls on all sides. The place is concentrated and isolated.

It seems that a great number of public servants joined these guilds, especially the guild of the *hastiferi*. An inscription informs us that lictors and public slaves, who were members of the guild, paid for the building of Bellona's temple on land given by the *decuriones*.[22] In A.D. 211 three patrons restored a shrine.[23]

18.   19.

21.   22.

Schola del Traiano, Guild of the Shipowners (IV v 15). This is the
largest and most impressive of all possible guild seats (fig. 23).
One enters from the Decumanus through a lavish vestibule,
originally flanked by four *portasanta* marble columns, of which
only one is left, and walks into a monumental courtyard which
contains a big water basin running through nearly the whole
length of the courtyard. At the far end of the courtyard, in a
part of the structure which dates from A.D. 250-300 (*ScO* I 238),
there is a *tablinum*-type sanctuary with an apse. In the apse was
found a statue of Fortuna. The pattern of the mosaic floor of
that *tablinum* shows that a *triclinium* was set up here for the
banquets of the guild. On the west side of the late addition in
which the sanctuary was installed there is a latrine with running water and accommodation for four persons. The structure

23.
Schola del Traiano -- seat of the shipowners'
guild. 1. Domus with peristyle.
Scale 1:700.

is too monumental for a private residence; obviously it was used for ceremonial purposes. It meets all the specifications of a guild site, and its type is closely related to guild sites like those of the Augustales and the Caseggiato dei Triclini.

The proximity of the guild house of the *fabri navales* across Decumanus and two inscriptions (Bloch 32 and 33) found inside the *schola* have been claimed as evidence that the building was of the *fabri navales*. [24] One inscription says that the *naviculariei* made a dedication of a statue to Pacceius: "[Pacceio L. f.]/q(uaestori) pr(o pr(aetore)]/naviculariei O[stienses]/quod is primus sim[ulacrum. . . .]/statuarium pro . . ." ("[To Pacceius, son of Lucius] quaestor with praetorian authority the ship-owners of Ostia, because he as the first a [sculptured picture?]," Bloch 32). The inscription is supplemented by the inscription *CIL* XIV 3603. Bloch points out that the inscription cannot be later than the Augustan age. Brickstamps, however, dates the oldest parts of the Schola del Traiano to A.D. 145-155 (Bloch in *ScO* I 226), considerably later than the inscription. A second inscription (Bloch 33) is the dedication to the L. Volusius Maecianus, who taught law to Marcus Aurelius. Among his many high posts in the civil service and the military command is that of *praefectus fabrum*. This is a strictly military command, which of course does not connect him with *fabri navales*. No *praefectus fabrum navalium* has never been recorded. [25] There are two kinds of *praefectus fabrum*, as is demonstrated by the inscription *CIL* XIV 298: "M. Antonio/M.F. Men./Severo/*prae-fecto fabr.*/IIvir quaest. aer./quaestori alim./flam. divi Vesp./*praef. fabr. tign.*/Ostiensium," where the plain title *prae-fecto fabr.* reveals that it is a purely military post, while the *praef. fabr. tign.* commanded the fire-fighting units of the guild. The *tribunus fabrum navalium Portensium*, which was found in the inscription in the guild site of the *fabri navales* (Bloch 31; cf. also *CIL* XIV 169) and which was one of the proofs that the shipwrights owned the site, was instituted by a special arrangement for Ostia, as pointed out by Waltzing.[26] There is also a significant difference between a *praefectus* and a *tri-bunus*.

The only indication of ownership by *fabri navales* would be that the two properties were close neighbours, across the street from each other. This is decisive in Becatti's reasoning (*ScO* I 149). The proximity of the two places seems, however, to work against the idea of single ownership. Both places are set up for specific guild activities. Why would the *fabri navales* need two places for the same purpose? And having a place of the grand-iose dimensions of the Schola del Traiano, why would they at a later date, at the time of Commodus, move to a smaller place? We are faced with the embarrassing problem of the duplicate facilities no matter how one visualizes the take-over of the one by the other.

It would be more natural to look for a different corporation as owner of the Schola del Traiano and for a wealthier group than the *fabri navales*. One wealthy profession was that of the *navicularii*, and it would be more realistic to focus on the inscription of the *naviculariei* (Bloch 32). The two inscriptions Bloch 32 and 33 most likely belonged in the Schola del Traiano and were not brought in later; the Schola del Traiano was no marble dump. On the other hand, the Augustan inscription must have been brought into the Schola from somewhere else, after the erection of the Schola at the time of Antoninus Pius. The only ones who would have been interested in moving that old inscription would have been the ones who owned it, the *naviculariei*. When a guild erected a statue to a benefactor they placed it in their guild house. The *fabri navales* could only have been interested in that inscription if it had been addressed to themselves, which obviously is not the case. It is addressed to *(Pacceio L. f.) q(uaestori) pr(o pr.)* by the *naviculariei.* Therefore it seems safe to conclude that the *navicularii* wanted to move the inscription to the Schola because the inscription was their private property and the Schola their private premises. The Schola was the guild seat of the *navicularii.*

The seat of the guild of the *navicularii* of Ostia is not known from other sources. It is erroneous to look for their *sedes* in the Piazzale delle Corporazioni, because this is a square for the foreign and out-of-town *navicularii et negotiantes,* to whom were added the local groups who served them *(restiones, stuppatores, codicarii, pelliones),* and the square must have been for business, not for guild activities.

These twelve guild sites have a number of features in common. Some of them have a monumentality that goes beyond that of private buildings. This is particularly obvious in sites like those of the *stuppatores* and the *fabri navales,* in the Serapeum, and in the site of the *fabri tignuari*(?) in V xi 1. These are dignified structures with courtyards surrounded by colonnades, where the effect of the sanctuary is enhanced by the frontal axiality of the plan.

A second group is constituted by the site of the *Augustales,* the guild of the shipowners, and the Caseggiato dei Triclini, which have the same approach. The difference is in the sanctuary not being a temple but a *tablinum*-type stateroom, those of the *Augustales* and the shipowners being upgraded by an apse.

A third group is formed by the Schola and temple of the *mensores* and by the temples in the Campo della Magna Mater. They have full temples, but the surroundings, although they may offer all the facilities that are wanted, have not been arranged with an artistic and architectural intent.

The so-called Basilica is the most condensed version of a guild site, where, practically speaking, everything is gathered inside the same four walls and the only concession to guild religiosity is a niche in the main hall.

It will also be noted that they all have ample meeting and

banquet facilities. Either there was a wing of the colonnade (*Stuppatores*, V xi 1, *Augustales*) or a special arrangement like a *schola* with an open yard (guild of the *mensores*, Serapeum, the so-called Basilica, and the *hastiferi*). Caseggiato dei Triclini in the present state has *triclinia*, which are a late addition; previously their banquets took place in the colonnade, like other guilds with similar facilities. *Fabri navales* may have met in or behind the temple.

Seats of Unnamed Guilds

The inscriptions give evidence of a considerably higher number of guilds than the twelve guilds that were studied above. It is inconceivable that the guilds outside this group of twelve should not have operated from some domicile or have been connected with some sanctuary in Ostia. Only a few of them, however, can be linked to locations in Ostia.

To move ahead it might be useful again to look at the same twelve guilds: they seem to have a number of characteristic features in common. These features were necessary for the activities and ceremonies of the guilds, and if there are other locations in Ostia which display similar characteristics they may have been guild seats.

Over the years several places in Ostia have been designated as guild seats by various students of that city. These potential sites and a couple of new ones will be discussed in what follows.

Domus di Marte (III ii 5) is a building of moderate size, located on the corner of the western Decumanus and the Cardo degli Aurighi (fig. 24). It has three *tabernae* on the Cardo and three on the Decumanus. The southern *taberna* on the Cardo served as entrance to the interior, where two rooms surround a central courtyard on the northwest and northeast sides. An opening as wide as the wall gives access from the courtyard to a *tablinum* in the northwest. Along the northeast side of the courtyard is a

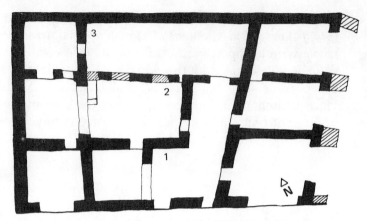

24.
Domus di Marte –The
House of Mars. 1. Entrance. 2. Central
hall with Mars altar
in the north corner.
3. *Schola* or banquet
hall.
Scale 1:300.

long hall running through the house and having the same
length as the entrance hall, the courtyard, and the *tablinum*. In
the northern corner of the courtyard is an altar with the inscription, "Marte/Aug/Sacrum" (Bloch 6). Brickstamps from A.D.
123-124 date the Domus to about A.D. 127 (Bloch in *ScO* I 137,
235). In about A.D. 300 *(opus vittatum)* the entrance to the middle
taberna on the Cardo was walled in and three niches were constructed in the new wall; a door opening then connected the
former *taberna* with the courtyard. The wide openings to the
eastern hall were closed, and the northwest end of the hall was
cut off and joined with the *tablinum* through a door opening.
There seems to have been a fountain in the north corner of this
hall. Bloch and Becatti (ll. ll.) both classify the Domus di Marte
as a guild site. This site, too, offers all the facilities that are
wanted by a guild: place of worship, hall for meetings and banquets, and a water supply. It is interesting that this hall has
been walled in similarly to the meeting hall of the *Augustales*.

There is nothing to indicate which guild should be considered as owner of the site. The dedication to Mars offers no clue,
since we have records of many guild dedications to Mars.

A guild house (V iii 1) which is classified as a *domus* (*ScO* I 236).
It is located at the north end of a block, bordered by Via della
Fortuna Annonaria, Via delle Ermette, Via della Casa del
Pozzo, and, on the south side, by an unnamed street (fig. 44).
The building is Hadrianic. One enters from the Via della For-

tuna Annonaria, the entrance is flanked by a *taberna* on either side, and the entrance hall is about the same size as each of the *tabernae*. To the left in the entrance hall was a conventional drinking fountain. The fountain is marked on Gismondi's plan (*ScO* I, sheet 8) and is seen in figure 45, but it was torn down in 1976. Behind the entrance is the main hall of the house, which goes through the whole depth of the house. Against the back wall, facing the entrance, is a *tablinum*-type sanctuary, whose walls consist of six piers with wide openings between them. On either side of the sanctuary is a side hall. In the middle of the main hall is an *impluvium* surrounded by four column foundations, giving an *atrium*-like floor plan. This is the *tetrastylum* of the guild.[27] The west wall of the main hall has nine windows and one door, which occupy the whole length of the wall; the east wall has, similarly, eight windows and two doors. At a later time some of the openings in the sanctuary wall were filled in, two tiny rooms were arranged at the east wall of the main hall, and a flight of stairs was built in the northeast corner.

The plan of this building makes it a public building: a large hall, with a sanctuary of the style seen in the sanctuaries of the *Augustales,* of the Caseggiato dei Triclini, and of the barracks of the *vigiles,* with walls that are nothing but windows, and with a large drinking fountain in the entrance hall, the like of which is seen only in public places. The building shows all the characteristics of a guild seat. There is nothing to indicate which guild may have been located here. In what follows this guild house will be discussed further (pp. 113-15).

Guild temple in the Terme del Filosofo (V ii 7). On Via dei Cippi a prostyle temple was erected, with seven steps leading up to it at the front (fig. 25). The entrance from Via dei Cippi led into a courtyard with a colonnade on either side; the temple was built up against the wall in the back. It was a guild house in the same style as those of the *stuppatores* (I x 4), the *fabri navales* (III ii 1 and 2), and the *fabri tignuari* (?) in their temple for Pertinax (V xi 1), all laid out with the same frontal axiality. This construction took place at the time of Alexander Severus (*ScO* I 237). Whether the temple was ever finished is unclear. In the fourth

25.
Guild temple in the
Baths of the Philosopher.
1. Foundation of temple.
2. Courtyard. 3. Hall
with benches along
south and west sides.
Scale 1:330.

26.
Aula del Gruppo di
Marte e Venere.
Scale 1:400.

27.
The Curia.
Scale 1:400.

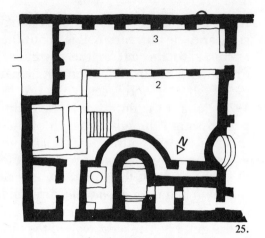

25.

century what building there was nearly disappeared and must have given way to a bath (*ScO* I 238). The southern colonnade was converted into a hall with benches along the south and west sides and with a niche built into the east wall. The intervals between the pillars of the colonnade were filled in (Becatti in *ScO* I 153, 155; II 28). Three Plotinus heads were found at and in the baths;[28] they point to a neo-Platonic congregation as the occupant of the hall in the last stage of the sanctuary-baths' existence, if indeed a sanctuary it was during that last stage.

No inscriptions or other kinds of evidence have yielded any information about the guild which originally built the temple. The building, however, has the plan and the harmony of a guild site.

The *Aula di Marte e Venere* (II ix 3) may have been a guild site, but there is nothing to indicate that it was (fig. 26). Early in the fourth century (*ScO* I 156, 238), a main hall with a large apse, equipped with three niches at the north end and a smaller one at the south end (total length, 14,30 metres; width, 8,50 metres), was implanted in a Hadrianic *insula* (II ix 2, *ScO* I 236) on the north side of the Decumanus. From this hall four steps led up to a smaller hall on the east side (6,25 by 6,25 metres), and the wide entrance is divided into three openings by two columns. The bigger apse in the large hall may have been a *nymphaeum:* there is a low wall across the baseline of the apse and a water-pipe along the northern wall on the inside. West of

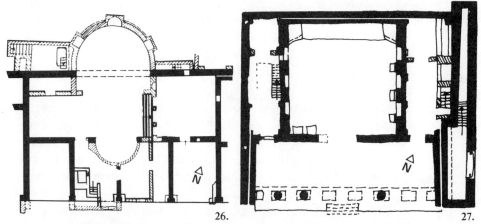

26.   27.

the main hall is a third, smaller one (4,35 by 4,67 metres). Those
are the main features.

The excavator G. Moretti (*NSc* V 17, 1920, 44 ff.) believed
it to be a Christian basilica, an idea rejected by P.A. Fevrier and
Russell Meiggs,[29] mainly on account of the non-Christian
inventory (Mars-Venus statue) and the lack of non-controver-
sial Christian monuments of any kind. Moretti has great difficulty explaining how the Mars-Venus group would have come
into a Christian church and how it could have been found
under the circumstances that were observed at the excavation
(o. l. 59-60). He leaves the question unanswered.

Becatti says that it probably is the *schola* of a guild (*ScO* I
156). What must have guided Becatti was the twin statue of
Mars and Venus, with portrait heads of Faustina and Marcus
Aurelius.[30] The style and plan of the building reminds us of the
plan of the original seat of the *lenuncularii*, which weighs in
Becatti's favour.

The *Curia* (I ix 4) was placed right in the centre of Ostia, with
the façade on the Decumanus and the forum on its left flank.
Having the basilica as next neighbour across the Decumanus, it
is where a *curia* would be expected to be placed (fig. 27). There
are numerous precedents for such a central location in other
ancient cities. It resembles a sanctuary in that it was built like a
hexastyle temple *in antis* and raised six steps above the street.
The six steps are built in the central intercolumnium. Behind

the vestibule is the main hall, with a narrow hall on either side. The main hall, which would be the meeting hall of the *decuriones,* has three niches in either side wall and a narrow platform built up against the rear wall.

The only reason that the Curia has been considered as the seat of the *Augustales* is that at a later date when Ostia had declined deeply, and the Curia was converted into different use, the side halls were partitioned off into rooms and other changes were made with the makeshift workmanship of the late period. In the one wall and in the vestibule were found fragments of the Fasti of the *Augustales* and of funeral inscriptions used as building material.

The original excavator G. Calza considered that the building might have been the seat of the *Augustales.* [31] He later rejected the idea and accepted the identification with the Curia, and in this he was supported by M.F. Squarciapino, G. Becatti, and Herbert Bloch. [32] Russell Meiggs, however, believed the building to be the seat of the *Augustales,* an opinion which he has confirmed recently. [33] Meiggs believes that the find of the Fasti in the building proves the ownership of the *Augustales* and that this interpretation is confirmed by the circumstance that "the so-called curia of Ostia is singularly unfitted to the needs of a council. It is small for a body of at least 100 members."

The find of Fasti fragments used as building material does not prove that the *Augustales* were located here. [34] Who would claim that the fragments of funeral inscriptions proved that people were buried in the same place? Furthermore, other fragments of the Fasti were found elsewhere in Ostia: the fragment Bloch 40 was found in the Casa degli Aurighi, Bloch 41 was found west of the Hercules temple, and two fragments were found in the colonnade of the Forum Baths and on the Decumanus at the Jupiter temple. [35] Although most of the fragments are found in the Curia or its vicinity, we have to admit that we do not know where they come from.

The size of the Curia seems adequate for its purpose. It measures 11,70 by 11,70 metres, for a total of 136,90 square metres. The highest number of *decuriones* that we hear of is 110

(Meiggs 181), which gives each *decurio* 1,25 square metres. Diocletian's Curia on the Forum Romanum measures 25,20 by 17,60 metres or 443,50 square metres. Allowing the same area of 1,25 square metres per senator, the Roman Curia would accommodate 356 senators. This Curia was rebuilt after the fire during the reign of Carinus and it duplicated the plan and dimensions of the old Curia Domitiani.[36] This old Curia served at the times when the number of senators was in excess of six hundred. With a *senatus frequens* the Roman senators would have had much less space than the *decuriones* of Ostia. Wooden benches accommodated the *decuriones* of Ostia, and civic records could be kept in the side halls and upstairs. These premises are as adequate as, for instance, the ones in Pompeii (close to 137 square metres, including the apse) and Timgad (158 square metres).[37]

The Mithraeum at the Porta Romana (II ii 5). Raissa Calza, in her charming book *Ostia*,[38] suggests that the *cisiarii*, who were organized in a guild (see above p. 58), must have had their seat somewhere in the neighbourhood of the Piazzale della Vittoria, where the *cisiarii* had their stand and where the big water trough for their mules and horses can still be seen. The Baths of the Cisiarii make their presence felt in that part of the city. Of course, if one looks for a sanctuary around the Piazzale della Vittoria, there is at the present time not much choice, since the area south of the Piazzale is unexcavated. The only sanctuary is the Mithraeum II ii 5,[39] which on its west side is connected with a hall, whose floor has one of the most beautiful polychrome mosaics of Ostia, from the middle of the second century A.D.[40] This hall again has a connection with the eastern-most *taberna* of II ii 6 (fig. 28). South of the Mithraeum, but without communication with it, is a small room with another beautiful mosaic from the middle of the second century[41] and with a niche in the rear wall, maybe serving the activities of the *cisiarii*. There is nothing about the whole plan which makes this Mithraeum different from other Mithraea in Ostia, and there is definitely nothing which would designate it as a guild site, except the proximity of the *cisiarii*.

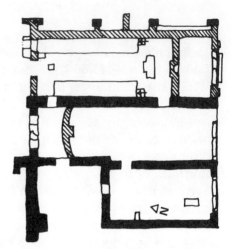

28.
Mithraeum at Porta
Romana.
Scale 1:300.

Caseggiato degli Aurighi and the adjoining sanctuary (III x 1 and III ii 12). Raissa Calza deals with the Cas. degli Aurighi (144-47), the use of which she does not understand, because as a whole it does not look convincing as a tenement house. In the northern cross-corridor she finds an indication of its purpose: the two vivid pictures of chariots and drivers wearing the colours of two of the circus factions suggest to her that this might be the seat of a large, wealthy sports corporation, like the youth organization. The sanctuary on the east side of the Cas. degli Aurighi looks like a Mithraeum,[42] but Calza explains that the objects and the sacrifice of a pig depicted in the mosaic floor are directly in conflict with the religion of Mithras and belong in the Hercules cult, the god who protects palaestras and sports organizations. Next to the sanctuary there is a kitchen, one of the three equipped kitchens found in Ostia, and in the courtyard there is water—all the necessities of a guild are on hand in the Casa degli Aurighi. There is no convincing evidence that this youth group had a meeting place here. However, *CIL* XIV 409 mentions that Cn. Sentius was *quaestor iuuenum* and *patronus iuuenum*, and the organization is also mentioned in S4448 and S4552, so it is known to have been around.

The Schola Iuuentutis in Pompeii is possibly the place where one gets the closest look at the *iuuenes,* and here a more military spirit seems to reign, compared with the one which meets us in the Cas. degli Aurighi. On the outside, on Via dell'-Abbondanza, trophies of arms are painted on the wall; inside, winged Victories carry weaponry, stylized candelabra have

Roman legionary insignia at the top and palm branches with which the victors would be crowned, and on one wall there are cabinets for weapons.

The identification of the Schola Iuuentutis is Matteo della Corte's; questionable is Amadeo Maiuri's Schola Armaturarum,[43] which could only be for the benefit of the same group. The Pompeian *schola* places the activities of the *iuuenes* on a very different level and makes it much easier to understand the fury with which the Severi turned upon them; they would be dangerous when they joined in the riots that supported the opposition (*Dig.* 48, 19, 28, 3). There are also grave doubts raised by the sanctuary with the three naves. It is listed with the Mithraea, because its plan is that of a Mithraeum, but Becatti lists many basic paraphernalia of the cult of Mithras which are missing in this sanctuary,[44] and M.F. Squarciapino mentions Jupiter Heliopolitanus or Jupiter Dolichenus as divinities who may have occupied the sanctuary.[45] The existence of the kitchen, which has been built together with the sanctuary, might point toward the cult of Jupiter Dolichenus or the cult of some Syrian god, since banquets were very important in those cults.[46]

What militates against a cult of Hercules in the Casa degli Aurighi is that a *spelaeum* is an extraordinary place to worship Hercules. It would be more apropos to look for an oriental god, since the environment with a Serapis sanctuary in the sister *insula* (Cas. d. Serapide), the Serapeum (III xvii 4), and the Mithraeum *planta pedis* (III xvii 2) only one block away show a strong oriental influence. The pictures of two racing chariots serve their own purpose: chariots with spirited horses are picturesque and decorative when bare walls need decoration.

A guild in the Forum Baths (I xii 8). On the south side of the palaestra of the Forum Baths is an elegant suite of rooms believed to be a guild (fig. 29).[47] Four *taberna*-like rooms face the palaestra, and through each *taberna* one can proceed to a hall which covers the whole combined width of the four *taberna* rooms. This hall is divided by two columns. Continuing west in the hall one passes a doorway that is as wide as the hall, and divided into three openings by two columns. Three steps bring one into another hall somewhat shorter and narrower than the

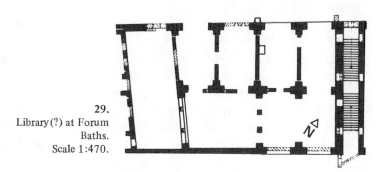

29.
Library(?) at Forum
Baths.
Scale 1:470.

first one. There are remnants of elegant floor mosaics. This building, however, is lacking many facilities that are characteristic of a guild. It resembles, rather, the locales for the different kinds of entertainment that were connected with the public baths, such as lecture halls and libraries. And there is nothing to indicate that there ever was a guild in this place.

The Temple in the Piazzale delle Corporazioni (II vii 5). The idea that the temple in the middle of the Corporation Square was a guild temple is voiced occasionally (fig. 30).[48] The idea originated at a time when there was no clear perception of the nature of the square. Actually, Piazzale delle Corporazioni is a misnomer. Only one of the many inscriptions uses the word *corpus:* the second stall has the inscription "corpus pellion Ost. et Porte hic" (S4549, 2). We have inscriptions in over a third of the stalls, and the general picture that is presented by them all is that of consular activity. The stalls are distributed by geography, not by professions. What would be different *corpora* locally are here sharing the same stall: *navicularii* and *negotiantes* from the same locality are sharing a stall in three cases; one stall is simply marked *stat. Sabratensium,* which covers everything. Of course the *navicularii* are the leading occupants because shipping was the backbone of the entire operation and the skippers wanted a cargo for the return trip, too. Of the local guilds we see only the ones who catered to the needs of the overseas skippers: *stuppatores, restiones,* who shared a stall, *pelliones,* and *codicarii.* The majority of the stalls were occupied by

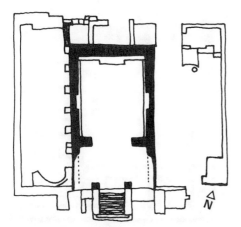

30.
Temple in the
Corporation Square.
Scale 1:500.

the representatives of overseas territories and places outside
the Italian peninsula. The square is a concentration of people
who have the same business and who have to deal with each
other and the local Romans. It is an exalted market-place with
an international flavour.

   It is hard to see a place for an individual guild's sanctuary
in these surroundings. One inscription speaks of a "corporatus
in templo fori vinari inportatorum negotiantium," which, however, may refer to a different place and to circumstances that
we cannot assess. [49] It is easy to agree with Russell Meiggs (288)
that the forum *vinarium* should be sought in Ostia not in
Portus. But we have no guarantee that what we call Piazzale
delle Corporazioni or Corporation Square is not what the
Ostians called Forum Vinarium. In the Piazzale delle Corporazioni one would rather look for a cult of a more general nature.
Raissa Calza suggests Annona or the *genii* of the corporations
or Ceres Augusta.[50] Ceres Augusta is already worshipped in
the guild temple of the *mensores frumentarii* in Via della Foce
(see pp. 55-56).

   The Domitianic temple was later flanked by buildings of
which only foundations are left and whose purpose is unclear.
There is nothing which would suggest the operation of a
guild.

   Of twenty-one real and potential guild seats that have
been surveyed here, fifteen can be identified as seats of known

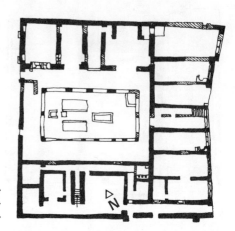

31.
Domus Fulminata.
Scale 1:630.

(twelve) or unknown (three) guilds. One difficulty: the *canno-phori* and the *dendrophori* were attached to the Magna Mater (Cybele) sanctuary. Many inscriptions concerning these two guilds are found inside the enclosure in the neighbourhood of the sanctuary, but it is not possible to point out the specific houses among the many badly preserved foundations (for the probable site of the *schola* of the *cannophori,* see above p. 69). Of the remaining potential guild seats two are highly questionable (Aula di Marte e Venere and the Mithraeum at the Porta Romana), and four, the Curia, the temple in the Corporation Square, the suite in the Forum Baths, and the Cas. degli Aurighi, seem less likely.

Any further search for guild seats becomes increasingly speculative. Raissa Calza wonders whether the Domus Fulmin-ata (which Meiggs calls House of the Thunderbolt) would not be the seat of some association rather than a private residence (fig. 31). Maybe it was not an official public corporation, sup-ported by the state, she writes, but some *collegium* with not too numerous a membership meeting in a choice and exclusive place. She thinks of the Bona Dea sanctuary across the street and mentions the possibility that an association that was con-nected with the cult had the Domus Fulminata as domicile.[51]

The Domus Fulminata was built at the middle of the first century A.D. (*ScO* I 234), and it has some distinctive and elegant features. The peristyle has a large fountain basin in the middle, a *biclinium,* an altar, a row of elegant rooms on the long north side of the peristyle, and on the other side an apartment with an entrance door from the peristyle. Above the apartment there

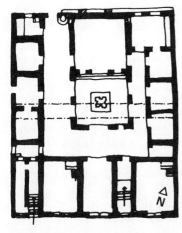

32.
Domus del Tempio
Rotondo.
Scale 1:450.

was an upstairs; in a corner downstairs there was a latrine with three units. It was a large building which served many people. It is puzzling that the south wing turns its back on the rest of the house and that only the north wing opens on the peristyle, but there is nothing which links it to a guild or an association, and there is no valid reason why it could not be a private residence.

An equally good candidate is Domus del Tempio Rotondo (fig. 32), originally built in the reign of Alexander Severus (*ScO* I 152, 237). It has several features in common with the seat of the *Augustales:* the western wing of the peristyle is twice as wide as the eastern one and is well designed for banquets; there is a well in the same wing inside the portico, which reminds one of the seat of the *stuppatores.* The *tablinum* is monumental and lifted out of the peristyle, and there is an elegant, centrally heated suite off the west wing of the peristyle, like the one in the seat of the *Augustales,* but there is no indication of a guild in this *domus*.

Finally, in his masterly publication of the building whose walls are decorated with *opus sectile* work, located outside the Porta Marina, Giovanni Becatti suggests that it must have been a guild seat (*ScO* VI 161 ff.). It may, and it may not. No inscription has been found to support this interpretation, nor are there any of the other features which must be considered characteristic of a guild seat. Moreover, the whole building complex differs from the usual type of guild centre. It seems, rather, to have been a building of a much more general character than a guild seat.

Notes

1. Described in great detail by Tengström, 19ff.
2. This inscription is published and discussed in the *Rendiconti dei Lincei*, as quoted, by dott. Antonio Licordari, who has called it to my attention.
3. I am thankful to Professor Guido Barbieri for having given me the text of this inscription, which is given in full on p. 115.
4. All these types of vessels and their different functions have been brilliantly explained by Lionel Casson in "Harbour and River Boats of Ancient Rome," *JRS* LV (1965), 31-39.
5. I am grateful to Professor Guido Barbieri and dott. Antonio Licordari for this information.
6. Waltzing I, 231ff., 304-06, 400-03, 420ff., 482ff.
7. See, for example, Calza, *NSc* V, 18 (1927), 237; *CIL* XIV, 2112, latter half. Waltzing I, 229-31.
8. Compare Herodian, ed. C.R. Whittaker (Loeb, 1971), II, 173, note 3.
9. Bloch, 7; Becatti, *ScO* II, 26.
10. Becatti publishes the guild seat in *ScO* II, 21ff.
11. The excavation is published by G. Calza in *NSc* VII, ii (1941), 196ff. and the statues by Raissa Calza, *ibid.*, 216ff.
12. In *Rendiconti morali dei Lincei* Series 8, vol. 26, fascicle 5-6 (1971), 472ff. See also pages 102, 120 of this study.
13. Becatti, *ScO* IV, 33; date on p. 36.
14. *Ibid.*, 35.
15. Becatti in *ScO* IV, 151-53.
16. Compare Squarciapino, *I culti orientali ad Ostia*, 19-20.
17. Meiggs, 368.
18. See Maria Floriani Squarciapino, *I culti orientali ad Ostia*, 1-18; G. Calza, "Il santuario della Magna Mater a Ostia" in *Memorie della Pontificia Accademia di Archeologia*, Series 3, vol. 6 (1946), 184ff.
19. *dendrophori, cannophori,* see Squarciapino, *I culti orientali*, 7-8.
20. Duncan Fishwick, "Hastiferi," *JRS* LVII (1965), 142ff.
21. Compare Waltzing's definition and description of *schola*, vol. I, 211-30.
22. Calza, "Il santuario," 198, la.
23. Calza, "Il santuario," inscription 5.
24. Raissa Calza, *Ostia* (Rome, 1965), 110; Becatti, *ScO* I, 149.
25. Waltzing II, 354-56; compare 388ff.
26. Waltzing II, 355-56.
27. Waltzing I, 229 with n. 4.
28. Calza-Squarciapino, *Museo Ostiense* (1962) 79 with note. Sala IX 4, 5, and 6.
29. Fevrier in *Mélanges* LXX (1959), 312; Meiggs, 396.

30. Felletti Maj, *Catal. d. musei e gallerie d'Italia; Mus. Naz. Romano, I ritratti,* 119, no. 236.

31. G. Calza in *NSc* V, 15 (1918), 223, and V, 20 (1923), 186.

32. Squarciapino, *AC* 12 (1960), 260; Becatti, *JRS* 51 (1961), 204; Bloch, *Gnomon* 37 (1965), 195-96.

33. 219-220; 2d ed., 594.

34. Calza's words are: "I frammenti di questi fasti furon trovati in gran parte in tardo muro a secco con altri, in genere più minuti e non pertinente ad esso, entro e immediatamente presso un edificio religioso prospiciente il decumano" (*NSc,* 1918, 223). One fragment showed the letters DM.

35. See inscriptions S4560-63, introduction.

36. Lawrence Richardson, Jr., "The Curia Julia and the Janus Geminus," *Röm. Mitt.* 85 (1978), 359-69 with references; Nash, *Pictorial Dictionary* I, 301 with references.

37. A. Ballu, *Les ruines de Timgad* (Paris, 1897), 143.

38. *Ostia,* 31.

39. See Becatti, *ScO* II, 45-46.

40. *ScO* IV, 44-45.

41. *Ibid.,* 45.

42. Listed as a Mithraeum in Calza's *Indice topografico,* 250.

43. M. della Corte, *Juventus* (Arpino, 1924), 60ff; one Adirans gives money to *vereiiai Pumpaiianai* (Buck, no. 4, I. 2); Amadeo Maiuri, *Pompeii, Itinerari* 3 (1967), 80-81.

44. Becatti, *ScO* II, 69-75.

45. In *I culti orientali di Ostia,* 63.

46. *Ibid.*

47. Meiggs, 415.

48. Meiggs, 329.

49. *AE* (1940), 54.

50. *Ostia,* 53-54.

51. *Ostia,* 136.

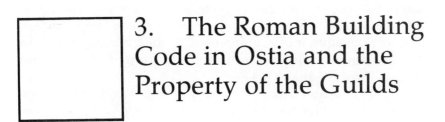

3. The Roman Building Code in Ostia and the Property of the Guilds

Basic Property Laws

From various sources we know some of the basic rules of the building code of Rome: Tacitus's annals and other literature, inscriptions, and the bits and pieces of the *Edictum Perpetuum* which have found their way into the *Corpus Juris Civilis*. [1]

At the beginning of the period which will be the subject of the following discussion stands the Great Fire in Rome, a turning point in the development of Roman urban life. It gave the Romans a fresh start and allowed Nero to plan and issue new regulations about construction in Rome. From Tacitus we are informed about some fundamental building rules which governed the relationship betwen the local government and the common citizen. The area, however, where most of the conflicts occurred was in the relationship between the individual citizens, when one property bordered on the next and conflicting interests clashed. This area is well illuminated by the comments of the *Digesta* that derive from many court cases. Much of the material in the *Digesta* is drawn from commentaries on the Edict, among which those of Ulpian are especially worth noting.

It is unfortunate that we are unable to study old Rome to determine how the law was applied or, rather, to what extent it was obeyed. As could be expected, Ostia is in accordance with that law and provides the only idea of the impact of the law in contemporary Rome.

1. A universal law, introduced by Nero after the Fire, dictated that neighbouring houses could not have a common wall between them: "aedificia . . . nec communione parietum, sed propriis quaeque muris ambirentur" ("the buildings must not have common walls, but each should be contained by its own walls," Tacitus, *Ann.* XV 43).

That law was usually obeyed in Ostia. Where two neighbouring properties were separated by a single wall, there was generally an open space on the one side, so that two buildings were not touching each other, or else, in reality, they were both parts of the same property. On the other hand, that single walls *(paries communis)* could separate houses in Rome may be inferred from the many times they are mentioned in Roman law. Their existence led to many complicated situations (*Dig.* VIII 2, 8; 13 pr. and 1; 19 pr. and 1; 25, 1; 40). However, it must be remembered that pre-Neronian buildings were not subject to the Neronian code.

By *paries communis* is understood a single-ply wall; this is made clear from the fact (*Dig.* VIII 2, 13 1) that one loses paintings and other precious wall coverings on such a wall if the neighbour's house is demolished, and one can only expect compensation for the value of ordinary wall covering or wall decoration *(vulgaria tectoria)*. But one can build an earthenware vault *(cameram ex figlino opere,* cf. Vitruvius V x 3), if it is constructed in such a way that it will remain standing when the wall is torn down; wooden stairs against the common wall are also permissible because they can be removed (*Dig.* VIII 2, 19, 1-2).

The existence, and the problems, of the common wall in Ostia is proven by the inscription Bloch 68: "hic paries/ad hanc altitudin/hac fine/communis est" ("This wall is common to this height and to this point in length"). The inscription was found in 1938 in the Terme delle sei Colonne. It would have been interesting if the exact location of the find had been recorded. The inscription says that only part of a wall, in length as well as in height, was *communis*. This would handsomely fit the single wall in the south end of the Baths where open peristyles are neighbours on the two sides and an old *horrea* building is on the third side. The *horrea* are from the early first century A.D., that is prior to Nero's building code (see Rickman 59, with references), while the Baths are from the time of Trajan (*ScO* I 127, 235; II 93). Buildings from the pre-Neronian era would be exempt from Nero's law, anyway. A survey of Ostian buildings shows that the number of single-wall separations of buildings is surprisingly small. Some of the separations only seem to be separations and are created by the modern registration in regions, *isolati,* and houses (III ii 8, and others) which has divided up buildings that actually are whole units, as in V iii 3, 4, 5. This will be discussed later. But the basic law is that real building units in Ostia are contained within their own walls.

2. The Roman *dominium* is absolute ownership, although there is no definition of it in Roman law. The Romans had respect for private property, and the right of ownership was virtually unlimited: "cuius est solum eius est usque ad coelum" ("The owner of the land owns it as high up as the sky").[2] The limitations imposed on ownership were imposed in the general public interest, but they were "alien to it and detract from its purity."[3]

Old laws command that if somebody builds a house on somebody else's land the house shall belong to the one who owns the land: "ex diverso si quis in alieno solo sua materia domum aedificaverit, illius fit domus, cuius et solum est" ("On the other hand, if somebody builds a house with his own building material on somebody else's land, the house will belong to the owner of the land," *Instit.* II 1, 30).

3. That a Roman could not block a neighbour's lawfully installed door needs no comment. Another point is the prohib-

ition against blocking or obstructing a neighbour's windows. In this matter the authority is divided between the private persons and the magistrates: first, the city had jurisdiction over that side of the houses which faced the streets and public areas. In *Digesta* XLIII 8, 2, 6, Ulpian in his commentary to the Edict testifies that, "cum quidam velum in moeniano immissum haberet qui [var. *quod*] vicini luminibus officiebat, utile interdictum competit: ne quid in publico immittas qua re luminibus Caii Seii officias" ("When somebody in his balcony installs an awning which takes some daylight away from the neighbour, this interdict is applicable: you shall not in a public locality place anything which will stand in the way of N.N.'s daylight"). A curtain on a balcony could take the light away from a neighbour, or, in general terms, "plane si aedificium hoc effecerit, ut minus luminis insula tua habeat, interdictum hoc competit" ("It is clear that if this building causes your apartment house to receive less daylight, this edict applies," *Dig.* XLIII 8, 2, 14). So much for the façade of the houses.

The same problem among the neighbours in the block was subject to private agreement. The basic rule, however, was that nobody could interfere with a neighbour's free enjoyment of his property by, among other things, blocking or obstructing his doors or windows. There are lots of examples of this in *Digesta* VIII 2 ("De servitutibus praediorum urbanorum"); see also *Codex Justinianus* III 34, 1 ("De servitutibus et aqua"). In addition to blocking sunlight, later it was ruled that the view from the windows could not be obstructed either. This protection of the *prospectus* was accepted as a right in the late Republic (Rodger 124-25). The difference between the two is spelled out: the light means that one can see the sky, and there is this difference between *lumen* (light, daylight) and *prospectus* (view, prospect) that "prospectus etiam ex inferioribus locis est, lumen ex inferiore loco esse non potest" ("Prospect can come out of low places, daylight does not come from a low place," *Dig.* VIII 2, 16). The difference is spelled out later in the building code of Constantinople. *Codex Justinianus* VIII 10, 12, 3 explains that *fenestrae luciferae* ("windows to give light") have to be six feet above the floor, but then a builder might, unlawfully, raise the floor inside the building so that the windows whose function it was to light the room become *fenestrae prospectivae* ("windows to provide a view") and allow the occupant of that room a view into the neighbour's property and intrude on his privacy. If, on the other hand, the occupants of the apartment could see the sea from their windows nobody would dare to obstruct that view (*Cod.* VIII 10, 12, 2; cf. *Novellae* 165, "De prospectu in mare").

A clear early example from Italy is given by the inscription *CIL* X 787 (3 B.C.), which testifies that the city council of Pompeii had to pay 3000 *HS* to the temple of Apollo for the right to block the windows between the *porticus* of the temple and that of the forum of Pompeii: "M. Holoconius Rufus D.V.I.D. tert./C. Egnatius Postumus D.V.I.D. iter./ex D.D. ius luminum/opstruendorum HS ∞ ∞ ∞/redemerunt. parietem-que/privatum Col. Ven. Corn./usque at tegulas/faciendum coerarunt." Rodger (29) points out that the words of the inscription are ambiguous: some scholars (Overbeck, Mau, Karlowa) believe that *ius luminum opstruendorum* means "the right to block lights" while others will translate it "the right to block up windows." This distinction is of no practical importance to the present discussion: the windows in Pompeii that are discussed here have been filled in with masonry.

It is tempting to measure Ostia against these laws. In Ostia we know next to nothing about the owners of individual properties. Some names are connected with certain houses (Annius's House, Buticosus's Baths, Horrea Epagathiana, Alexander Helix's tavern), but in such a way that it is not obvious what the person's name means to the property. Among many things, it could mean ownership or a sports hero's memorial. However, we know that guilds had acquired full corporate rights under Antoninus Pius and that they invested in real estate. Furthermore, we know about some places in Ostia which were guild property, and by appraising the guild's attitude toward the adjoining property—whether they respect it or violate it—we could tell about ownership. If their actions

were flagrant violations of neighbouring property and, consequently, of the law, it is likely that the guild owned that neighbouring property.

The Themistocles Complex

The Themistocles Complex. In the corner of Via degli Augustali
and the Decumanus in Ostia there is a complicated set of buildings: a collegiate temple, east of it a plain *insula*, and south of
the temple and *insula* the complex structure which has been
called the largest single building at Ostia.[4] It has a very desir-
able location, with one façade on the Decumanus across from
the theatre and the compound of the four small temples; to the
south are the Baths of the Swimmer, to the east are *horrea*, and
to the west is the distinguished meeting place of the *Augustales*,
and also the biggest and, presumably, most odorous *fullonica*
found so far in Ostia, which seems to indicate that the inhabi-
tants of the *tabernae* in the Caseggiato del Temistocle, after all,
could not have been overly discriminating.[5]

The site of the Themistocles complex has a triangular
shape. The eastern property line and the western façade on the
old and original Via degli Augustali converge because of the
streets in this part of Ostia. From Via degli Augustali to Via del
Sabazeo, they lead to a gate in the southeast corner of the Sullan Wall. Consequently, all boundary lines of the buildings in
this part of the city are oblique (the building block with the
Sabazeum, the Hortensius *horrea*, the Artemis *horrea*, and the
Themistocles complex) and point in the general direction of the
south gate. The street in front of the Themistocles building,
which led to the gate, must have been blocked in the first century A.D. by the Baths of the Swimmer (Terme del Nuotatore
V x 3).[6] Also the second, more westerly branch of the same Via
degli Augustali and the third street, Via del Felicissimo, were
cut off by the baths. The new pattern, set up by the baths, is
acknowledged by the construction of the building V xi 1 in

Hadrianic times. Presumably not until Via delle Ermette is there a street going south to the wall. However, about all this we shall not have certain knowledge until the southeast corner of Ostia is excavated.

The original Caseggiato del Temistocle was a wedge-shaped structure which covered the whole lot and had a front on the Decumanus.[7] It is naturally divided into an east wing comprising a row of apartments, contained by the walls A and B, and a west wing consisting of a row of *tabernae* along the west side, between walls E and F-G, and of an area of storage space and accommodations behind the *tabernae*, between walls C and E (fig. 33). These two wings were independent buildings.

The East Wing. The four wedge-shaped apartments increase in length as well as in width from south to north. When one compares the plan of the most northern apartment with the others it becomes clear that its north end has been cut off by the *insula*. If that apartment was proportionately as long as the preceding two apartments it would have reached the short, thick east-west partition wall (L in fig. 33) in the *insula*, and north of it there would still be space for a *taberna* with *porticus* comparable to the *tabernae* in the neighbouring block to the east, V xi 4. The direction of the short east-west partition, wall L, is dictated by the floor plan of the apartments in the east wing. It is parallel with all the partition walls in the apartments, and its orientation differs from the other east-west walls of the *insula*. The south wall and the north wall of the *insula* are twisted slightly in order to create a frontal effect on the Decumanus and correspond to a similar effort to correct the obliquity of the temple plan.[8] The short partition wall of the *insula*, then, most likely contains an original wall of the east wing. The west wall of the *insula* and the wall C line up perfectly. Wall B is not visibly preserved under the *insula*, but the main extension of the east wing seems clear.

The walls A and B are only 0,45 metre thick. The east wing can only have been one storey high. The three northern apartments have the floor plan of the standard *medianum* apartment.[9] The *medianum* (see fig. 11, room 3) is paved with *opus*

33.

The Themistocles Block. The temple and the *insula* face the Decumanus. The Caseggiato del Temistocle faces Via degli Augustali. The east wing is contained by walls A and B and originally stretched as far north as wall L. The east wing was probably distributed in ten to eleven rooms, north of which was a *taberna*. The remaining part of wall B shows ten original door

openings, four of which are blocked. Corresponding to the ten doors were ten rooms. An eleventh room at the northern end was given to the *insula*. The west wing was confined by walls C and F, with wall E as the spine. Its western half was *tabernae*; its eastern half had accommodations and storage space lighted by windows up high in wall C. When the tem-

ple and the *insula* blocked all access to the Caseggiato del Temistocle, one entered from Via degli Augustali. Facade G was added to wall F and supported a gallery and stairs, thus creating access to the upper floor(s).
Scale 1:500.

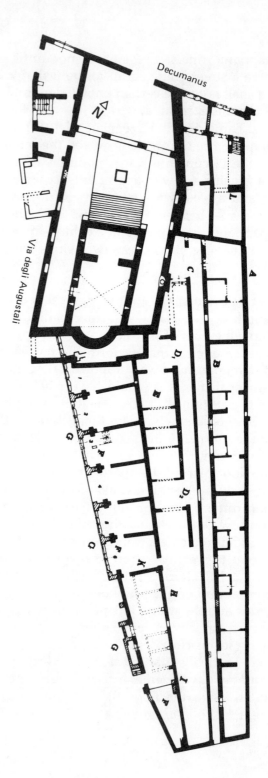

spicatum (brick set in the herring-bone pattern), and there is a catch basin, connected with the sewer system, right inside the entrance doors. All other apartment rooms where pavement is preserved are paved with white mosaic with a black border following the walls. This indicates that the *medianum* had an open skylight in the roof, which was an important source of lighting. The low height of the building may also be indicated by a very doubtful window in the wall C, which is part of the west wing of Caseggiato del Temistocle (fig. 34). Wall C is 0,60 metre thick, which points to a house of more than one storey. Wall C is preserved to a height of up to four metres, and it would not make sense to put in a window to light some of the west wing if all of Caseggiato del Temistocle were under one roof and, consequently, the hallway in front of the apartments were covered, as was once suggested.[10] Since, on the other hand, the east wing was only one storey high it would not shut out the light from a window in the west wing.

If the window in wall C may be subject to legitimate doubt—it has no finish along the edges and may simply be a hole cut much later—there is another and stronger indication that windows were installed in wall C. In the Commodan wall H, toward its south end, there is a window opening, 0,60 metre wide, starting 2,08 metres above the floor (fig. 35). It serves a room in the west wing which is part of a five-room apartment where the individual rooms are clearly marked by the white mosaic floors with black borders along the walls. The partition walls have disappeared and are only discernable by the gap between the mosaic floors and by the marks left on wall H. This room was also the one through which one entered the apartment. The entrance door was placed in the Severan front (wall G), and this added an extra small hallway to the other hallway which was running in front of the room and which gave access to the other rooms of the apartment. To get light for the entrance room became a problem: there simply was not enough space for a window in the west wall beside the front door. So the entrance room was the only one of that apartment which could not get light from the west. Therefore this window was made in the east wall of the room and placed up high in order to give more light to the room and also to create a direct line for

34.
Rough cut in wall C.
It is questionable that
'there was a window
in this low position.

35.
Entrance to southern
apartment in the west
wing, facing the Com-
modan wall H, with
window opening.

36.
The north side of the
window opening in
room 3 of apartment
in east wing (for plan,
see fig. 11).

34.

37.
Angiportus between
wall B (to the right)
and wall C (to the
left), looking north.
Photo: Bill Barazzuol.

38.
Facade of *tabernae* on
Via degli Augustali.
The lower Severan
addition supported
a gallery, which gave
access to the floor(s)
above the *tabernae*.

39.
Remains of steps at the
south end of wall G.
Photo: Martin Kilmer.

37.

the light flow, which started from a more elevated window in
wall C.

Furthermore, to revert to the east wing and the apartment
which has been described as apartment 8 (pp. 41-43), the vertical sides of the window opening in room 4 (fig. 36) are twisted
toward the south in order to pick up the most possible light
from that side, a technique which is duplicated in the neighbouring block (V xi 4) by a loophole on the east side of the passage from the Decumanus into the yard. The turning south of
the window opening was motivated by the high wall in front of
doors and windows in the east wing, which reduced the
amount of light considerably (fig. 37).

The West Wing consists of a row of *tabernae* on old Via degli
Augustali and behind these a space was taken up by accommo-

35.

36.

38.

39.

dations and storage. The outer walls were 0,60 metre thick (C, E, F), while walls D1 and D2 were only 0,45 metre. The width of the outer walls indicates that the building could be three storeys high, while the apartments (between D1-D2 and E) were light inside constructions whose walls had no load-carrying capacity, even though they might rise to the same height as the rest of the west wing. The spine of the west wing is wall E, with walls C and F distributed symmetrically on either side: those three walls made the west wing.

The building originally went all the way up to the Decumanus. Details of this are lost, buried under the collegiate temple. The main entrance must have been from the Decumanus, with stair(s) to the upper floor(s). Also, the *angiportus* between the two wings clearly points to an entrance from the Decumanus. The great change came at the time of Commodus when

a guild decided to build a temple facing the Decumanus.[11] The guild in question, as will be demonstrated, was the owner of the whole Caseggiato del Temistocle.

The temple has already been dealt with (p. 64) and does not need much explanation. It is the type that is known in Ostia in the collegiate temple (I x 4) by the Tempio Rotondo, the temple of the shipbuilders (III ii 2), the temple under the Baths of the Philosopher (Terme del Filosofo V ii 6) and the Serapeum (III xvii 4). It was recognized as such right away, for it has the paraphernalia required for the activities of a guild: the banquet facilities, with running water in a fountain on the west wall of the courtyard.

The new temple cut away half of the west wing and blocked the old access from the north. In order to get into the west wing the owners had to make a new approach through the east wing, where the *insula* had not yet been built. That new approach was through the *angiportus* of the east wing, and by cutting through the wall C and setting in a main entrance with a doorstep (fig. 33 at letter C) they made an entrance directly into the corridor between walls C and D1-D2. This is one indication that the east wing and the west wing were under the same ownership.

Behind the temple, at the south end, an *intercapedo* was built to separate the *tabernae* from the temple, for no other apparent purpose than fire protection. The *intercapedo* was added later: it was built after the new front had been added to

40.
Caseggiato del Temistocle – House
of Themistocles. Reconstruction
design is by Maria Antonietta
Ricciardi. The actual remains of
the walls are shown darker than
the reconstructed parts. The only
firm elements in this reconstruction
are the thickness of the wall, which
allows for three to four storeys
in the northern half of the house
and the presence of the outside
stairs, together with the purpose
for the stairs. The facade features
a gallery that gave access to the
second floor after the house had
lost its direct access from the
Decumanus and that was used
after the raising of the level of
street and floors deprived the
ground floor of much of its usefulness. The walls of the *intercapedo* and the temple must also
have constituted the north wall
of the house (to the left in the
picture). The south end of the
house, of which most is left out
in the picture, can hardly have had
the same height as the northern
half, since the walls F, H, and I
south of the last *taberna* are only
0,45 metre thick. The reconstruction
is not quite to scale in that the
width of the north end of the
house has been contracted considerably.

the *tabernae*; a small corner of one new front protrudes on the
south side of the *intercapedo* wall, and soundings in the ground
reveal other rests of that same front. While all the walls from A
to F are Hadrianic, the frontal addition to the *tabernae* G and the
wall H, which is an extention of E, are Commodan-Severan
brick; the wall H (8,90 metres) is continued by wall I (16,10
metres), which is a characteristic late piece of masonry made of
a mixture of various materials.[12] The cross wall K is *opus reticulatum* and presumably part of the oldest building.

This addition to the front of the *tabernae* is interesting: it
was made at the same time as the temple (or the *insula*). The
front was brought forward 1,75 metres at the most northern
pillar and 1,40 metres at the south end (fig. 38). Traces of steps
at the south end (fig. 39) explain it all: the pillars supported a
balcony which was running along the whole front of the *tabernae*. The steps at the south end are the beginning of the stairs
that led to the balcony (see reconstruction, fig. 40). It is the
same kind of access to the upstairs rooms that existed in the
courtyard of the Caseggiato del Larario, where the stairs were
inside the building.[13] The different lay-out in the Caseggiato
del Temistocle accounts for the lack of inside stairs in that
house. Only one flight of stairs is recorded in the third *taberna*
from the north; its location inside the Hadrianic door opening
shows that it antedates the addition to the front of the *taberna*
(fig. 41 a and b). This reorganization of the Caseggiato del
Temistocle must have been undertaken to create more space,

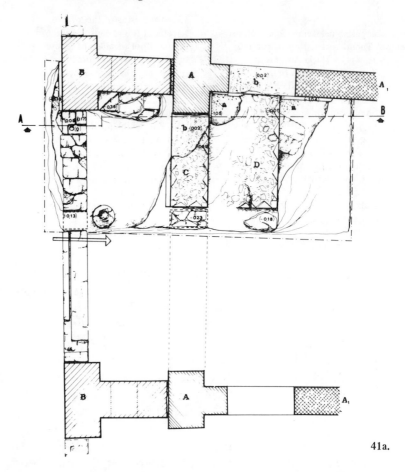

41a.

since the erection of the temple and the *insula* had cut away close to half of the area of the Themistocles complex.

The section between the east wing and the *tabernae* goes back to the oldest building (fig. 42). The walls D1 and D2 are built for the sole purpose of creating some living space between walls D1-D2 and E. At the time of Gallienus these rooms and the apartments in the east wing were decorated at the same time and in identical style.[14] That is more evidence that all of Caseggiato del Temistocle was under one ownership.

No sooner was the temple finished than a new building project was started. The owners of Caseggiato del Temistocle wanted to take advantage of its valuable location on the Decumanus to build an *insula*, which may have been a revenue

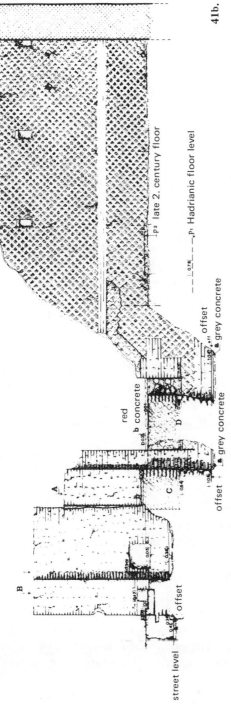

street level · offset

red · b concrete · grey concrete

offset · grey concrete · offset

P¹ late 2. century floor

P² Hadrianic floor level

41b.

41.a. and b.

Excavation in the third *taberna* of the Caseggiato del Temistocle – House of Themistocles – by Soprintendente prof. Valnea Santa Maria Scrinari and prof. Maria Antonietta Ricciardi (March 1980). The latter recorded the excavation and drew the accompanying plan (a) and elevation (b).

Broken lines indicate the border-lines of the excavation. A1 (cross-hatched): Hadrianic *opus mixtum*. A (narrow diagonal lines): Hadrianic *opus testaceum*. B,C,D (wide diagonal lines): Severan brick or concrete work. Only in the third *taberna* is there any trace of stairs to the floor above. These *tabernae* differ sharply from the usual *tabernae* in Ostia, in which there are individual stairs to the floor above. The stairs in *taberna* 3 belong to the Hadrianic house: they start well inside the Hadrianic door opening. After the construction of the new facade the stairs were apparently given up. At the same time the ground level was raised as in most of Ostia in the post-Neronian period, here by 0,78 metre so that the height of the ceiling was reduced to less than 1,83 metres (the distance from the p2 floor to the under-side of the ceiling beams; see elevation drawing). The *tabernae* were now low and badly lighted, and access to the upper floor(s) was more convenient from the new gallery.

property. In Severan time the east wing, which is a Hadrianic structure, was truncated at the north end to make space for that *insula*. [15] A building procedure like this could only be followed by somebody who owned the east wing, or else the builder would be building on the neighbour's land and block his doors (cf. p. 93 ff.). It will be argued later that the interference goes beyond any reasonable easement. There is, however, another indication that the east wing and the *insula* were in the hands of the same people. It is a well-known phenomenon that in Commodan-Severan masonry the bonding courses could be marked by a red coat of paint or by a red glazed brick face. This red line is seen in several places near the bottom of the walls of the *insula* as well as in many other places in Ostia. [16] But this red line is never used in Hadrianic masonry.

However, in a second operation red paint has again been applied to a course in the *insula* and, for the first time, in the apartment wing: in the *insula* there are faint traces of red paint on a course in the east wall about one metre above the lower red line; the paint has flowed down and tinted the mortar below the course and is now best seen on the mortar; in the apartment wing red paint has been applied to the second course of the brick platband of the *opus mixtum* in the Hadrianic wall A; there are traces of the paint in the first and second apartment and also on the west side of the corridor (wall C), 1,51 metres above the base of the lower platband. The paint is applied in the same manner and probably at the same time in both places, before the walls were stuccoed. This seems to indicate that the work was done by the same work crew in both places, after the *insula* had been finished and when they repaired the damage done to the apartment wing, when its north end was cut off. This red line must have had a different meaning from that applied to the bonding courses.

To summarize the building history: Originally the so-called Caseggiato del Temistocle was a building which extended all the way to the Decumanus. It consisted of two wings: a one-storey east wing and a taller west wing which were separated by an unroofed *angiportus*. The main entrance must have been from the Decumanus, and stairs to an upper storey, or to upper

42.
Looking north between wall C (to the right) and wall E (to the left). Between the two walls one sees the ends of walls D1 and D2. To the far left are the remains of walls F and G. In the background, between walls C and E is the wall of the temple and the *intercapedo*.
Photo: Bill Barazzuol.

storeys, in the west wing must have been located in the northern half. The west wing had more than one storey—the three bearing walls are 0,60 metre thick. It is customarily assumed that 0,60-metre walls at the ground floor in Ostia mean that the buildings were three to four storeys high.[17] The west wing consisted of a row of *tabernae* with an upstairs, and behind it between walls E and C was a space lit by windows in wall C, above the roof level of the east wing. It can be debated whether an upstairs existed between walls C and E in the part of the building which is preserved; if there had been one, there would have been evidence of a floor-ceiling on wall C, which in places is preserved to a height of four metres. Inside, the walls D1 and D2 were added to create some accommodation, and this could rise to more than one storey; the whole area south of wall K (before walls H and I were built) could be used for storage, with a wide gate on Via degli Augustali for handling material (tools, hoists, material for forms, and other material used by ancient builders, if this was the property of the *fabri tignuarii*).

In Commodan times a collegiate temple was superimposed on the north end of the west wing, leaving the east wing intact. To offset the loss of direct access to the west wing from the Decumanus the owners installed a main entrance at point C, which was reached from the Decumanus through the *angiportus* in the east wing.

Not long afterwards, in Severan time, the *insula* V xi 3 was built, cutting off all connections between the Caseggiato del

Temistocle and the Decumanus. This made the newly built north entrance at point C completely useless, and the main entrance was now from Via degli Augustali. More serious was the apparent loss of space and access to the upper storey(s). Close to half of the Caseggiato del Temistocle was lost. An addition was made to the front of the *tabernae* in order to build a balcony and stairs to the upper storey(s). Wall H was erected, and more accommodations were created in the southern tip of the west wing between walls H and F-G. The exact timing of these alterations is difficult to establish because they were so close together; the interval between the temple and the *insula* may be only one or two decades.[18]

In an article in the *Rendiconti dei Lincei, Scienze morali* (1971, ser. VIII, vol. xxvi, 472-78) Fausto Zevi has argued that the collegiate temple was dedicated by the *collegium fabrum tignuariorum Ostiensium* to Divus Pius Pertinax, not later than A.D. 194. He bases his argument on a dedicatory inscription of which half has been found in the neighbourhood of the temple, while in 1924 the other half was found being used as building material in the west end of the city at the corner of Via della Foce and the Decumanus. With all due reservation about the mobile nature of inscriptions in Ostia, Fausto Zevi finds the topographic coincidence of the one half of the inscription and the temple being so near to each other too tempting: the inscription has been the dedicatory inscription of the temple.

This explanation may be correct, and it may not. The *collegium fabrum tignuariorum* already had a guild site in the Caseggiato dei Triclini by the Forum, and the site had everything that may be expected, and needed, in a guild seat: a sanctuary, water supply, banquet space, cooking facilities—all of which were also present in the collegiate temple. The Caseggiato dei Triclini, however, does not have the practical facilities (storage, accommodations) which are in the Caseggiato del Temistocle (see p. 104) and in the guild site of the *lenuncularii*, of the *stuppatores*, and the unidentified guild V iii 1-5. The guild of the *fabri tignuarii* had numberous members, as their somewhat fragmented *album* shows (CIL XIV S4569), and may have needed larger than normal facilities.

The temple, the *insula*, and the Caseggiato del Temistocle can only be understood as one unit. It has already been pointed out that the east wing, the west wing, and the *insula* were under the same ownership. That is even clearer in the case of the temple; the building of the temple constitutes a much heavier encroachment on the Caseggiato del Temistocle than did the *insula*. It all goes beyond a reasonable easement—the erection of the temple and *insula* constitutes a radical change: the Caseggiato del Temistocle is completely crushed. This would constitute a flagrant violation of Roman property laws, and it would only make sense if the owners of the temple—the guild—had owned all three components V xi 1, 2, and 3 from the beginning. Such an ownership seems natural, since at the time of the construction of the temple and the *insula* the guild members had enjoyed rights as legal persons for some time, that is, they could own property, including slaves, and receive legacies, a development which, from a slow start in the beginning of the second century, had gained speed and enjoyed special favour under Marcus Aurelius.[19] More examples of this will be seen in the following.

It must be assumed, then, that the Themistocles complex is guild property. That makes the whole complex easier to understand. In the first place it is clear that we are not faced with a standard apartment building. It lacks, first of all, a decent approach; the apartments are rather inaccessible. There are no wide doors on the street, let alone the monumental entrances with staircases that might be expected in a three-storey Hadrianic housing project—the type which is common in Ostia. There were stairs in the third *taberna* but they were eliminated when the gallery was added to the front (fig. 41). There are no indications of inside wooden stairs, but it is certain that there has been some upstairs space above the *tabernae*. The built-up centre, between walls D1-D2 and E, stopped at the south end of wall D2, with the line of wall K indicating the boundary. The south end of the building may have been open storage space or industrial installation related to the professional activity of the guild. The walls H and I are later additions, so that the south end was originally confined by the walls F and C plus the short south wall.

The entrance to this building is either through the last *taberna* to the south or through the corridor between walls B and C, a lay-out which does not consider either convenience or style. It has the utilitarian appearance of a guild. But the most interesting part of this building is the row of *tabernae*. They are unique in that each *taberna* is connected with its two neighbours by doorways. This remarkable plan can be studied in four other places, all of which have a similar combination of architectural elements, as will be described. It can be argued, furthermore, that all these places are guild sites and that a *taberna* arrangement of this sort is guild style. It is a demonstration of the old nature of the Roman guilds—the brotherhood of the members and the concentration of members of the same profession in the same area. From antiquity through the Middle Ages craftsmen of the same profession would settle in the same street or neighbourhood so that everybody would know where to find them. That is why we find street names like Clivus Argentarius, Via inter Falcarios, Vicus Unguentarius, Frumentarius, Lorarius, Lanarius, Inter Lignarios (Street of the Silversmiths, Sicklemakers, Salve Merchants, Grain Merchants, Leather Merchants, Wool Merchants, Wood Merchants); we know, also, that goldsmiths were in Vicus Tuscus.[20]

Their *tabernae* were interconnected as an expression of the guild brothers' status. A guild was a closely knit group. It was a real brotherhood: some guild members called each other brother (*frater*), and they could not testify against each other. All guild brothers owned all guild property in common, they shared a common cult, and they had a common burial place. They had many common meals. As Waltzing points out, the frequent meals contributed to creating "l'esprit de corps." To some of the brothers the guild was their only family or their closest relative.[21]

The plan of the *tabernae* demonstrates that communal approach. It differs from the plans of the hundreds of other *tabernae* in Ostia and elsewhere in which the units are carefully separated and each made a world unto itself. In the Caseggiato del Temistocle, privacy and individual ownership do not exist. The doors to the street may be closed, but behind the doors everything—*tabernae* and the space behind them—seems to be accessible to everybody in the family. That is why only one flight of stairs (or two?) was needed for the upstairs above the *tabernae,* where other, non-collegiate *tabernae* have individual stairs to their private *cenacula.*

What else was done in the complex is impossible to establish. The building is a non-luxurious place, which suggests the environment of humble people. It is in drastic contrast to the elegant living quarters in the neighbouring seat of the *Augustales* across the street. That a bust of Themistocles has been found here would say nothing about the activities of the house, even if we were satisfied that the bust originally belonged in the house. Besides the inelegant apartments in the east wing there are some basic accommodations behind the *tabernae* and also much storage space. There are other guilds in Ostia that have similar undetermined grey areas for storage and primitive accommodations, and it seems ideal for guilds that owned slaves.

Four Guild Seats and Their Property

The Seat of the Augustales (V vii 1, 2, 4, and 5) is located on the Decumanus west of the Themistocles complex. That it is the seat of the *Augustales* is well documented by finds in the building: a statue on whose base is an inscription to "A. Livius Chryseros Sevir Augustalis Quinquennalis" and statues of Empress Sabina (Hadrian's consort), Emperor Maxentius, and Fausta (Pudicitia), Maxentius's sister. East of the apse is found still another inscription to a *sevir augustalis.*[22] The message of these finds confirms what can be read out of the building itself, and it has all the characteristics of a guild site: the sanctuary, with its later addition of an apse, the water supply in the middle of the peristyle, and the much wider east wing of the peristyle, which obviously was their banquet hall (fig. 43).[23]

The precise date of the seat of the *Augustales* is rather irrelevant.[24] However, the two different building stages are of interest to us. First, the late republican *domus* under the seat of the *Augustales* and the row of *tabernae* on the Decumanus (V vii 1) is dated to Antoninus Pius (*ScO* I 235); next, into this was

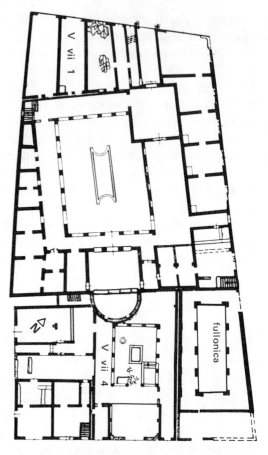

43.
The guild seat of the *Augustales* and the *tabernae* on the east side were built at the same time. Note that the *Augustales* have blocked the doors and windows of the *tabernae* on the north side (V vii 1) and have built an apse into the peristyle of V vii 4. The *fullonica* V vii 3 is separated from the *Augustales'* seat by a double wall. Scale 1:630.

built the guild seat about A.D. 150-165 or, as Herbert Bloch says (*ScO* I 227), the third quarter of the second century A.D.

The interesting thing is that the seat of the *Augustales* has cut off the row of *tabernae* on the Decumanus and blocked the windows and doors that face south. They did not even fill in the openings from the inside of the *tabernae*. Moreover, in the third century the *Augustales* added an apse to their collegiate sanctuary, an apse which cut into the peristyle of the old *domus*. It is obvious that the *Augustales* owned both these neighbouring buildings since the *domus* originally, besides the peristyle, also comprised an *atrium*, which now has been covered by the collegiate building. It was all one lot. The *fullonica*, which has its own outer wall on the west side and on that part of the north side which borders on the Augustalian property, was independent of the guild property. On the northeast corner of the *fullonica* the wall is single-ply because there was no building on the side of the Augustales; there was only a flight of stairs under open air. Conversely, the seat of the *Augustales* comprises the courtyard with the surrounding rooms, the sanctuary, and the row of *tabernae* on the Via degli Augustali. All this was built in one operation by the *Augustales* and is contained within the same outer wall.

It is worth noting that this building was constructed at a time when the guilds of the *Augustales* were upgraded and expanded (Becatti in *ScO* I 143), and at the same time it should be noted that as time passed the guilds of the *Augustales* assumed more and more the appearance of professional guilds and do not seem to differ from them in legal status.[25] Consequently there is nothing strange about the interconnected *tabernae* on the Via delgi Augustali: it is guild style. The *tabernae* on the Decumanus (V vii 1) pre-date those of the *Augustales* and were presumably not built by a guild; there is no inside communication between them. Only the guild *tabernae* were built so.

The City Block V iii 1-5 looks like a guild seat with appurtenances (fig. 44). V iii 1 is classed as a *domus* of Hadrianic age (*ScO* I 232, 236) and is discussed elsewhere (pp. 76-77). It has an *impluvium* surrounded by four column bases, which suggests an *atrium*. In the back is what looks like a *tablinum* with a room on either side. Two small rooms and a flight of stairs along the east wall are a much later addition and are of no interest to this discussion.

However, there is a drinking fountain at the entrance (fig. 45); the east wall and the west wall each have ten windows or door openings, which do away with the privacy of a *domus*, and the *tablinum* originally had no solid walls; and besides the opening in front there were two openings in each of the two side walls. The *tablinum* looks like a sanctuary of the same type as the ones in the seat of the *Augustales*, of the *fabri tignuarii*, in the Caesareum of the *vigiles* (II v 1), or in the Schola del Traiano. The sanctuary, the drinking fountain, and the *atrium-*

44.
The guild complex in Via della Fortuna
Annonaria. One notes the drinking foun-
tain in the entrance of V iii 1 and the
two blocked doors in the north wall of
V ii 2. The two apartments V iii 3 and
4 have been discussed above, pp. 27-32.
Scale 1:600.

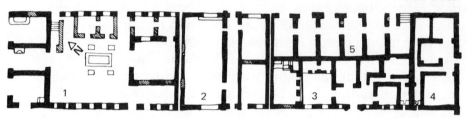

like room with the many windows look most of all like those in
a guild seat. The guild most likely owned the whole block
isolato iii. That they owned the next house to the south is
understood from the way in which they blocked the doors of
that Trajanic building (V iii 2), a building which seems to constitute a storage or work area.

The three units V iii 3, 4, and 5 are one building erected at
one time and in one operation. It is discussed at length on
pages 27 to 31, but for the sake of clarity a few details are
repeated here. The whole construction is enclosed by one wall,
and the division into two *insulae* and a *caseggiato* is not convincing (*ScO* I 232). The three components all have common walls,
which would have been an infraction of Roman law if they
were separate houses at the time of Hadrian. All the walls,
outer walls as well as the walls which separate the three components (V iii 3, 4, and 5), are 0,60 metre thick. This thickness
indicates a height of three storeys. All claims that the two residential units V iii 3 and 4 were only one storey high, while V iii
5 had three floors, are unfounded, especially when it is stated
that V iii 3 and 4 were "lacking internal stairways."[26] Evidence
of stairs to the upper floor(s) of V iii 3 can be seen (fig. 4). Furthermore, in the *taberna* wing V iii 5 the most southern room is
a stairway leading up.

Finally, a sign of the unity of iii 3, 4, and 5 is the telling
detail that room 7 of iii 3 originally was a *taberna* directly connected with the *tabernae* of iii 5 and that the walls of the *tabernae*

45.
Remains of drinking
fountain in the entrance
of the guild complex
V iii 1-5. The fountain
has now been taken
down.

of iii 5 and of room 7 of iii 3 were sheer brick, in contrast to the
opus mixtum of all other rooms of iii 3. The easy access from one
part of this southern complex to the other is reminiscent of the
easy inside communication in the Themistocles complex. It
should be noted that the corner of the wall that one passed on
the way through the *angiportus* from iii 5 to iii 3 is rounded so as
to make the passage easier. All this, together with the interconnected *tabernae*, points to a guild as owner and occupant of this
property. Which guild was the owner-occupant is unknown.

The So-called Basilica (I ii 3). This building was called a basilica
by Paribeni (1916). The place was badly excavated in 1850, but
at the beginning of World War I Paribeni and Calza returned to
do further excavations.[27] Whatever the original purpose of the
basilica may have been—and it is doubtful that it really was to
be a basilica—from what we know now it must have been a
guild seat.

    A marble plaque (19 by 25 centimetres) found in the Aula
del Buon Pastore mentions the *corpus (lenunculariorum) traiectus
Luculli*. It reads: "IMP.CAES. M. ANTO/NIO.
GORDIANO/PIO. FELICI. AVG/CORP. TR. LVCVL" ("To the
imperator Caesar Marcus Antonius Gordian, Pious and Lucky,
Augustus the guild at Lucullus's Crossing," unpublished,
Ostia inv. no. 7906). M. Antonius Gordianus is of course
Gordian III (238-244).[28] It is fair to assume that the basilica was
the seat of the guild of the *lenuncularii*.

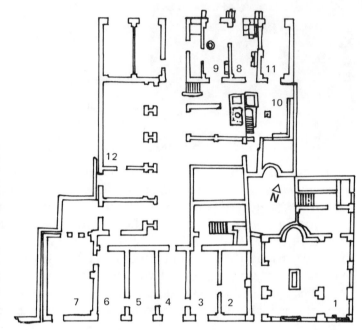

46.
The guild seat of the *lenuncularii*. The so-called Basilica (room 1) and the *tabernae* were built in one operation. The guild property comprised the whole rest of the building, including the *popina* (8-11), all of which is inside the same wall. Scale 1:540.

It must be kept in mind that the five guilds of the *lenuncularii* in Ostia[29] must have offered services of the greatest importance to the operation of the port of Ostia; neither persons nor goods could move without their co-operation. *Corpus scaphariorum et lenunculariorum traiectus Luculli* (*CIL* XIV 409) must have controlled a section of the ferry service on the Tiber, of persons as well as goods (*scaphae, Dig.* XIV 2, 4 pr.). The ferry service was needed much more after the Claudian and Trajanic harbours had been finished and, consequently, much of the activity had moved from the mouth of the Tiber to Portus. An enormous traffic between Portus and Ostia followed, and the ferry service must have been fairly lucrative.

The basilica has been described on page 65. The guild style may be recognized in the five interconnected *tabernae* immediately west of the basilica (fig. 46, rooms 2 to 6). The basilica contained a sanctuary in its niche at the north end; the Aula del

47.
Guild seat of the *stuppatores*.
1. Republican tabernae. 2. Augustan
tabernae. 3. The wing with the
shops of the guild. 4. The courtyard. 5. The Mithraeum. The two
rooms marked with an a were closely
connected with the guild activities,
such as banquets and meetings.
Scale 1:500.

Buon Pastore is a later addition. North of the basilica was an
open courtyard, in the middle of which is a fountain with a
marble basin (fig. 46, 10). The west wing of the Caseggiato del
Termopolio was presumably a row of *tabernae*, of which all
inside partitions are now missing (fig. 46, 12); here was storage
or accommodations of the kind that are found in other guilds. It
is interesting that the façade of these *tabernae* has been brought
out about 1,30 metres into the yard by the addition of pillars in
front of the doorposts, to which they have been connected with
a short piece of wall. It is interesting because the same kind of
addition has been made to the *tabernae* of another guild, the
Caseggiato del Temistocle. In the courtyard north of the basilica is a cellar that most likely was for cold storage of food-
stuffs—the same installation as was found in the guild seat V iii
3 and in Domus del Protiro V ii 5. There is no need, with Paribeni, to think of a sanctuary of some unknown divinity.[30]

Here there is everything needed by a guild and encountered in other guilds. And everything mentioned is contained inside the same building and confined by the same wall. I ii 3, 4, and 5 are all one building. There are double walls along the whole west side, except for the small, open courtyard north of the first *taberna* (fig. 46, 7) where no wall was necessary, because the two buildings did not touch each other. Along the east side there is a double wall between the north wing on the Via di Diana and Caseggiato del Balcone Ligneo. South of that north wing lies an open courtyard where a double wall was not required, but there are double walls again south of the courtyard.

Paribeni has given an account of the development of the whole block I ii through six stages, and it is significant that the *tabernae* and the basilica are built in the same stage at the same time.[31] The same combination of interconnected *tabernae* and official guild centre was built by the *Augustales*; the two features that belong together in guild activities are built together. It is equally significant that the development from that time on comprises the entire complex I ii 3, 4, and 5, or, better expressed, "although the structure was completed piecemeal, the later additions probably represent the steady completion of a single design. The over-all plan of the building is far too unified to be the product of haphazard construction."[32]

One problem remains: the two buildings in I ii 2 and 6 seem to be built on the public square at the Lar altar. The various buildings that we are looking at are not the result of a long development: all the buildings are Hadrianic, with the oldest brickstamps being from the years 113-115 (*ScO* I 215-16; 235) and all built within a few years of each other. Paribeni's building schedule is, first, the basilica and the *tabernae* (o.l. 405 ff.); next, I ii 2, east of the basilica (o.l. 411); then the house of the *thermopolium* (o.l. 413); and last the house I ii 6 east of the *thermopolium* (o.l. 419). We do not know if the ground on which I ii 2 and 6 are built was public. Being inside the old Castrum, it could be, with a high degree of probability. But we have no way of knowing what arrangement had to be made with the Curia to build there. If one builds on public ground, and the building was a hindrance to the public, its removal could be demanded. But if the house was no hindrance, it stayed and the owner was assessed a land tax, a *solarium* (*Dig.* XLIII 8, 2, 17). It looks as if the house I ii 2 blocks the eastern door openings of the basilica, if indeed doors they were. But we have no way of knowing whether the *collegium* was the builder of I ii 2 or what rules were applied in a special case like this.

However, the question is of academic interest. The main observation that can be made is that the basilica with the *tabernae* and the Caseggiato del Termopolio is a single, self-contained unit: the south wing and the west wing served the guild; the courtyard with its perennial fountain and the *popina* offered some of the basic services needed by the guilds. The *popina* in Via di Diana was undoubtedly the property of the guild brothers.

The Guild Seat of the Stuppatores (I x 3 and 4). This guild seat was described and discussed above (pp. 61-62). That the *stuppatores* owned the guild seat seems reasonably well documented. That they, furthermore, owned the adjoining row of *tabernae* to the north seems equally obvious. The water basins in the *tabernae* and those outside the doors on both sides of Vico del Pino, as well as the various pounding rocks, represent some of the most important means for the production of *stuppa* (oakum) from flax (Pliny *N.H.* 19, 16-18), and the presence of this equipment in the *tabernae* can hardly be explained unless there are *stuppatores* in the neighbourhood. Both the inscription from the Mithraeum and the contents of the *tabernae* point to *stuppatores*. [33] The *taberna* wing is not separated from the guild seat, since there is only a single-ply wall between the two, while the adjoining wing to the northwest (I x 2) is meticulously held apart by a double wall; I x 2 is shown to be an independent building. Becatti found rests of baths under the guild seat (*ScO* II 27), and it was probably the bathing establishment which joined the two properties (the baths-guild seat and the *taberna* wing), because the big basin in the southernmost *taberna* probably is a converted *frigidarium* basin. It might be a fair conclusion that the *stuppatores* took over the baths—a wise move on their part, since a lot of water was piped into baths. They also built a vaulted corridor for rain-water piped into the big basin from

the guild's roof—another proof of joint ownership (fig. 47).
The *stuppatores* built the guild centre but not the *tabernae*; consequently only two pairs of *tabernae* have inside connections.

Conclusions

Those who owned the Caseggiato del Temistocle were also
those who built the temple and the *insula*. The Caseggiato lost
half of its area, its main access, and its inner communication.
The dismemberment of the Caseggiato del Temistocle would
violate the Roman laws against building on a neighbour's land,
against blocking the access to his property, and against having
a single-ply wall as separation between two buildings. Moreover, much evidence of a technical nature points to a single
owner. If all was legally one building, all transactions would be
legal.

The *Augustales* must have owned the whole block in which
they built, except, possibly, the *fullonica*. The *fullonica* has its
own walls on the two sides where it borders on the guild site.
The *Augustales'* ownership of the whole block, except of the *fullonica*, is more likely, because the property originally was a
domus which went from street to street, north to south. Their
guild seat was built in one operation together with their *tabernae*. The *tabernae* along the Decumanus must have been part of
the purchase, since the *Augustales* blocked their windows and
doors. Later they built their apse into the peristyle toward the
south. If they did not own it all, they would violate all the same
laws that would have been violated in the Caseggiato del
Temistocle. Later they also built an *insula* (for revenue?) in the
southwest corner of their land.

The so-called *domus* V iii 1 was a guild seat which owned
the adjoining house V iii 2 and could block its doors; V iii 3-5
was one building, showing the criteria of guild property. V iii
1-2 with the sanctuary and the place for official guild activities
and V iii 3-5 with the place for the more practical and professional part of the guild enterprises complement each other and

belong together. The proximity of these two halves, V iii 1-2 and V iii 3-5, and especially their existence in one city block made it likely that it was all owned by one guild.

The so-called Basilica was built together with the *tabernae* in one operation, in the same way as the seat of the *Augustales*. The whole block of the basilica, the *tabernae*, and the Caseggiato del Thermopolium was enclosed by a common wall and developed uniformly. It was one building owned by the guild.

The guild of the *stuppatores* owned their guild seat and, in addition, the *taberna* wing to the northeast, I x 3 and 4. They took over the baths, which had annexed the *taberna* wing. They demolished the baths and build their ceremonial seat in their place and integrated what may have been a *frigidarium* basin, which had been built in the south end of the *taberna* wing, into their oakum-making operations.

One remarkable feature is common in these guild seats: an integral part of them is a row of *tabernae*, and if they are built by the guilds for guild purposes they are connected with each other through inside doorways.

Notes

1. Years ago, M. Voigt made a rather summary survey in his "Die römischen Baugesetze," *Ber. d. Verh. d. Sächs. Ges. d. Wiss. in Lpz. Phil.-hist. Klasse* (1903), 175-98. A new study by Alan Rodger, *Owners and Neighbours in Roman Law* (Oxford, 1972), sorts out the complexities of servitude laws. Much material and many fine observations are in Z. Yavetz, "The Living Conditions of the Urban Plebs in Republican Rome," *Latomus* 18 (1958), 500-517.

2. Buckland, *Main Institutions of Rome Law*, 103.

3. Rodger, 2.

4. Packer, 10.

5. Unpopularity of *fullonicae*, Martial 6, 93, 1.

6. *ScO* I, 234.

7. See Becatti in *ScO* I, 149.

8. Becatti l.l.

9. About this terminology, see "The Medianum and the Roman Apartment" in *Phoenix* 24 (1970), 342ff.

10. Packer 194-96; *ScO* I, 134.

11. Becatti in *ScO* I, 147; compare 237 col. 2 and fig. 33.

12. Compare *ScO* I, fig. 34.

13. Calza in *NSc* (1923), 184; *ScO* I, 205-06.

14. Van Essen in *Bull. Com.* 76 (1956-58), 178.

15. *ScO* I, 237, col. 2; see also fig. 34; a base of Hadrianic masonry *ScO* I, 236, col. 2. The Hadrianic masonry is presumably the remainders of the walls of the east wing, not the whole *insula*.

16. *ScO* I, 205, col. 1, and 206, col. 1.

17. For more about walls and heights, see "The Roman Apartment," note 26.

18. To differentiate between H and G and the collegiate temple is difficult. The measures of the length, the thickness of the bricks, and the thickness of five courses of masonry may not mean very much but here they are:

Tempio Collegiale:
    bricks fifteen to twenty-four centimetres long; three to four centimetres thick
    five courses 23 to 25,5 centimetres
    bonding courses 1,50 metres apart
Commodan wall H:
    bricks eleven to twenty-nine centimetres long; 2,8 to 3,5 centimetres thick
    five courses 23 to 26,5 centimetres
    one bonding course of *sesquipedales* fifty-three centimetres above the floor

Commodan wall G:
  bricks thirteen to twenty-eight centimetres long; 2,8 to 3,8 centimetres thick
  five courses 23,5 to 25,5 centimetres

The bonding courses would place the temple and the extension wall H close together in time, with the distinction that wall H is less carefully crafted than the temple. The front addition to the *tabernae* and the wall H could have been built at the same time to make up for the loss of the northern half of the west wing.

19. Waltzing I, 449ff.; II, 438-55; 431ff. The whole question of *collegia* as legal persons is discussed by Waltzing in II, 431ff., and, recently, in great detail and on a much broader base by Francesco M. de Robertis in his *Storia delle corporazioni e del regime associativo nel mondo romano* (Bari, 1972) II, 235ff.

20. More material in Lellia Cracco Ruggini, "Le associazioni professionali nel mondo romano-bizantino," in *Settimane di studio nel Centro italiano di studi sull'Alto Medioevo* 18, Spoleto (1971) 70 n. 30; cf. Friedländer, *Sittenges. Roms* (or: *Roman Life and Manners*) vol. 1 ch. 3 iv, 2.

21. Waltzing I, 329; compare 37 and 322ff.

22. *NSc 7*, 2 (1941), 203ff.; 216ff.

23. The guild site has been described on page 62.

24. The data supplied to us are rather confusing. Becatti (*ScO* I, 143-44) says that the guild seat is built 150-65 in a Hadrianic *insula* and a first century B.C. *domus*. The *fullonica* (V vii, 3) dates to Anton. Pius. The *insula* V vii 5 to Marcus. *ScO* I, 237, dates the Caseggiato V vii 1 to Anton. Pius. G. Lugli in *La tecnica edilizia*, 611, dates the guild seat to Marcus. G. Calza in *NSc* 7, 2 (1941), 202-03, found brickstamps of the year 125 in the *tabernae* to the north and in the seat. In the *tabernae* he also finds brickstamps of Julius Apollinaris (#1203, about A.D. 130-50) and of Flavius Aper, cos. II A.D. 176. Herbert Bloch finds the stamps of Jul. Apollinaris and Flavius Aper in the guild seat, not in the *tabernae* (*ScO* I, 227).

25. Waltzing I, 125, says that "les Augustales formaient souvant de véritables corporations (corpora, collegia), organisées comme celles des artisans"; compare I, 39, 83, de Robertis, 254, note 74, Meiggs[2], 217.

26. Packer, 11.

27. *NSc* 5, 13 (1916), 143; 399-400.

28. I am grateful to Professor Guido Barbieri for having given me this reference. The inscription was found in February 1951 and is first referred to by Becatti in *ScO* I, 132.

29. Waltzing II, 73ff.; Meiggs, 296-98; *CIL* XIV, 352, 4144.

30. o. l., 402-03.

31. o. l., 408.

32. Packer, 127.

33. This interesting guild property will be discussed at greater length in *American Journal of Archaeology*, 1982.

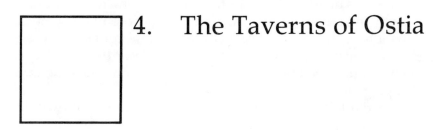

4. The Taverns of Ostia

Tönnes Kleberg's Work: The Ostian Evidence

The characteristic counter with a barrel-vaulted basin at the bottom is the surest indicator of the Ostian tavern; that is, if all other conditions are right. The same bar counter can also be seen in a few guild seats, and it is necessary to take a close look at the surroundings before one decides to which of the two institutions an individual counter belongs, tavern or guild.

The guild fountains have been discussed elsewhere. Here the taverns or bars or restaurants will be studied, and the study must of necessity follow in the footsteps of Tönnes Kleberg, the Swedish archeologist who in three consecutive books on Roman tavern life has given a treasury of information on the position of Roman inns and innkeepers in Roman society, on taboos and prejudice, on human frailty and depravity. The three books are, first, his thesis of 1934, which was written under the inspiration of the old masters Axel Boëthius and Matteo della Corte. It was then amended and translated into French in 1957 and, finally, again published in a condensed and popularized German edition in 1963.* They are all variations on the same theme, but each of them adds something new as the author, progressing from one edition to the next, also progresses in tavern wisdom. He concentrates on Pompeii, where he finds 120 taverns and twenty hotels, he glances briefly at Herculaneum, and in Ostia he notices fourteen of the thirty-odd taverns that were excavated when he went through Ostia for the revision of his thesis in preparation for the French edition. His mention of the Ostian taverns is interesting in that he is the first to study them as a group. He does not pay much attention to the difference between Pompeian-Herculanean taverns and those in Ostia, although he feels that some differences are rooted in political dictates and, consequently, in a changing lifestyle.

In the following section there is a survey of the existing bars or taverns. The words bar, tavern, restaurant, and inn are used rather indiscriminately about the same kind of *taberna*, and the terminology will be discussed later. It may be tricky to make safe identifications of the taverns, because so many of the original criteria were of an ephemeral character and have disappeared over the years since the excavation. A tavern was also too humble and lowly a place to claim too much attention during the excavation, and the diaries of the Ostian excavations are rather laconic, owing to the conditions under which the excavators were forced to work. What mostly was recorded—and recorded very satisfactorily—were the sculptures and the inscriptions. Many of the details that Kleberg could observe have now disappeared completely. In some cases, however, the excavators have tucked fragments of the equipment from the bars away among the rubble under the *subscalaria*, and

---

* Tönnes Kleberg, *Värdshus och värdshusliv i den romerska antiken*, Gothenburg 1934; *Hôtels, restaurants et cabarets dans l'antiquité romaine*, Uppsala 1957; *In den Wirtshäusern und Weinstuben des antiken Rom*, 1st edition, Darmstadt 1963.

here, for instance, a few fragments of mortars can be found.

The taverns now appear in various states of preservation. The majority of them have enough interesting details to warrant a plan as well as a photograph attached to the description of them on the following pages. The plans are made to scale, and in the text of the description only the more relevant measures are given.

A small group of taverns appear now as bare *tabernae*. All the details that could be recorded during the excavation and that are shown on Gismondi's plan have now disappeared. In these cases Gismondi's plan will be shown, because it is our only source. The six taverns in this group are numbers 5, 9, 25, 30, 31, and 37. Another small group shows only a floor mosaic, or wall or ceiling pictures, housed in an uninteresting and bare room. In this case a photograph of that feature will be illustration enough. This group contains taverns number 12, 13, 14, 15, and 22.

Survey and Interpretation of Ostian Taverns

The taverns in the Via di Diana in the House of the Thermopolium (I ii 3-5) and in the House of the Mills (I iii 1) were located in a comparatively busy part of the city. The Forum is nearby and so is the river with all its activity. The *horrea* along the river on both sides, east as well as west, brought many people to the district, and there may have been accommodation for strangers in the Casa di Diana.

The two taverns in the House of Mills are neighbouring *tabernae* on the north side of the street, but they are independent of each other and have no interior communication.

1. The eastern tavern (fig. 48): one enters directly from the street into a rather small barroom (4,85 by 4,85 metres). The bar counter is immediately inside the door to the left and blocks one-third of the opening (one metre). An original bar counter was built up against the west wall to the left (2,20 by 0,84

48.
Tavern 1.
Scale 1:100.

49.
Tavern 1.
Counter with water
basin and substructure
for a water heater built
against the west wall.

50.
Tavern 1. Free-standing
counter with water
basin.

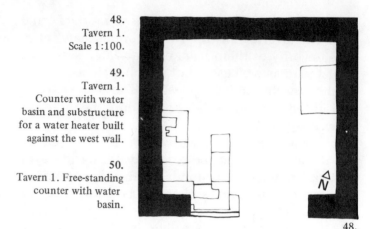

48.

51.
Tavern 2.
Scale 1:125.

52.
Tavern 2. Free-standing
counter with water
basin.

metres), with a 0,50-metre basin at the bottom, while the
northern part of the counter top (0,85 metre) has the substructure for a water-heater (fig. 49). The north end of the water
basin is filled up with masonry. This original counter has
apparently been given up and replaced by a new one, which is
shaped like an inverted L, so that a 1 by 0,30 metre wing is built
parallel with the street and partly on the doorstep, of which
only the western end is preserved, while the main part of the
counter protrudes 2,03 metres into the room. The main counter
is 0,48 metre wide and has in its base an 0,81-metre-long water
basin (fig. 50). On the east wall near the northeastern corner is
a masonry base (1,30 by 1,04 metres, 0,28 metre high), the purpose of which is unknown. The height of the counters varies

49.

50.

51.

52.

from 0,91 to 1,02 metres; the lower part of the substructure for the water-heater is 0,73 metre high; and the shelf between the two counters is 0,46 metre high.

2. The western tavern, the immediate neighbour of the previous tavern, measures 5 metres north-south by 4,45 metres east-west (fig. 51). There is a full 3,07-metre doorstep with a groove for a sliding shutter and a *cardo* hole for a swinging door in the east end. In the eastern (right) side of the room is a bar counter 1,02 metres inside the southern wall (fig. 52). Its measurements are 0,49 by 0,95 to 1,08 metres, 0,90 metre high. The basin at its bottom is 0,50 metre wide. There is a gap between the counter and the east wall, which was filled by a masonry pillar. Together with a pillar 0,54 metre north of the counter it

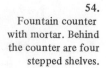

53.
Tavern 3. Main entrance
from Via di Diana, with
masonry benches on
either side.

54.
Fountain counter
with mortar. Behind
the counter are four
stepped shelves.

55.
Tavern 3. Wall painting
advertising fruit and
vegetables sold in the
tavern. Below the
painting are four
stepped shelves over
a side table.

53.

presumably created the base for a water-heater (see plan). This northern pillar now measures 0,34 by 0,56 metre, one metre high, and has at the northern edge a 0,36 by 0,14 metre, 0,12 metre high, addition, in the well-known pattern of water-heater bases. Gismondi's plan, sheet 8, indicates three other bases in the northeast corner, of which nothing is now left; the plan does not agree with the preserved masonry.

3. The best known of all Ostian taverns is the so-called *thermopolium* in Via di Diana (I ii 5). It was excavated in 1915 by Paribeni.[1] Excavations in this block had already begun in 1850, and as the *thermopolium* stands now it has been heavily, but cautiously, restored. The *taberna* has its façade on Via di Diana, which elsewhere (p. 119) has been claimed to be the property of the guild of the *lenuncularii*. It is one of the biggest taverns in Ostia (fig. 46). From Via di Diana one enters the main room (room 8 of the plan), passing between two benches that flank the entrance on the outside (fig. 53). The door is about as wide as the room, half of the entrance is blocked by the L-shaped bar counter, which has a water basin at the bottom of each of its two wings. At the time of the excavation a piece of lead water-pipe was still left in the south end of the counter, but it has now disappeared. Behind the counters and built up against the east wall are three stepped shelves; a mortar found in the tavern is placed on the counter top (fig. 54). In the middle of the same east wall is a marble side-table with a shelf under the table-top and three shelves built up against the wall, stepwise over the table-top. Over the side-table is a fresco showing vegetables

54.   55.

and fruits sold in the bar: green olives, a turnip, eggs or peaches in a glass with water (honey water if they are peaches), and two red cheese—or watermelons—hung from a nail.[2] It is worth noting that no meat is shown in this fresco (fig. 55).

The *taberna* to the right (on the west side, room 9 of the plan) was part of the bar. Paribeni called it the kitchen of the bar.[3] A *focus*, which may have been the base for a charcoal fire serving a water-heater or cooking in general, is built up against the east wall. Near the middle of the room, close to the west wall, is a huge storage jar, a *dolium*, dug into the ground. It is the type of jar found in wine or oil *horrea*; it would hold upwards of two hundred gallons. In this case it was presumably used for the wine that was part of the perennial *conditum*, the most frequently sold commodity in Roman bars. The *taberna* east of the main room may also have been part of the bar (room 11). Door openings lead from the main barroom and the eastern *taberna* out into an open courtyard with a small fountain, a square marble basin with a lead pipe in the middle from which a water jet must have shot up (room 10). The yard was walled on all sides, and a long masonry bench is built along the east wall. On the west side is a flight of stairs leading to a cool underground pantry with a marble shelf on the west wall, an arrangement which is seen elsewhere in Ostia and which Paribeni, at first, considered a sanctuary.

Of the various objects found in the bar during excavation (among them, fragments of small columns and terracotta lamps), only a long, narrow marble slab with three bronze

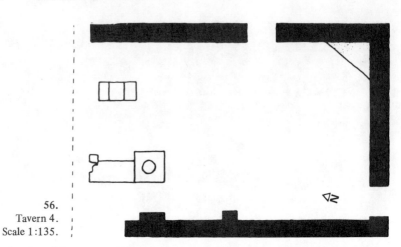

56.
Tavern 4.
Scale 1:135.

hooks is of interest. It completes the picture of the tavern and reminds us of the Pompeian wall-painting of guests in a *popina sellariola*,[4] which contains a long, narrow rack with spikes from which sausages, fruit, and other *cibaria* are suspended.

4. The tavern in I x 2 in the oldest part of the city, by the city market, in one of the oldest buildings, and dating to the time of Augustus, makes the most old-fashioned impression of all Ostian inns (fig. 56).[5] The whole *taberna* front is lost, but the façade line must have been 0,50 to 0,60 metre north of the old bar counter (fig. 57). The three walls to the east, south, and west are still preserved in heights varying from 0,40 to 2,30 metres. A door (1,04 metres) in the east wall connects with the next *taberna*, and another door in the southwest corner (one metre) opens into one in the south.

In the northwest corner is a well-head (1,02 by 1,03 metres), with a circular opening in the middle (0,48 metre), built in brick and tufa blocks, *tufelli* (fig. 58). The depth of the well is unknown. The distance from the top of the well-head to the water surface is 1,60 metres (Winter 1977). Below the top of the latest well-head (0,62 metre) is an older one in sandstone, which has been in use for a long time to judge from the rope marks along its edge, left by the rope used in drawing water. The addition to the well-head was made necessary when the Flavians raised the level of the city (see pp. 9-10).

A counter, built in the same material as the new well-head, extends from the well-head to the front of the *taberna*; the front of the *taberna* east of the inn indicates where the façade

57.

58.

59.

57.
Tavern 4. Facade on
the Decumanus.

58.
Tavern 4. Old well with
original counter.

59.
Tavern 4. In front, the
old well with counter;
in the background, the
newer fountain counter.

must have been. This counter measures 0,70 by 1,50 metres.
The northeast corner of the counter has been reinforced with a
fragment of a sculptured marble slab brought in from some
other building. Neither counter nor well-head are preserved to
a height (0,35 to 0,65 metre) which is near the original one; all
traces of stucco or marble covering, if any, have disappeared.

East of this well counter are the remains of an orthodox
bar counter with a vaulted basin in the base built of brick and
mortar (0,62 by 1,22 metres, fig. 59). Preserved are the vault
with part of the water basin (0,51 metre) and the two pillars,
which survive to unequal heights (up to 1,13 metres), while the
whole centre of the counter top above the vault and all covering, be it stucco or slab, are missing.

It would be fair to assume that the well with the counter in front of it represents an older phase of the tavern which goes back to the time before the construction of Claudius's aqueduct. Some time after the aqueduct had been built, a new bar fountain was installed in the bar and provided a welcome change from the brackish water of the well to the sweet (but hard) water from Acilia. Presumably, then, the well water was used only in emergencies or for other purposes than for the *conditum*.

5. On the east side of Via del Pomerio is a line of old *tabernae*[6] with a portico in front, so constructed that there is one column in line with each *taberna* wall (I x 2). In the third century the space between the *taberna* walls and the columns was walled in, so that the *tabernae* were extended all the way up to the street. The sixth *taberna* north of the guild seat of the *stuppatores*, by having these two 2,69-metre extensions added to the front, reached the dimensions of 10,52 by 4,50 metres. In the southeast corner are the remains of stairs to the *cenaculum* above, consisting of a landing (1,24 by 1 metres) with, according to Gismondi's plan, three steps in front. The individual steps cannot be seen now, but what remains fills a 0,86 by 0,90 metre area. In the northeast corner, 1,37 metres from the east wall, a short (1,45 metres) and thin (0,23 metre) partition wall was built, which now at its highest point is 0,85 metre.

On the extended part of the south wall are some paintings. That part of the wall shows the remains of three panels with a Victoria holding a wreath raised in her right hand; a mask; and a heifer or deer and a round tripod table, all painted in red on white ground, except the table, which is golden. The date of the painting could be about the middle of the third century.

Of special interest to this study, however, is the counter that Gismondi's plan shows on the left, inside the entrance and built up against the wall (fig. 60). It is the type of counter that is repeated several times in other places (see following tavern numbers 8, 16, 20, 21, and 23). In all these places Gismondi uses the same symbol as in this number 5, and the counters are all there to allow a comparison between the symbol and the real thing. It is obvious that at the time this *taberna* was excavated a

60.
Tavern 5 is only remembered thanks to
Gismondi's plan. Its location across from
the Macellum and the fish market and
a few steps south of the Decumanus
seems ideal for a tavern.

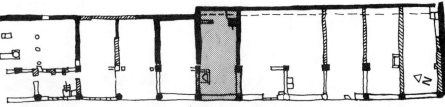

Via del Pomerio

similar construction existed here. A slight elevation in the
ground where it was located is all that is left. Gismondi's plan
is the sole evidence of that counter; the location across from the
macellum, the fish market, and the very busy corner of the
Decumanus leaves no doubt that this was a tavern.

6. The Forum Baths bar is at the west end of the palaestra
of the Forum Baths. It is located on the northeast corner of
housing block I xii 10, which is built between the Cardo Maximus and the palaestra and is shaded by a portico on the east
side. One enters from the north side as well as from the east
side through wide *taberna* doors, both with travertine doorsteps
(fig. 61). The one from the north is partly blocked by a bar
counter (3 by 0,50 metres) built in block and brick, with a barrel
vault over the 0,82-metre basin. It seems to be a product of the
third century. It has been somewhat restored, and fragments of
white marble slabs have been reattached to the counter top and
sides as covering. A mortar has been fastened to the counter
top (fig. 62). There were two openings to the room on the west
side of the barroom and a wide opening to the room to the
south.

In Via delle Terme del Mithra are two taverns (I xvi 1) in
comfortable proximity of the Baths of Mithras:

7. The first one is the first *taberna* on the right side of Via
delle Terme del Mithra. It is one deep room (9,40 by 4,30
metres); in the southeast corner there is a 1,47-metre opening
leading to the room on the corner of Via delle Terme del Mithra

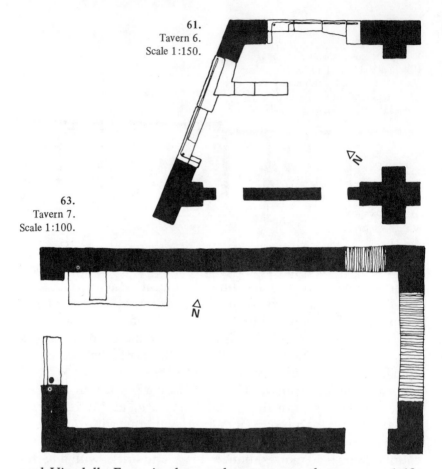

61.
Tavern 6.
Scale 1:150.

63.
Tavern 7.
Scale 1:100.

and Via della Foce; in the northeast corner there was a 1,18-metre opening which was later blocked. In the eastern wall was a 3,05-metre opening which was later walled in with *tufelli* in *opus reticulatum* over a platband. Of the front doorstep only the southern end (1,34 metres), with a cut-out for a *cardo* door, has been preserved (fig. 63).

Two things indicate that this was a bar. First, right inside the *taberna* door, on the north side, there is a pile of rubble, the east end of which is preserved well enough to give the measurements of the counter at 2,90 by 1 metres, and, approximately *in situ*, two marble slabs, which were the components of the water basin. Second, among the rubble found in this tavern are three fragments of a mortar (displayed on top of the pile of

62.
Tavern 6. Counter built over the front step; mortar on the counter.

64.
Tavern 7. Remains of counter, with the marble slabs of the water basin. Three fragments of a mortar are on top of the rubble pile.

rubble in fig. 64). The location of the plundered and vandalized counter at the entrance to the *taberna* and the presence of a mortar can hardly be understood, unless this place was a bar.

8. Three doors farther north is the second bar. The room is about the same size as the previous one (9,50 by 4,25 metres), and in the southeast corner there is a doorway which connects with the adjoining *taberna* to the south (fig. 65). Built up against the north wall and blocking part of the entrance is a bar counter (1,05 by 1,40 metres, one metre high), with a basin below and three stepped shelves above. The shelves are now rather dilapidated (fig. 66). Gismondi's plan (sheet 2) shows that the middle of the shelves was recessed in a half circle, of which few traces now remain. Farther off the entrance, close to the south

65.
Tavern 8.
Scale 1:100.

66.
Tavern 8. Counter
with water basin.

67.
Tavern 8. A big tufa
container dug into
the ground is in the
way of a *dolium
defossum.*

68.
Tavern 9.
Scale 1:200.

wall, is a tufa storage jar partly dug into the ground. Its size is
considerable: 0,90 metre across the top and 0,48 metre deep. Its
purpose is not clear (fig. 67).

9. In II ii 2 (east), with entrance from Via dei Magazzini
Repubblicani, there was a bar (fig. 68). The building is basically
from the time of Hadrian, with repairs and changes from the
middle of the third century.[7] The bar is a rather deep room
(9,15 by 5,65 metres). A 2,92-metre-wide door is the entrance;
two rectangular pillars, 5 metres from the entrance, divide the
barroom in half. In the rear wall, at the southwest corner, a
door opening (1,02 metres) has been cut crudely through the
wall at a later date, without being finished. In the corner to the
left inside the door and built up against the east wall was the

66.

67.

68.

bar counter, the bar fountain with a shelf on top. Today, there is only a pile of dirt and rubble in that corner, but on Gismondi's map (sheet 5) it is shown in the form that is well known from other counters in Ostia (see previous no. 5). This *taberna* is located in a place where one would expect to see a bar, near the Baths of the *cisiarii* and the busy square of the Porta Romana.

10. In II ii 2 (west), in the same house as no. 9, there is a tavern in the street between the Horrea Antoniniana and the Baths of the *cisiarii* (fig. 69). The front step goes from wall to wall (4,85 metres). Its central section is missing and the south end section (1,04 metres) has a cut-out and a *cardo* hole for a door while the northern section (2,22 metres) is grooved to

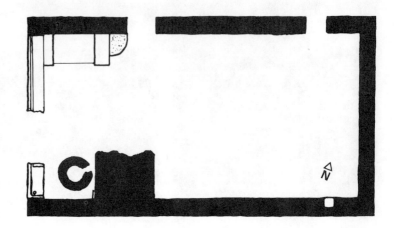

70.
Tavern 10 viewed from
the street.

71.
Tavern 10. Remains
of counter with water
basin.

72.
Tavern 10. *Dolium
defossum*. Behind
it are remains
of an undetermined
structure.

73.
Tavern 10. Lamp niche
in southeast corner.

accommodate the *taberna* shutter (fig. 70). To the left, inside the door opening, are two upright sides of a bar counter which measures 1,94 by 0,90 metres and about 0,88 metre high, with space at the bottom for a 1,23 by 0,90 metre water basin (fig. 71). The corner between the right side of the bar fountain and the wall is filled by a short pillar rounded on the outside; next comes a 0,88-metre-wide door opening, a rough, late work. At the east end of the same wall is another door opening, 0,66 metre wide.

On the right side, inside the door, is seen the top of a *dolium* which is dug into the ground so that the rim is level with the surface. The diameter of the rim is one metre, with a 0,59-metre opening in the middle; about a quarter metre of the rim is

70.   71.

72.   73.

missing on the east side (fig. 72). Immediately behind the
dolium, further into the room and built up against the south
wall, are the remains of a brick structure, the dimensions of
which can be measured along the south wall (1,77 metres) but
which diminish in height from south to north, so that the
south-north extension cannot be measured precisely (1,30 to
1,40 metres). This structure may have been covered with marble slabs, a fragment of which (0,25 metre wide, 0,06 metre
thick, height cannot be stated) is left at the bottom of the inner
corner on the west side; this piece is moulded and shows traces
of red paint on the outside. It is probably the structure which
Kleberg calls *fourneau* (*Hôtels* 43). The measurements in Gismondi's plan (sheet 5) do not correspond with the dimensions

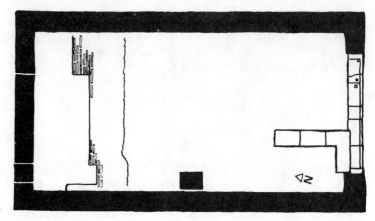

74.
Tavern 11. The profile
of the north wall is
drawn at the north
end.
Scale 1:120.

which can be verified today. In the back of the room, 0,72 metre from the east wall, there is a 0,30-metre-wide and 0,31-metre-high lamp niche in the south wall, one metre above the floor (fig. 73). The depth of the tavern room is 9,50 metres (by 4,88 metres wide), so that lighting would be needed early in the cavernous deep of the tavern, especially since the street in front is very narrow and light must have been shut out by the *horrea* on the other side of the street.

This bar is Kleberg no. 3. When he described it in 1934, he could record details that have disappeared now. Besides the *fourneau* mentioned above, and which may have been a second bar counter or a *focus*, Kleberg saw *tuyauterie*, of which no trace is left.

11. There is a bar on the eastern Decumanus, with entrance from the Portico del Tetto Spiovente (II ii 6), in the fourth *taberna* west of the Mithraeum (fig. 74). The doorstep is still there, with a 0,78-metre bed and *cardo* hole for a swinging door cut out at the east end and a groove cut for the *taberna* shutter. The room is 10,10 by 5,15 metres. The L-shaped bar counter (3,10 by 0,85 metres), with a 0,85-metre basin at the base, is placed in the orthodox position inside the door on the left side (fig. 75). The leg of the bar counter presents a 1,35-metre façade on the street. Against the west wall, 4,62 metres north of the south wall, a tufa block (0,62 by 0,72 metres, 0,48 metre high) has been set up, which may have helped to support a *focus*. In the back wall, Gismondi's plan shows a window

75.
Tavern 11 seen from
the Decumanus.

opening at the east end and a loophole at the west end. What can be seen now is a 0,66-metre window opening; of the east window only the east side is left (see profile of north wall on fig. 74).

Outside the barracks of the *vigiles* (II v 1) there were three bars: two on the south side of the entrance, one north of it. All that is left of the walls is the outline, given by a shallow foundation with one or two courses of a brick wall and best preserved around the central bar. Whether the two southern bars actually were one or two is uncertain, but since there seems to have been a solid, common wall without a door opening between the two and since there is little connection in the patterns of the two mosaic floors it is likely that they were two bars.

12. All three bars are built as lean-tos to the barracks of the *vigiles*. On the barracks' walls are marks of their beams and roof tiles that have been fastened with cement. The southern bar (no. 12) has a simple, black mosaic floor; in its southwest corner is written, with white *tesserae,* "ΠΡΟΚΛΟΣ / ΕΠΟΙ-CEN" ("Proklos made it" or "Proklos had it made") in a white frame (*tabula ansata,* fig. 76); the inscription is so oriented that it is best read by whoever enters from the east.[8] Becatti dates the mosaic floors in this and the following bar to the first years of the second century.[9]

76.
Tavern 12. Southwest
corner of mosaic floor
with inscription.

13. The central bar has a black mosaic floor; in the middle of it is a chalice designed in white mosaic line-drawing and framed by a double-mosaic-line rectangular frame (fig. 77). The chalice is viewed upright by someone entering from the north and coming from the entrance of the barracks. In the southwest corner, close to the wall of the barracks and facing east, is written with white *tesserae* in a single rectangular frame "[Pro]CLVS/FECIT M C S I" ("Proculus, soldier of the cohort, made it at his own expense").[10]

14. The northern bar is paved with white *tesserae* with a few black ones accidentally thrown in. A picture of a chalice is set in the middle of the floor in black *tesserae,* surrounded by a black double-*tessera,* rectangular frame, which again is set inside a big five-*tessera,* rectangular frame; this outer frame is so large that, inside it, there is space for a smaller rectangular frame above the framed chalice and a broad, black mosaic band below it (fig. 78). The picture of the chalice is turned so that it is seen correctly by someone entering from the south, coming from the entrance of the barracks.

The three bars are by far the smallest bars in Ostia; their measurements are (north-south by east-west): no. 12, 2,28 by 1,90 metres; no. 13, 3,20 by 1,90 metres; no. 14, 3,52 by 1,95 metres. The only indication that these three rooms were bars are the pictures of the chalices, a decoration which is also found in other bars (no. 15 and no. 32), and their location at the barracks. The way the entrances to the bars are designed, if one

77.

78.

77.
Tavern 13. Mosaic floor
seen from the north.

78.
Tavern 14. Mosaic floor
seen from the south.

79.
Tavern 15. Mosaic floor
seen from the east.

79.

can judge from the orientation of the decorations, shows that
the bars were established to cater to the *vigiles*. They could have
made use of that catering service, since there were not less than
four hundred *vigiles* stationed in Ostia.

The inscription "Proclusfecit M. C. S. I." most likely
should be read "Proclus fecit m(iles) c(ohortis) s(ua)
i(mpensa)." For the not uncommon extension of MC as *miles
cohortis*, see the inscriptions in *CIL* XIV 214; S4509, 4 and 6;
S4526 c, which all come out of the barracks of the *vigiles* in
Ostia. "S(ua) i(mpensa)" was proposed by Vaglieri.[8]

The inscriptions indicate that the person who laid the
mosaic floors, or had them laid, did not own the place; no
property owner will stress that he himself paid for improve-

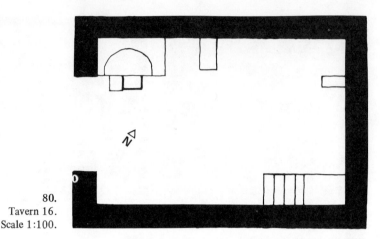

80.
Tavern 16.
Scale 1:100.

ments on his property. The situation is analogous to the one in Piazzale delle Corporazioni, where several groups laid mosaic floors *de suo*. This again indicates that the two or three bars at the barracks were held as a concession, comparable to the concessions at the amphitheatre of Pompeii: "Permissu aedilium Cn. Aninius Fortunatus occup[at]" ("Held by Gnaeus Aninius Fortunatus by leave of the aediles," *CIL* IV 1096) is an example; 1096 b and c, 1097 a to c, and 1115 are other examples, to which more could be added.

Did the *vigil,* or ex-*vigil,* Proclus hold the concession to the two southern bars that have his name written in the mosaic? The words *Proclus fecit sua impensa* or *Proklos epoiesen* certainly reveal his economic interest in the bar. J. C. M. Toynbee sees Proclus as an itinerant Greek mosaic layer; Becatti calls him the "mosaicista che rivela un greculo."[11]

The expression that *Proclus epoiesen* or *fecit* does not necessarily imply that he did it with his own hands, and neither does the inscription necessarily say that he was a mosaic layer. It says, however, that he was a *miles cohortis,* that is a *vigil,* and although we shall hardly ever know the complete story of Proclus's involvement with the bars in front of the *vigiles'* station in Ostia, he appears at the time of the laying of the mosaic floor to be the concessionaire of the bars, after an arrangement with his superiors and, perhaps, also the Curia.

15. Where the portico of the Baths of Neptune meets Via della Fontana the bar of Fortunatus is located (II vi 1). The

81.
Tavern 16. Tavern
fountain counter with
overflow basin in front.

direct access from the Decumanus to Via della Fontana has
been blocked by the bar, and a bypass was established east of
the bar. There is a wide *taberna* entrance from the portico from
the south, with a travertine threshold, and there is a narrow
door from the east from the bypass, a wide window opening in
the north wall, and a narrower one in the west wall. The whole
bar measures 6 metres north-south and 4,60 metres east-west.

There is nothing left to prove that this was a bar, except
the fragments of the mosaic floor: a coarse white mosaic, on
which is reproduced a chalice in black *tesserae*, with the inscription, "[. . .]Fortunatus/[. . .]atera quod sitis/Bi" (picture of
chalice "Be," fig. 79). Vaglieri supplements the inscription:
"[hospes inquit] Fortunatus [vinum e cr]atera quod sitis bibe"
("The host Fortunatus says: drink wine from the crather if you
are thirsty").[12] This mosaic, combined with the location in the
portico, close to the baths, seems to remove all doubt that this
was a bar.

16. On the east side of Via delle Corporazioni, exposed to
the afternoon sun, is a bar measuring 6,85 by 4,45 metres (II vi
5); four steps and a landing (1,27 metres high), built in masonry
in the southeast corner, indicate that the innkeeper had an
upstairs *cenaculum* (fig. 80). In the left corner, right inside the
entrance (2,65 metres), is the bar counter (1,88 by 1 metres, 1,20
metres high) with a water basin (1,25 by 0,77 metres, with
rounded back wall, fig. 81). Most likely there were shelves on
its top. The water basin is interesting in that a smaller basin

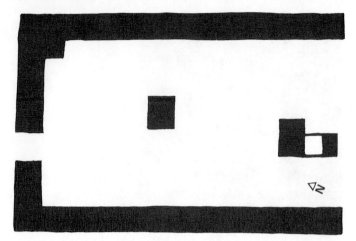

82.
Tavern 17.
Scale 1:110.

(0,50 by 0,35 metres) built in marble slabs is installed in front of it to take up the overflow of water. To the west of it is a 0,36 by 0,36 metre base. On the north wall, one metre from the counter, are remains of a pillar (0,85 by 0,45 metres), which, together with the side of the counter, must have supported a *focus* for cooking or for a water heater. In the back of the room, built against the east wall and exactly one metre from the north wall, there is the lower part of another pillar (0,64 by 0,28 metres), whose purpose cannot be determined. Gismondi's plan in this place indicates what may have been a bigger basin, of which, however, all traces have now disappeared.

17. A tavern is established in II ix 2 on the Decumanus, in the second *taberna* east of the small temple on the corner of Via dei Molini (fig. 82). Not much is left of the tavern except the bar counter (0,75 metre at the north end, 0,45 metre at the south end, by 1,62 metres long), with a barrel vault for the water basin (fig. 83). It is built of brick and placed as close to the street as possible, to the left in the entrance. It is stripped of most of its stucco covering and seems now to stand somewhat high, because the present ground level is lower than the ancient floor level.

The entrance to this bar is nearly as wide as the whole room. The doorstep has disappeared completely. The room measures 8,75 by 5,05 metres. In the rear wall (at the north end) is a 0,99-metre-wide door opening to a back room. The bar-

83.
Tavern 17. Fountain
counter in the entrance,
seen from the
Decumanus.

room is divided in the middle, both ways, by a 0,73 by 0,54 metre brick pillar.

18. Although this bar (III i 10) is known only in its fourth-century version, its roots go back to Trajanic days. It has a place in the architectural expansion of northwestern Ostia, which followed immediately after the construction of Portus. Here Trajan tried in a hurry to create cheap accommodation for some of the many people who suddenly flocked to Ostia. It is the kind of habitation for which the name Casette-tipo, "standard housing," has been coined. This development (III i 9, 10, 12, 13) covers a considerable area in northwest Ostia. It is not without a certain impersonal, paramilitary appearance, and it is difficult not to think of an imperial master plan for it all. Becatti describes the development in *Scavi di Ostia* I.[13] To his list of examples should be added III xvi 4 for its spare motel-like plan, which seems to have been repeated in a different place in Ostia, in the east wing of Caseggiato del Temistocle. In this last case the plan was abandoned in the third century, and the rooms were distributed in four apartments.

The special building complex that interests us here, III i 9-10, is the most grandiose of them all. It seems to be a precursor for the Case a Giardino in that three (four) wings surround an area in which an *insula* has been built but the major part of that area is still left open, presumably with some greenery in it. It is understandable that in an area with such a concentration of

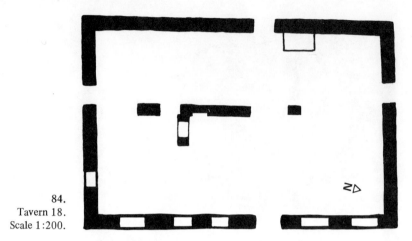

84.
Tavern 18.
Scale 1:200.

people and with limited facilities for housekeeping, as it appears, there must have been a need for public catering. Some of the buildings that we are looking at may have been hotels. There can be little doubt, then, that the ground floor—the whole ground floor—of III i 10 was a bar or restaurant.

One enters from the east through a wide (1,42 metres) main door (fig. 84). Besides the door there are five windows in the east façade. The room inside is 14,90 metres long, measured along the east wall, and 13,95 metres along the west wall; it measures 8,25 metres across at the north end and 9,24 metres at the south end, tapering off from south to north. The room is divided from south to north by a row of four pillars that are the same distance from the west wall (3,63 to 3,79 metres), but the northernmost one is over one metre closer to the east wall than the last one in the south end.

The bar counter is the barrel-vaulted type and is built out from one of the pillars so that it stretches full length into the room (fig. 85). It measures 1,64 by 0,55 metres, is 1,10 metres high, and has a 0,90-metre basin. There are water-pipes leading up to the counter from the northeast as well as from the south; a primitive drain takes the overflow away, directs it under the pillar, and continues as a somewhat makeshift covered drain on the west side of the pillar, running in a northern direction. There is a mosaic floor in most of the bar, of different patterns that indicate an original separation into three different rooms.

85.
Tavern 18. Fountain
counter. At the bottom
of the basin are two
lead pipes. A break
in the floor to the
right of the counter
shows a lead pipe lead-
ing up to the counter.
Cf. fig. 133.

Across from the main entrance there is a narrower (1,16 metres) door opening to Via Calcara. Right north of the door is a second 1,60 by 0,90 metre water basin, of which only the bottom remains. The south wall has a window and a door (one metre); the door was cut in unceremoniously at a later time and never finished, and a similar door (1,05 metres) was cut in the north wall. Both of them were more for the convenience of the western half of the bar, their distance from the west wall being, respectively, 2,95 and 2,40 metres. There is no evidence of a *focus*, but the abundance of water shows that the place could handle many people, and it is only matched by the bigger bars like Alexander Helix's or the Diana bar.

North of this inn in what must have been an *angiportus* an extra fountain is built in front of the wall. A piece of lead pipe was still left in its north wall as late as the summer of 1975, when it must have fallen to a souvenir hunter.

19. When the handsome Casa delle Volte Dipinte (III v 1) was built in the time of Hadrian (about A.D. 125-128), there was a *taberna* in the northern corner of the building.[14] This *taberna* was equipped as a bar in the third century, if it was not already a bar differently equipped.[15]

The evidence suggests that the Casa was probably a hotel. First, all the rooms on the ground floor were equipped with doorsteps with *cardo* holes that could be locked individually, and that points very much in the direction of a hotel, especially since the doors all open to a long corridor through the centre of

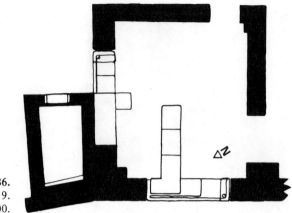

86.
Tavern 19.
Scale 1:100.

the house. The only exception is what may have been the man-
ager's apartment immediately south of the *taberna*: the inner
door between his two rooms shows no *cardo* holes in the doorstep. Private apartments in Ostia demonstrate that there was
only an outer entrance door and, in larger apartments, a door
which could close off the family's inner sanctum. There were
no other doors. Secondly, both floors of the Casa have a
kitchen, a bath, and a latrine, which makes it look still more
like a hotel. It offered a traveller all the animal comfort he
needed. The cooking facilities were especially important since
travellers bought and cooked their own meals.[16]

The identification of the Casa delle Volte Dipinte with a
hotel looks more convincing when it is considered that its
closest neighbour to the north across the street, the so-called
Insula Trapezoidale (III iv 1), could have been a *stabulum*.[17] In
antiquity the same professions, like the guilds, would seek the
same locations.

One enters the barroom from both streets, from northeast
as well as from northwest (fig. 86). There is a full doorstep in
the northwest entrance, with a 0,70-metre cut-out and a *cardo*
hole for a door and a groove for the sliding shutter. At 4,35 by
3,71 metres, it is one of the smaller bars in Ostia. The bar
counter at 2,45 by 0,55 metres (1,10 metres high) occupies half
of the length of the room (fig. 87). The counter is built in brick
and covered with marble slabs, of which much is still preserved, and it has the usual water basin at the bottom. Right

87.

88.

87.
Tavern 19. Counter
seen from the north-
west entrance.

88.
Tavern 19. *Lacus*, with
opening for drawing
water.

89.
Tavern 19. Bar counter,
with barman's narrow
entrance.

89.

outside the northeast corner of the Casa was added a fountain, a covered *lacus,* from which water was piped into the bar. Before the building of the *lacus,* the northeast entrance of the bar had been reduced from 2,64 metres to 1,20 metres and closed with a brick and block wall. The wall was built on top of the doorstep, burying more than half of it.

The *lacus* outside the bar is not a very careful job (fig. 88). It is badly out of line with the façade of the Casa, and the basin is not squared off. It was added sometime in the fourth century, after the brick and block wall had been built. At 2,70 by 1,85 metres, it compares in size with, for example, the *lacus* in Casa di Diana, and apparently it looked after the water supply of the neighbourhood, including the bar and the *stabulum* in

90.
Tavern 20. Counter
with stepped shelves;
the indented pattern
of the shelves has been
preserved in the
restoration.

front of the Casa. For this purpose, an opening like a window was installed in the traditional way in its east wall and was framed with travertine, which had been recovered from other buildings; the top piece of the frame had been a doorstep. Through this window, which is 1,15 metres above the ground, they dipped water needed for people and horses. A smaller basin inside the staircase of the Casa delle Volte Dipinte may have taken care of the kitchens and baths in the house.

Inside the bar a square brick pillar is built up against the brick and block wall as an addition to the bar counter and is separated from it by an opening that allowed the barman to get behind the counter (fig. 89). The floor in front of the counter is paved with *bipedales*, the rest of the floor with yellow brick in the herringbone pattern, *opus spicatum*.

There are stucco patches on all walls, with some red and white paint. Bianca Maria Felletti Maj has studied all the paintings in the Casa delle Volte Dipinte.[18] The interesting part of the decoration of the bar is the picture on the southwest wall. It is very mutilated, but the following can be seen: to the left is what looks like an *aedicula* with an urn(?) and a lid equipped with a knob handle. In front of the *aedicula* stands a young man in a yellow toga. He stretches his right arm toward the urn, with the palm of his hand turned upward. He faces a group of three men who are moving toward him, two of them with their right hands held out. The third man may have held his hand out in the same way, but since most of his body from the knees

91.
Tavern 21. Remains of
counter. The shelf pat-
tern is similar to that
of tavern 20.

up has been lost, along with half of his face, we cannot know
the position of his hand. He wears a cape with a *cucullus*.
Above the *aedicula* is written:

[. . .]ELICIS
[. . .]ONE . CA[. . .]

Above the three men in the group is written, respectively:

[. . .]VIOL IA[. . .]   AGATETUC[he . . .]   SEX PERPERNA
TADA . PANE[. . .]

Next a young man appears with a wreath around his head. He
is dressed in a tunic, with some garment slung over his left
shoulder, and is turning away from the previous group,
toward the centre of the picture: a *clipeus* where a bearded,
Antoninus Pius-type man is depicted. This man is shown in a
shoulder portrait and is dressed in a tunic. Below him is written
"[Pa?] NCRESTU[s]." To the right of the *clipeus,* on a lower
level but higher than the other people, there is a girl's(?) head,
above which is written "IODOTE." Then a wall of a house and
a balcony appear. One person must have been on the balcony;
Felletti Maj listed his hand, which held something and can still
be distinguished. A third person, of whom only the right third
had been saved, was addressing the person on the balcony and
was raising his right hand while his left hand was holding an

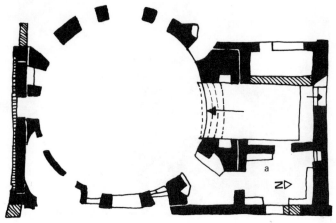

92.
Tavern 22, in the Baths
of the Seven Sages.
The tavern (a) was
converted into an *apody-
terium* equipped with
benches along the three
walls and had direct
access to the rotunda
of the baths.
Scale 1:250.

unguentarium. Above the railing of the balcony is part of an inscription, "[. . .] ALTANA IS[. . .]."

The fresco is too fragmented to make sense, and the inscriptions are too laconic and mutilated to give any information. It is even doubtful that a well-preserved fresco could have told us something: it seems to address a very inside group. One could ask what this picture is doing in this particular bar. Felletti Maj has dated this picture to the time of Antoninus Pius, "maybe toward the middle of the century" ("*verso la metà del secolo*," o.l. 31). She differs only slightly from van Essen's dating in Bullettino Comunale 76 (Roma 1956-58, 157): about A.D. 140.

That is one date. But on the other hand, the bar, as we know it now, cannot have been opened up till later. It was hardly begun before the wall that reduced the door opening in the southeast wall had been built. Felletti Maj compares its masonry with the *opus vittatum* of the Domus di Amore e Psiche, which she dates to "maybe the second half of the third century" (o.l. 31). This date seems a little early compared to the customary date of the beginning of the fourth century (*ScO* I 238). This is a minor discrepancy, because it will be clear, anyway, that there is a wide time gap between the wall decorations and the beginning of the bar. The find of a Maximinus Thrax coin in the mortar of the tavern counter during recent repairs (*NSc* XXIV, 1970 Supplement 42) does not contribute much to the dating. It gives a *terminus post quem* (A.D. 235) but not much

93.
Ceiling of tavern 22.
Note the two wine jars.
Scale 1:630.

more, because coins in the Roman world had a long life. The paintings, then, have nothing to do with the bar, and their presence in the bar offers no help to interpret them—presumably not even if a case could be made for the existence of a previous bar in the same *taberna* but differently equipped.

20. Outside the Porta Marina, on the west side of the street, are two bars that are built in the same style and installed in the same house (III vii 3). The better preserved of the two is the southern one, located immediately south of the entrance to the Domus Fulminata. It is just one deep room (9,50 by 3,45 metres) with a door opening nearly as wide as the whole room. In the door opening, partly blocking the entrance, is the bar counter (1,84 by 0,90 metres), built in brick with three stepped shelves on top. The two upper shelves are deeply indented in the centre (fig. 90).

21. The other bar is the second *taberna* north of the entrance to Domus Fulminata. It has about the same dimensions as its sister to the south (no. 20), 9,30 by 3,80 metres. The bar counter is placed inside the entrance to the left, in the same pattern as no. 20. Only the inner pillar with the corresponding part of the three stepped shelves and the water basin is left. It comes out 1,38 metres from the south wall and was originally 1,77 metres long (fig. 91).

22. In the Baths of the Seven Sages (III x 2) there may have been a bar (fig. 92). There is nothing left of the bar but some pictures on the walls and the ceiling. These pictures were

94.
Tavern 23. The entrance
from the outside is
through the wide door
opening to the south-
east. The doors to
the northwest and
southwest lead to the
many rooms behind
the tavern.
Scale 1:110.

painted in a *taberna* in a Trajanic building, with entrance from Via Calcara. When the Trajanic building was torn down, part of this *taberna* was integrated into the Hadrianic Baths of the Seven Sages. Equipped with benches along the walls, it served as an *apodyterium*. The difference between this *apodyterium* and others is that this one has decorations of a non-balneal character on the walls. High up on the southwest wall the two Greek Sages Solon and Thales are depicted, and on the northeast wall, at the northwest corner, is Chilon; each figure is sitting in his chair. Above the head of each is written a line of his good advice to the public on how to improve digestion and elimination. There would be plenty of space on the rest of the walls for the missing Sages; that the frieze continued is shown by the word "Prieneus" on the northeast wall, at the northern corner. Below the line of Sages there was a lower line, which is now very fragmentary. On the southwest and the northwest walls, round the northwest corner, are four heads, painted on a smaller scale than the Sages and accompanied by some inscriptions, now mutilated. In a frieze above the Sages, of which most has been lost, one sees wine jars in jar stands, one on the southwest wall and two on the northwest wall; above one of the latter is the word "Falernum." On the ceiling are two more wine jars.[19]

What has suggested that this was a bar are the decorations on the walls, especially the wine jugs on the walls and ceiling (fig. 93). Was it a bar? Not the pictures of the Seven Sages with their rowdy humour but the pictures of the wine jugs would be

95.
Tavern 23. Tavern
counter with remains
of stepped shelves. The
masonry points toward
the early fourth cent-
ury. The wall painting,
which was covered by
the counter, is from
the third century.

the only hint. All the criteria, however, on which we depend
for identification of bars have disappeared. It was certainly not
a bar after its integration into the baths.[20]

23. In the northeast corner of III xiv 1, in a building from
the time of Antoninus Pius,[21] there may have been a bar. It is
located on the corner of Via tecta degli Aurighi and Via sud
delle Casette Tipo, with entrance from Via tecta degli Aurighi.

This *taberna* is distinguished by its smallness: it measures
north-south 4,15 metres by east-west 3,68 metres (fig. 94). In
the southwest corner a fountain counter is built against the wall
so that it covered the third-century wall decorations (fig. 95).
The counter measures 1,35 by 1,02 metres with a 0,95 by 0,86-
metre basin.

Via tecta degli Aurighi does not seem to have been a public thoroughfare: there is a doorstep with a door-check at both
ends of it. But there is direct access from the *angiportus* between
the Baths of the Seven Sages and the Casa degli Aurighi, with
its big latrine on the corner. Other bars in this district are one
on the corner of Cardo degli Aurighi and Via di Annio (no. 24),
one on the corner of Via del Serapide and Via della Foce
(no. 25), and one in the housing plant east of the Baths of the
Seven Sages (no. 18). Despite this, the location so close to the
Baths, which apparently was a well-frequented place, looks
like an attractive position.

There is, however, no other evidence that this was a bar
than, possibly, the counter. It is a bar-style counter, as evi-
denced by the stepped shelves, but its position is uncommon,

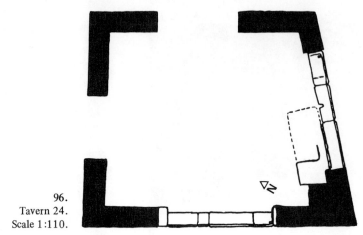

96.
Tavern 24.
Scale 1:110.

if not unseen, since it is placed in the back of the room, far from
the entrance. This type of counter usually had to have been
combined with a wooden counter close to the entrance. But the
wing where the bar is located has the character of an industrial
building: the low vaults, the bake oven, the huge, round
storage jars, and the rectangular vats seen in bakeries (for
example, in Via dei Molini). In all, there are twelve rooms that
have inside connections, and it seems that all the equipment
was installed at about the same time, after the middle of the
third century, since it covers the wall decorations.[22] The bar
fountain could have been set up for the working crew, if there
was a big one, and its placement would have been more cove-
nient for people who approach it from inside the building than
from without. The small dimensions of the place would be no
objection, because there are smaller places in Ostia. The problem is whether this fountain served the general public or a
closed group of people.

24. In Annius's House (III xiv 4), on the corner of Cardo
degli Aurighi and Via di Annio there is a *taberna* (5,90 metres
north-south by 5,35 metres east-west), with entrances from
both streets and with wide doors to the rooms north and east of
the *taberna* (fig. 96). The entrance from the south is partly
blocked by a structure in masonry, now badly decayed, which
in length can be measured at 2,40 metres and in width at the
east end at 1,10 metres (fig. 97). In the middle of this structure,
Gismondi's plan (sheet 6) indicates a rectangular basin, compa-

97.
Tavern 24. Remains
of counter in southern
door opening. The
southern wall of water
basin is preserved for
about half of its ori-
ginal length.

rable to the ones in Alexander Helix's bar (no. 32, figs. 110, 113). This basin, however, can hardly be verified today.

The southern doorstep measures 3,65 metres; it is the standard *taberna* doorstep with a groove for the shutter and, at the east end, space and *cardo* hole for a swinging door. The counter takes up 1,95 metres of this door space. The position of this structure to the left in the entrance points to a bar counter and combined with the location of the *taberna* it suggests a bar.

25. A *taberna* on the corner of Via della Foce and Via del Serapide (III xvii 5) has a wide *taberna* entrance (4,07 metres) from the portico on the north side (fig. 98). This entrance still has its doorstep, with a groove for the shutter and space cut out for a 0,67-metre *cardo* door, at the east end and to the left when one enters. Another door opening, 2,99 metres wide, with a 0,35-metre fragment of the doorstep at the north, gave access from Via del Serapide. The *taberna* measures 5,60 metres north-south and five metres east-west. In the south wall there is a 1,01-metre door to a *subscalare*, and a 0,95-metre door in the southwest corner to a western room.

Gismondi's plan (sheet 1) gives the outline of a structure positioned in the right side of the northern entrance and pointed into the room from the doorstep, which reached over halfway toward the rear wall, about 3,50 metres. Every trace of that structure has disappeared today; not even an elevation in the ground can be seen. But since Gismondi's outlines are

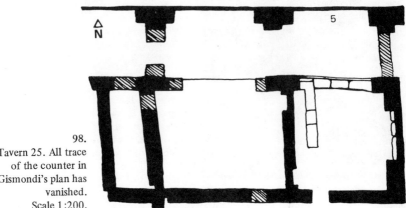

98.
Tavern 25. All trace
of the counter in
Gismondi's plan has
vanished.
Scale 1:200.

identical to the ones that are shown in nos. 1, 2, 6, 11, 19, 26, and 27, all containing orthodox bar counters, it is probable that the vanished structure in III xvii 5 was a bar counter. Again, the street-corner location, combined with the placement of the counter, is a strong indication that this *taberna* was a bar.

26. The bar of the Baths of the Pharus (IV ii 3) is the first bar inside the Porta Laurentina and must have drawn its customers partly from the visitors entering the city and partly from the clients of the Baths of the Pharus (fig. 99). A side door in the entrance to the Baths opens into the bar; the *taberna* front, however, is on the portico on the Cardo Maximus, facing northeast. In the northwest wall there is a narrow opening into a *subscalare*; in the southwest wall a door opening, later closed with brick. The bar counter is set up in the door opening on the Cardo Maximus, parallel with the northwest wall, so that there is working space for the barman between the counter and the wall.

The bar counter is covered with marble slabs of different colours and grains; the water basin is conspicuous in that it protrudes into the room in front of the counter—the only one of this type found in Ostia (fig. 100). In the northwest corner are the remains of two marble shelves supported by a brick pier on the outside and by grooves in the wall on the inside, the equivalent of stepped shelves in other bars. The floor is covered by a mosaic of an indiscriminate mixture of black and white *tesserae*. It should be noted that a mortar was found in this bar.

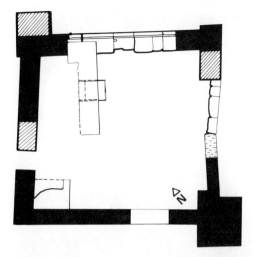

99.
Tavern 26.
Scale 1:115.

27. Five doorways north of the entrance to the Baths of the Pharus is the second bar on the Cardo Maximus (IV ii 3, fig. 101). A wide *taberna* door gives access from the portico, and the bar counter is placed in the back of the room toward the southwest corner. In the corner are shelves of marble slabs, two on the southwest wall and two on the southeast wall. The counter is in the usual style, with a water basin under a barrel vault that is covered with grayish and pink marble slabs, has gray as a base, and on which pink panels are divided by white marble bands, all heavily fragmented and restored. The floor is covered by a black and white mosaic, originally set in a pattern of white circles on a black background; later on, after repairs, the *tesserae* were laid back without plan or pattern. One notes that the floor has been broken up to repair the water line leading up to the bar-counter basin (fig. 102); for this repair the workmen broke through an undisturbed part of the floor where the original pattern of the mosaic was preserved, and when they filled and closed the ditch they simply relaid the *tesserae* in a disorderly way, without any thought of the original plan. In front of the bar counter there is a drain-hole with its ancient marble cover. On the walls are patches of stucco with yellow and red paint.

As well as the entrance from the portico, there is another in the northwest wall, providing access from the *angiportus*. In the southwest wall is a wide opening. Mosaic flooring covers the whole opening, which indicates that there was no door; a door would have needed a doorstep, and it is fair to conclude

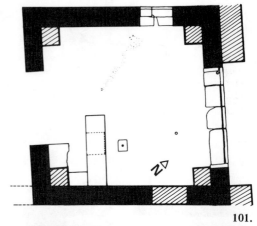

100.   101.

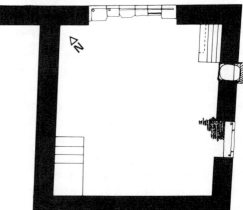

103.

that the back room was part of the tavern. In the northeast
corner of the back room are the remains of a brick pavement in
the herringbone pattern. Moreover, there is a door with a travertine doorstep in the southwest wall, which opens out into
the courtyard and which has a *lacus* a few steps away. That
door replaced a much wider *taberna* door. A third opening,
leading to the *angiportus*, has been completely filled in.

This tavern seems to have had two rooms in which to
serve the customers. A walled-in doorway, which opened
between the main bar room and the neighbouring *taberna* to the
southeast, was not functioning during the last phase of the
bar's life, and the neighbouring *taberna* and its back room were
not included in the bar.

100.
Tavern 26. Counter
with protruding water
basin. The marble
covering of the counter
has survived better than
any other in Ostia and
is complete enough to
give an impression of
the standard of Ostian
bars.

101.
Tavern 27.
Scale 1:120.

102.
Tavern 27. Tavern coun-
ter, restored with frag-
ments of marble slabs
recovered around it. The
repairs to the mosaic
floor show that the wate
line to the counter basin
has been replaced.

102.

103.
Tavern 28. The well
in the southeast wall
existed before the
house was built and is
located outside the
house. See fig. 105.
Scale 1:115.

104.
Tavern 28. Northeast
corner of tavern with
basinless counter and
the vaulted opening to
the well.

104.

28. Thirteen doorways north of the entrance to the Baths
of the Pharus is the third bar on the Cardo Maximus (IV ii 3),
which in appearance is different from other taverns in Ostia but
which supplements our understanding of Ostian taverns. One
enters through a wide *taberna* door from the portico on the
Cardo Maximus. The tavern is just one room (fig. 103), and in
the western corner, on entering, one notes the four masonry
steps which are the start of the stairs to the barman's upstairs
cenaculum. As well as the main entrance there is a side-door to
an *angiportus* in the southeast wall. The eastern corner is occupied by a high base (1,05 metres), on top of which are three
stepped shelves (0,31 metre), all built in masonry (fig. 104).

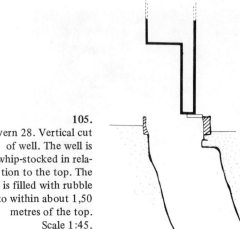

105.
Tavern 28. Vertical cut
of well. The well is
whip-stocked in rela-
tion to the top. The
well is filled with rubble
to within about 1,50
metres of the top.
Scale 1:45.

The front of the base is recessed 0,17 metre and is framed by a
0,27-metre pilaster on the one side and six courses of brick (0,31
metre) on the top. This whole structure is like the combination
of water basin and stepped shelves seen in some taverns, with
the great difference that here there is no water basin under the
shelves. There is no water basin because it was not needed: in
the same corner as the shelves is a vaulted opening in the
southeast wall which allowed the barman to draw water from a
well below the wall (for vertical cut, see fig. 105). The well in
the winter will fill to about 1,60 metres from the top. The top
1,60 metres of the well shaft is leaning toward the tavern. The
well top is bordered by a travertine frame which protrudes 0,18
metre into the adjoining *angiportus.* Below the leaning part of
the well shaft is a perpendicular well casing of unknown depth.
Apparently, the well existed before the *insula* of Hercules was
built during the third quarter of the second century.[23]

This whole arrangement shows that the counterfeit bar
fountain was a concession to tradition: it was hard for *caupones*
to think of any other way of stowing glasses and other vessels
away than on stepped shelves, and they also thought that there
had to be some kind of counter. One may wonder why this
shelf and counter ensemble was not put up as a frame around
the well head, which would have made a perfect combination.
One drawback, however, would have been that the bar operation would have moved back from the door where the main

action must have been. A wooden counter in the door presumably would serve the majority of the customers, who were sitting or standing in the portico.

This tavern demonstrates that water was a very essential commodity in a tavern. What may have been the oldest tavern in Ostia, the one in I x 2 (no. 4), at the old market-place outside the Porta Occidentalis of the Castrum, also originally depended on a well inside the tavern for the *calda*.

The floor covering of tavern no. 28 was yellow brick set on edge in the herringbone pattern; a patch of it is still there, close to the side-door.

29. The so-called Caupona del Pavone (IV ii 6) is located on the south side of the quiet street, Via del Pavone, between a building of Hadrianic date (IV ii 7) and the handsome Caseggiato dell'Ercole of the time of Marcus Aurelius.[24] The building of the inn dates to the Hadrianic period, with some subsequent rebuilding in the later Severan age (210-235), or, as the *opus mixtum* and the mosaics would indicate, closer to the middle of the century. To masonry and mosaics must be added the wall paintings, which Carlo Gasparri dates to the beginning and not later than the first twenty years of the third century.[25]

It is not a tavern in the ordinary sense: it is secluded in the far end of the building, as far removed from the street as possible (fig. 106). One enters a corridor from the street, and inside the entrance to the right is a staircase to the upper floors. With a wall thickness of about 0,60 metre the building could be three to four floors high; there are rooms on both sides of the corridor, four on each side. The last of the rooms to the right is actually a kind of antechamber, which leads to the tavern on the right, while on the left one may enter a courtyard.

The tavern room (fig. 107) measures 4,98 (southwest wall) to 5,08 (northeast wall) by 4,30 (southeast wall) to 4,57 (northwest wall) metres. One enters the tavern room through a 1,84-metre opening (which originally was 2,80 metres) in the northwest wall. The tavern counter is projecting from the northeast wall, 2,12 metres long by 0,64 metre wide and 1,20 metres high, with a 0,47-metre water basin at the bottom. Behind the counter, 0,63 metre, are two brick pillars which support three stepped shelves built into the east corner of the tavern. These

106.

This may have been the Peacock Hotel. The floor plan differs from that of the Casa delle Volte Dipinte. Tavern 19. The two wings on either side of the central corridor have direct access to the street. The upstairs also has access to the tavern room c through the same corridor. The dining-room is b; a is the courtyard with benches (continued next page)

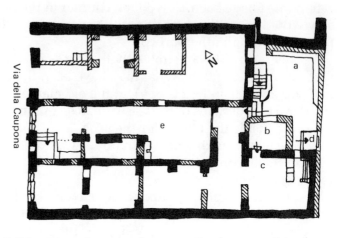

shelves are 2,06 metres long and, respectively, counting from below, 0,15, 0,16, and 0,19 metre wide, and also, successively, 0,14, 0,15, and 0,16 metre above their preceding step. There is one window in the northeast wall (0,85 metre wide, one metre high); a ledge around the top of the walls indicates that the height of the ceiling was 3,03 metres. The floor is paved in a black and white mosaic in an imaginative pattern that Becatti dates to the middle of the third century.[26] By the north corner of the room a narrower door (0,91 metre) leads down one step to a small, well-decorated room which has no other exit and which apparently was a small dining-room. From the ante-chamber a door gives access to the courtyard with its brick benches along the northeast and southeast walls. In the south corner is an *aedicula* with a peacock painted on its back wall; it is generally considered a Lar altar. It was an open courtyard and for that reason was originally separated from the neighbouring Hadrianic (*ScO* I 236) building IV ii 14 by just a single-ply common wall.

The equipment of the tavern room is identical to the many other taverns of Ostia, and it is combined with a courtyard with benches in the same manner as the tavern in Via di Diana (no. 3). Its location, however, sets it apart from the majority of taverns in Ostia. It was not a tavern where people dropped in. It was offering tavern services but, apparently, to a limited number of persons—first of all, presumably, to those who lived in the house. It is hard to reject the suggestion that the house IV ii 6 was a hotel.[27]

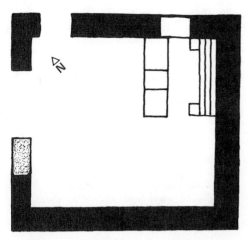

along the two walls;
d is the Lar altar with
the picture of the pea-
cock that gave name
to the tavern.

107.
Tavern 29. Room C of
fig. 106.
Scale 1:100.

30. There was a tavern (IV v 7) on the south side of the
western Decumanus, in the second *taberna* west of the fish market. To enter one passes a 3,40-metre doorstep with a conventional 0,70-metre space for a swinging door and a *cardo* hole
(fig. 108). The dimensions of the tavern are 4,81 by 7,12 metres.
In the back wall is a 1,20-metre door to the *taberna* behind,
whose main entrance (2,87 metres) is from the *angiportus* on the
southwest; no doorstep is left. This second *taberna* measures
4,24 by 9,70 metres, and from it one walks into a *subscalare*, the
third and last room. Two holes in the sides of the door opening
between the first and the second *taberna* show that the door
could be barred from the inside of the inn.

In the first *taberna*, Gismondi's plan shows two fountain
counters. Immediately to the left inside the front door the plan
gives the contour of a fountain counter of the type which is
built with a wall at its back. Since Gismondi's plan here is the
same as that shown in tavern no. 5, where further references to
other similar counters are given, tavern no. 30 must have had a
similar counter placed here. Furthermore, it is still possible to
see enough marks of the fountain on the east wall to determine
its approximate outline.

A second counter is shown further back in the room on the
right side. When one compares Gismondi's plan of it with
those of nos. 1, 2, 6, 11, and 19, which are all well preserved, it
is a natural conclusion that there was one of the same type
here—a counter with a barrel-vaulted water basin. The docu-
mentation in favour of a bar is very strong: besides the plan of

109.
Tavern 32. The *popina* of Alexander
Helix. Main entrance from the Decumanus;
minor entrances from the portico to the
left and from outside the city wall to the
right. The bar counter with twin water
basins is to the left in the main entrance,
behind it are a *focus* and then three stepped shelves. In the middle of the room
is a free-standing water basin; the floor
has been broken up to repair its water
line. In the southwest corner is an unidentified structure; its irregular plan
was original, since the pattern of the
mosaic floor follows its double corners.
Was it a *lararium?* The mosaic floor shows
three groups of human figures. Behind
the main room is a second room.
Scale 1:115.

108.
Tavern 30 (to the right, marked 7) and
Tavern 31 (to the left, marked 10).
Scale 1:400.

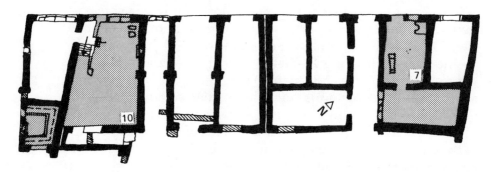

the bar counters one must consider their placement inside the
taberna. The one in the orthodox position in the entrance to the
left is especially convincing.

Gismondi's plan is the best proof that this place was a bar.
To this it must be added that the location between the Baths of
the Seven Columns and the *macellum* fish market, on the main
street of Ostia, is as good as any in Ostia.

31. South of the entrance to the Baths of the Seven Columns there is a tavern of which Gismondi's plan (fig. 108) is
the only evidence (IV v 10). One enters from the Decumanus
through a 2,94-metre door at whose south end a 0,74-metre
fragment of the doorstep is left. While the west wall measures
4,74 metres, the east wall is 8,71 metres long as the room grows

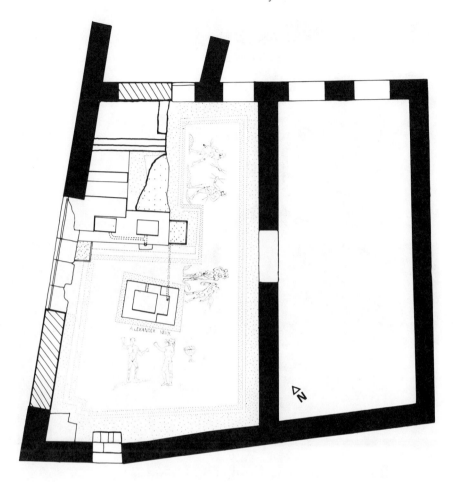

in width toward the east because of the oblique south wall, where a 1,84-metre *subscalare* is also added to the tavern. The north wall is 11,87 metres. In the south wall is a small door with a few steps opening into the staircase, so that one joins the stairs at a higher level than the tavern floor. In the southern corner is a 2,65 by 1,30 metre latrine. In the north wall was a 1,02-metre doorway which connected the tavern with the entrance to the baths; it is now blocked by a 1,32 by 0,38 metre pillar, 0,75 metre high. A 0,56 by 0,25 metre niche fills in the door opening. In the orthodox position, on the left side of the *taberna* door, the tavern fountain is indicated. Gismondi shows the two pillars in the same way as in nos. 17 and 18, where full

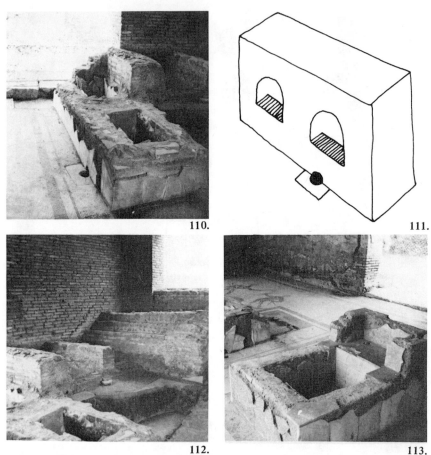

110.   111.

112.   113.

bar counters with barrel-vaulted basins are seen.

32. The tavern of Alexander Helix is on the east side of the
Decumanus Maximus in the middle of the old location of Porta
Marina (IV vii 4). It is named for one Alexander Helix, and his
name was written, at the beginning of the third century, in the
mosaic floor above the picture of two boxers.[28] Whether the
name refers to a famous boxer of the day or whether it is the
name of the proprietor of the bar is unknown, and immaterial.
It was one of the biggest taverns in Ostia and must have been
about the busiest of those that we know, located as it is where
the traffic from the seashore meets that from the centre of
Ostia. The western Decumanus is the main street in downtown
Ostia.

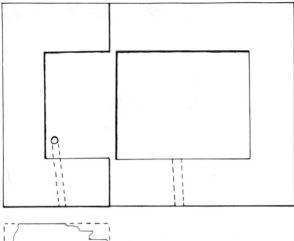

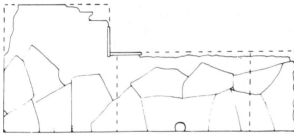

110.
Tavern 32. Lower half of the bar counter with twin water basins. Drain hole in front of the nearest basin. In the background is the *focus* structure.

111.
Tavern 32. Reconstruction of counter with twin basins.

112.
Tavern 32. Stepped shelves behind bar counter and *focus.*

113.
Tavern 32. Free-standing fountain. The lead pipe can be seen in the corner of the shelf to the left. The fountain presumably had the same function as that in the middle of the courtyard of the Diana bar (Tavern 3).

114.
Tavern 32. Plan and profile of fountain in fig. 113.
Scale 1:20.

The tavern consists of two rooms (fig. 109). The first room is large and has entrances from the Decumanus, from the portico north of the tavern, and from the square outside the Porta Marina. This front room contains the trappings so characteristic of bars: first and foremost the bar counter with the basin at the bottom (fig. 110). In this bar the counter has a double basin which is well preserved, while the top of the counter has disappeared. It was probably a standard counter with a barrel vault over each of the basins (reconstructed in fig. 111). There is an inside drain connecting the two basins, and from the eastern basin water drains out at the bottom into a catch basin built in the floor next to the counter (for details, see fig. 109). Behind the counter is a *focus* and up against the north wall there are

115.
Tavern 32. The repairs
to the mosaic floor
from the fountain
to the entrance from
the portico indicate
that the fountain and
the bar counter were
fed by the same
water line.

three shelves in masonry arranged stepwise (fig. 112). Near the middle of the room is a water basin larger than those in the counter and probably not covered (fig. 113). At the east end is a shelf, with the remains of a lead pipe coming out in one corner, walled in on the three sides but open toward the basin (for plan and vertical cut, see fig. 114). A drain at the bottom lets the water out onto the floor and into the same catch basin that served the bar counter. The repairs in the mosaic floor (fig. 115) show that the water was piped into the water basin from the portico to the north. In the southwest corner of the bar, the corner to the right of the main entrance, is a base or substructure serving some unknown purpose (fig. 116).

The whole room is paved with white mosaic with a black double border along the walls and the basins; at the entrance from the portico the mosaic shows two grotesque Egyptian dancers with crossed double sticks in their hands; in the middle of the room, nearly in front of the door to the back room, a Venus with an amoretto who hands her a garland is shown; in front of the entrance from the south and behind the two above-mentioned boxers, over whose heads is written "Alexander Helix," is standing a chalice of the same type as is seen in the so-called Fortunatus bar and in two bars outside the station of the *vigiles* (nos. 13, 14, and 15).

The second room is east of the main tavern room and somewhat smaller (4,25 by 9,55 metres). It has an entrance in the middle of the west wall. In the north wall are two windows facing Via della Caupona di Alexander; in the east wall across

116.
Tavern 32. Structure in
southwest corner may
have been a Lar altar.

from the entrance is a smaller door into a *subscalare*. The second
room may have been a dining-room.

33. North of the Caupona di Alexander Helix (no. 32), on
the east side of the Decumanus where the afternoon sun was
shining and where the customers were protected by a portico,
are four taverns, all in a low state of preservation.

The second *taberna* from the south, in the housing block IV
vii 3, is not quite rectangular because the east wall and the west
wall converge toward the north. The north wall is 6,50 metres
as opposed to the 7,30 metres of the south wall; the width of
the *taberna* is 4,35 metres (fig. 117). In the southeast corner are
the dilapidated remains of the stairs to the *cenaculum* above.
What is left of the stairs consists in a 1,13 by 0,92 metre landing,
to which four steps are leading. The steps protrude 0,90 metre
into the room, but they are too dilapidated to have their length
measured. In the northeast corner is a one-metre doorway into
an unexcavated back room. The tavern door is 2,96 metres with
a 0,64-metre space for a swinging *cardo* door cut-out. The bar
counter is pointed from the street into the room. It is built in
brick. The front of the counter rests on the doorstep, but only
the front pillar is preserved to a fair size. The opposite end of
the counter has disappeared, and of the water basin only three
slabs are left (figs. 118 and 119).

34. Nine doors north of no. 33 comes the next tavern (IV
vii 2). It is a deep room (12,80 by 6,13 metres, see fig. 120). The
2,98-metre-wide *taberna* door has a 0,72-metre space with a
cardo hole for a swinging door at the north end. The door is

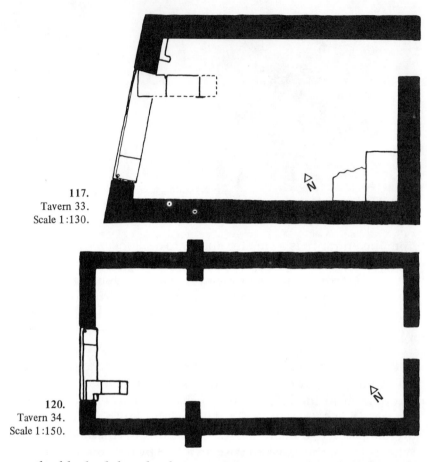

117.
Tavern 33.
Scale 1:130.

120.
Tavern 34.
Scale 1:150.

partly blocked by the bar counter, measuring 1,60 by 0,50 metres, 0,95 metre high, which starts on the doorstep and is directed into the room. The counter is built in rubble and cement (fig. 121); the brick vault over the water basin is preserved, but nothing is left of the possible marble lining. In the far end of the room is a 1,30-metre doorway into a back room which is unexcavated.

35. Seven doorways north of no. 34 is the next tavern, 12,75 by 3,75 metres. Its south side is encumbered by a *sub-scalare*, so that only part of the 1,95 metres that the *sub-scalare* covers can be added to the tavern, and this small space is further reduced by two pillars that are 0,60 metre thick and, respectively, 2,22 and 1,48 metres long (fig. 122).

A bar counter built in the 2,92-metre doorway is not much more than a rubble pile, one metre long and 0,73 metre at the

118.

119.

118.
Tavern 33. Entrance
with remains of tavern
counter.

119.
Tavern 33. The three
remaining slabs of a
water basin.

121.
Tavern 34. Free-stand-
ing tavern counter.

121.

highest point. The north end of that counter is still cohesive. Among the rubble that is piled up in the *subscalare* is half a mortar (fig. 123). In the rear wall is a door to the back room; much of the masonry at the door is broken down so that the door opening, which originally must have measured about 1,15 metres like other similar doors in the same house, now measures 2,29 metres.

36. Two doors north of no. 35 is the last tavern in the Caseggiato della Fontana a Lucerna. The dimensions of the room are 12,70 by 5,80 metres; a 0,74 by 0,95 metre pillar, however, cuts it in half both ways (fig. 124). A door in the rear leads to a back room. A bar counter has gone from the doorstep leading into the room, but, besides some scattered rubble, only the two long sides of the water basin are still standing; the third side is flat on the ground, and the fourth is missing (fig. 125).

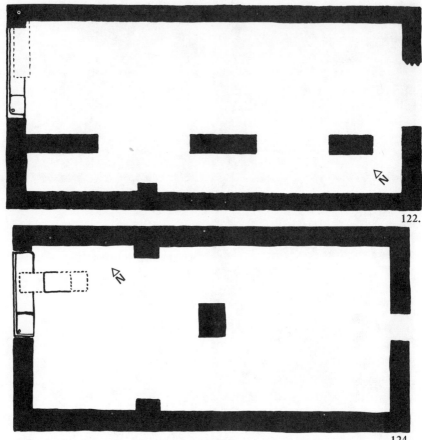

122.

124.

37. The *taberna* in V iv 1, on the corner of Semita dei Cippi and Via dell'Invidioso, has a wide (2,68 metres) *taberna* door on the west side and a narrow (1,18 metres) door on the north side, so that there was access from both streets. The dimensions of the room are 4,99 metres north-south and 4,71 metres east-west. Gismondi's plan (sheet 8) shows a structure on the left side when one enters the *taberna* through the western door, a structure which must have been a bar counter since the same design in II ix 2 (no. 17) represents a bar counter (fig. 126). Traces of foundations or substructures are indicated along the south wall, but today nothing of the kind can be observed on the spot and Gismondi's plan remains the only proof that there was a bar here.

122.
Tavern 35.
Scale 1:125.

123.
Tavern 35. Remains
of tavern counter. Half
a mortar is part of
the rubble in this
tavern.

123.

124.
Tavern 36.
Scale 1:100.

125.
Tavern 36. Remains of
tavern counter and
water basin.

125.

The location of the *taberna* on a street corner with the
counter in place at the door and the proximity of the Forum
Baths and the Baths of Invidiosus are persuasive signs that this
was a bar.

38. The short Via dell'Invidioso never amounted to very
much. Starting at Semita dei Cippi it was a well-paved street
for one block up to Via del Sole, where it petered out and was
cut off by the buildings which later contained the seat of the
Augustales. This means that one could get through as far as Via
del Mitreo dei Serpenti but no farther. What can be seen now
between Via del Sole and Via del Mitreo dei Serpenti is a narrow passageway between the Hadrianic buildings V vi 5 and 4
and, still narrower, between the Hadrianic V vi 2, south of the

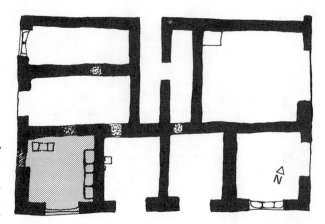

126.
Tavern 37, on corner
of Via dell'Invidioso
(north) and Semita
del Cippi (west).
Scale 1 :230.

eastern Via dell'Invidioso and, north of it, the Caseggiato del
Sole V vi 1 of the time of Antoninus Pius. The Caseggiato del
Sole burned down and was never built up again; this must
have happened about A.D. 300, since the masonry that walled
in the ruin is in *opus listatum*.

Before that happened a *taberna* had been added to the
south end of Caseggiato del Sole (V vi 1). It measures 8,39 by
3,44 metres (figs. 127, 128). It was basically a low addition to
Caseggiato del Sole: the east wall is 0,44 metre thick, the south
wall 0,37 metre. It must have had a light (wooden?) upper
storey, since there were stairs in the northeast corner of the
tavern: there is a 0,33-metre-high landing, with a 0,52-metre-
high step leading further up and remains of steps leading to the
landing (fig. 129). The *taberna* addition has been substantially
lower than the Caseggiato del Sole, whose south wall measures
0,60 metre (this wall being the north wall of the *taberna*). There
is a 1,03-metre doorway in the south wall of the *taberna*, giving
access to the southern *angiportus*. In its north wall is a 0,85-
metre-wide door opening to a *subscalare* in Caseggiato del Sole.
The front entrance from the west is lacking the front step, and
the width of the original opening cannot be determined
because the northern doorpost is missing; the opening is 3,06
metres (fig. 128).

Between the entrance and the door to the *subscalare* there
are two, maybe three, water basins. The first, from the east, is a
0,52-metre-wide, 1,02-metre-high niche with a vaulted top and
a rounded back wall (fig. 130); at the bottom it is 0,42 metre
deep, the bottom being 0,45 metre off the floor. The water was

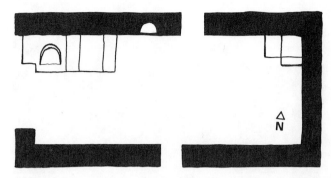

127.
Tavern 38.
Scale 1:110.

piped in from behind. That this was a typical drinking fountain is confirmed by a comparison with the drinking fountains in the collegiate temples of the *fabri tignuarii* and the shipwrights (V xi 1 and III ii 2), and in others. Next to this fountain comes another in the traditional style of the taverns; here the top has disappeared, but the barrel vault above the water basin is still there (fig. 131).

The last basin now has a straight front facing the *taberna*, while the rear side is rounded (see plan). Gismondi's plan (sheet 8) indicates that the basin of this third structure was circular at the time of excavation. That may have been the case; the width of this basin seems to have tapered off from top to bottom, and this shape can still be distinguished in the north end of the basin.

The drinking fountain in the form of a vaulted niche excludes the possibility of this tavern being an industrial plant. It is found in places where many people used to come, and several sources of water are not a rarity in Ostian taverns. The second fountain needs no further comment, and if the third basin is a round container it is not rare in the later bars. In tavern no. 8 is a round container dug into the ground, and a *dolium* is dug into the ground in no. 10. Their functions are not clear. The function of the *dolium* in no. 3, the so-called *thermopolium* in Via di Diana, must have been to store wine, an application which looks very unlikely in this case: wine jars were always dug into the ground.

The location of these three structures in the left side of the entrance is in the tavern tradition, and the presence of two

128.

129.

130.

131.

128.
Tavern 38, looking east into the tavern. The fountains are to the left at the entrance; stairs to the *cenaculum* are in the far left corner.

129.
Tavern 38. The stairs in the northeast corner lead to the *cenaculum.*

130.
Tavern 38. The niche may have been a drinking fountain.

131.
Tavern 38. The orthodox counter fountain and, in front of it, another big basin comparable to the *dolia defossa* elsewhere.

public baths, the Forum Baths and the Baths of Invidiosus, in the immediate proximity of this *taberna* makes it very probable that it was a tavern.

Notes

1. Paribeni, "Scavi dell'isola ad est dell'area sacra del tempio di Volcano," *NSc* V 13 (1916), 143; 399-428, esp. 416-17.

2. Kleberg, *Hôtels,* 55; Raissa Calza, 214.

3. o. l., 416.

4. o. l., fig. 13, with comment 114-15.

5. *ScO* I, 234, col. 1.

6. From the time of Augustus *ScO* I, 234, col. 1.

7. *ScO* I, figs. 32, 34; p. 238, col. 1.

8. *CIL* XIV, S4755b.

9. *ScO* IV, 63, notes 78 and 79. "il fondo nero farebbe propendere per una datazione al III sec. piuttosto che al II sec. . . . . nei primi anni del III sec. d. C."

10. *CIL* XIV S4755a.

11. J.M.C. Toynbee in "Some Notes on Artists in the Roman World," *Coll. Latomus* vol. VI (1951), 43-44. Becatti in *ScO* IV, 63.

12. *CIL* XIV, S4756. *NSc* (1909), 92ff.

13. *ScO* I, 125-26.

14. *ScO* I, 235.

15. Felletti Maj in *Bollettino d'arte* 45 (1960), 52.

16. Petronius 9,2; 16,1; Apul. *Met.* I, 24 (compare 25); portable dining equipment *Dig.* 34, 2, 40; Plut. *Anton* 9,8; Kleberg, *Hôtels,* 98-99, 62; Lionel Casson, *Travel in the Ancient World,* 198ff.

17. Becatti in *ScO* I, 137; what a *stabulum* was is explained by Kleberg, *Hôtels,* 18-19.

18. *Monumenti della pittura antica scoperti in Italia. Sezione terza.* "La pittura elle-nistico-romano. Ostia." fasc. I-II (Rome, 1961). The "ambiente X" = the bar is described on pp. 21ff. The date of the decoration of the wall is on 31ff.

19. All published by Calza in *Die Antike* XV (1939), 99-115.

20. Kleberg, *Hôtels,* 134, n. 52, is not convinced that this was "eine Kneipe," as Calza says.

21. *ScO* I, 237.

22. Van Essen in *Bull. Com.* (1957) 175; 177. On pages 173 to 177 van Essen has dealt with the paintings in this building and has distinguished several periods.

23. *ScO* I, 226; brickstamps A.D. 161-75.

24. *ScO* I, 236, 237.

25. Compare Becatti in *ScO* IV, 176, and Carlo Gasparri in "Le pitture della caupona del pavone," *Monumenti,* as note 18, fasc. IV (Rome, 1970), p. 32.

26. *ScO* IV, 176-77 and table 54.

27. Raissa Calza, *Ostia,* 80.

28. Becatti in *ScO* IV, 205ff.

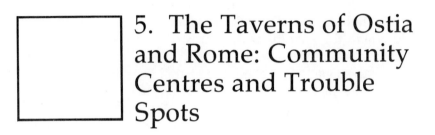

5. The Taverns of Ostia and Rome: Community Centres and Trouble Spots

The Functions of the Taverns of Ostia

The bars of Ostia present themselves as simple *tabernae*, which could have served a different trade with a different inventory: the rooms are no different from other *tabernae*. They have a tendency to be on street corners. Eight out of thirty-eight, a good one-fifth of the bars considered here, are on street corners, which constitutes a high proportion for one profession. A look at a map shows that there is only one district of the city where there is a real concentration: along the western Decumanus up to the Castrum and the Macellum there are eleven bars that can be identified, nearly one-third of all Ostian bars (28 percent). Of those eleven bars there are three in a row at the south end of the Decumanus Maximus, in or outside the Porta Marina, which corresponds with the pattern in Pompeii: places with refreshments for travellers as soon as they reach the city. There are fewer places at the Porta Romana for travellers from Rome. What is surprising is the low number of bars at the baths, although literature and Pompeii show that *popinae* were to be found *iuxta balnea publica* ("next to the public baths").[1] The Forum Baths and the Baths of Invidiosus have only three bars: a small one on the corner of Semita dei Cippi and Via dell' Invidioso, one at the bottom of Via dell'Invidioso, and a big one with two to three rooms at the corner of Cardo Maximus and Via del Tempio Rotondo. Speaking of baths, however, one has to remember that they were also served by ambulant vendors, as testified to by Seneca.[2] There are two bars close together across from the Baths of Mithras, there are three to four bars in the neighbourhood of the Baths of Trinacia, but we know of only one in the vicinity of the Baths of Neptune (Fortunatus's bar), unless one includes the bars at the entrance to the barracks of the *vigiles*. There are three bars in the immediate proximity of the Baths of the Cisiarii. Three bars are found close together in Via di Diana, which is understandable since they are located in a rather sterile neighbourhood of *horrea* and officialdom, with many people around.

Kleberg expresses his surprise that Ostia has such a limited number of bars compared to the situation in Pompeii.[3] One has to consider the difference between the two cities. Pompeii was buried at a moment when the city was pulsating with life; Ostia shows us the later phase of a dying city which was allowed to decay and to be depopulated and then to be pillaged by raiders and eroded by time. On the western Decumanus one counts eleven bars over a distance of nearly four hundred metres, and in Pompeii Kleberg counts eight taverns over a distance of seventy-five metres, right inside the Porta Stabiana.[4] It would not be unreasonable to assume that Ostia, of course, had a higher number of taverns during its more vital periods but that all trace of many bars has disappeared since the special bar equipment, the counter in particular, was made of wood. A partially excavated bar on the north side of the Decumanus in Herculaneum has a wooden bar counter blocking most of the wide *taberna* door. On top of the counter are tumblers and goblets still partly buried in the mud that submerged the whole city.

132.
Relief from a mausoleum in Isola Sacra.
To the left a vessel is being towed into
Portus, past the light-tower; to the right
is a tavern scene.
Photo: Soprintendenza, Ostia Antica.

What we have now in Ostia is what was built in masonry. But many of those masonry counters were poorly built and have not been able to resist decay and destruction. A fair number of counters easily recognizable at the time of their excavation have since disappeared.[5] This condition makes one wonder how many have disappeared before the excavation started.

The bar counter, which could also be called the bar fountain, is in many cases our only proof of the presence of a bar. Two styles exist: some counters (or fountains) are placed with their backs against the wall, with a water basin built into the base and stepped shelves on top. To modern people they look like a fireplace. They are most often placed in a corner right inside the door, so well out of the way that there would be space for wooden counters in front of them. There are eleven of this type of fountain counter in Ostian bars. The vast majority are of the second style, the free-standing counter, which is a counter in the real sense, with a vaulted water basin in its base that is accessible from both sides of the counter. There are twenty-four counters of this type.

This kind of counter is radically different from the counters that we know in Pompeii and Herculaneum. But it is an important part of Ostian taverns. This is shown clearly by a relief from a tomb in Isola Sacra (fig. 132).[6] The relief shows two scenes: on the left side is a merchantman being towed to Portus by a *lenuncularius tabularius*; Portus is indicated by a picture of the pharus, and the two vessels, reduced in size, are moving in that direction. To the right is a tavern scene. The right side of that picture shows two men sitting at a table, one drinking out of a tumbler, the other holding out his hand to receive a tumbler from the barmaid who is walking up to him and holding the tumbler in front of her with both hands. Between the girl and the thirsty sailor, a dog is standing on its hind legs, resting its front legs against the side of the table, and begging for a hand-out from the sailor. The left side of the picture is what interests us here. It shows a bar fountain with three stepped shelves above it. On the shelves are tumblers, a jar, and a flask. Is this a free-standing counter with stepped shelves behind it? It looks as if it is built against the wall, like the first type described above. Going farther to the left in the picture, one is looking at the end of a counter that together with the other counter would form an L-shaped counter. Some cases of similar counters are seen in Ostia. This counter might even have two water basins, one in each half, as in the counter of tavern no. 3, the so-called *thermopolium* in Via di Diana. The dolphin is placed as a decoration on the end of the counter—it brings a fresh smell of the sea into the tavern and it may very well be the signboard of the tavern. The date of the relief is somewhat controversial; Thylander prefers a Hadrianic date whereas Calza argues for the middle of the third century.[7]

Another characteristic feature of these counters is that they are mostly placed right in, or by, the entrance, often blocking part of the doorway. There are only three bars in Ostia where the fountain counter is placed toward the back of the room. The reference here is only to bars or taverns, not to the *stabula*, the hotels. One reason for the placement of the counter right at the entrance is that tavern guests would sit outside on the benches, like the ones in front of the *thermopolium* in Via di Diana, or on benches or chairs on the sidewalk and they would clutter the passage. Martial complains that the impudent *institor* had taken over all of Rome, that the black *popina* occupied all streets, and that wine bottles were hung on the pillars of the portico (as signboards for the *popina*).[8] Apparently, it was all done in the same manner as in modern Italy. It was very handy to serve outdoor customers if the counter was right in

133.
Lead pipe at the bot-
tom of water basin
in tavern 18.

the doorway. An intriguing detail is that the Ostians placed the counter on the left side of the doorway or the barroom—only two counters in Ostia were put on the right side. Two taverns have two counters each, one right and one left.[9] Was this the force of habit?

The function of the counters, especially the basins at the bottom, has often been misinterpreted;[10] it has been believed to be an oven or a place to wash dishes. However, it should be stressed that the main purpose of the counter basin was to secure a constant water supply, since water was maybe the most important commodity that bars served their customers.

There are several things that point to the counter basins as water suppliers. First, a piece of lead pipe was found lodged in a hole leading into the counter basin of tavern no. 3;[11] in tavern no. 18 (III i 10) several lengths of pipe leading up to the basin are still visible in the floor near the counter and at the bottom of the basin (fig. 133); tavern no. 27 (in IV ii 2) shows in the break of the mosaic floor, which again has been repaired, that the water line to the counter basin has been replaced or repaired (fig. 102); in the bar of Alexander Helix the free-standing basin in the middle of the room still displays a length of lead pipe, inset in the masonry (fig. 113), while the mosaic floor shows the same repairs to the pipe which supplied the counter as did the previous bar. Finally, the last bar north of the Baths of the Pharus (no. 28) shows a bar counter built against the wall, but the base of the counter has no basin in it since there is a whole well to the right of the counter, with all the water supply that the barman might need (see fig. 104 and above no. 28).

Water was needed in great quantities in the bars, either for *frida (frigida)* or *calda (calida)*. [12] Of the two, the *cal(i)da* was by far the more important: hardly anyone would drink his wine unless it was mixed with water warmed in an *aenum*, "quod supra focum pendet; hic aqua ad potandum calefit" ("which hangs over the fire; in it drinking water is heated," *Dig.* 33, 7, 18, 3). There is testimony about this in many places. A guild law commands that for their banquet the *magister cenarum* together with the wine should supply "caldam cum ministerio" ("hot water and service," *CIL* XIV 2112; II 16). Apuleius tells how Fotis has everything ready for her and Lucius's nocturnal orgy: "calices boni iam infuso latice semipleni" ("big glasses already half full of wine were ready"), then Fotis enters and "aqua calida iniecta porrigit bibam" ("having filled up with *calda* handed it to me to drink," *Met.* II 15-16). Martial (I 12, 3-4) mocks a drunkard: "iam defecisset portantes calda ministros/si non potares, Sextiliane, merum" ("The waiters would already have run out of *calda*, Sextilianus, if you did not drink your wine undiluted"). [13]

A particularly popular drink for centuries was the *conditum*, which was ordered as a refreshment and was the social drink of the bars. It was spiced wine, and the taste for spiced wines has been preserved in Italy to this day. The recipe for the mixture is given to us through many sources. [14] Basically, it is wine, hot water, honey, and ground pepper, to which other ingredients could be added; the list of spiced wines of the Romans is a long one. Pliny (see note 14) mentions that the *piperatum* is another name for *conditum*, and this particular ingredient accounts for the surprising find of mortars in some of the Ostian bars. There are mortars in two of the bars (now fastened to the top of the bar counter), and fragments of mortars are still around in a few other bars to remind us that pepper was minced here for the *conditum*. The relief from Isola Sacra (above fig. 132) shows what must have been stacked on the stepped shelves of the bars; the mortars reveal what some of the servings were. In a number of bars are *foci* where cooking could be done and water could be heated. There is no record of water heaters being found in Ostian bars. What has just been mentioned here, however, is all that is needed for the *conditum*.

No other bar equipment is known from Ostia, but from various other sources we know what one could expect. In *Digesta* (33, 7, 13), Julius Paulus, at the beginning of the third century, discusses what would be understood by inventory of a *taberna cauponia*. He makes a legal distinction between the whole *caupona* business, which would include the unfree *institores*, and the *taberna*, the business place alone. If it is the *taberna*, one would expect to find the following items: *dolia* (the bar storage jars, possibly *dolia defossa*), *vasa* (crocks), *ancones* (drinking vessels or vases), *calices* (goblets), *trullae* (ladles, to ladle wine out of jars), *urnae aereae* (bronze water pitchers), *congiaria*, and *sextaria* (measures containing a *congius* and the sixth of a *congius*). This inventory covers the operations of a tavern in Via di Diana (no. 3), to the ladle or dipper to get the wine out of the jar, to the various drinking vessels and pitchers, to the measures used to mete out the wine to the customers, either to consume on the spot or to take with them. The *sextarius* seems to have been a standard amount of wine for one person, if one can trust the famous relief and inscription from Aesernia (*CIL* IX 2689), which, in picture and text, illustrates a customer's departure from the inn and his settlement with the inkeeper. The first item owing is, in the innkeeper's words, "habes vini sextarium unum" ("You got a *sextarius* of wine").[15] From other sources other names can be picked up: Copa 7 speaks of *cyathus;* verses 29 to 30 give the traveller the choice of *vitrum* or *crystalli calices;* Petronius's *Cena* 95 mentions *furca de carnario* and *veru* (meat fork and spit); but nowhere is there substantial information about the services already mentioned.

Tavern Styles

One cannot help noting that the Ostian taverns differ in appearance, that they vary in size, and that they also represent different types of establishments. Looking at them individually and at their immediate surroundings, one understands that they could not all serve exactly the same purpose. Tönnes Kleberg dedicates the first chapter of his book about hotels, restaurants, and taverns in the Roman world to an analysis of the terminology that describes different groups of Pompeian taverns. Ostia plays a very small part in his analysis as he had very limited material to work with. But that does not detract from the high value of his semantic study, the core of which is an examination of linguistic usage drawing on the whole range of Latin literature. The main result of his research is that there are six important names for establishments in this category: *caupona, deversorium, hospitium, popina, stabulum,* and *taberna*. [16]

These six words are distributed three ways:

The *caupona, deversorium, hospitium,* and *stabulum* denote what modern languages would call hotels: houses where travellers could put up for the night and at the same time could have their meals and could drink. A *stabulum* originally meant a stable, and in this connection it stands for a hotel where one could stop in with one's horse. As Latin literature shows, however, it did not matter whether one brought a horse or not! A *caupona* was a hotel which catered to all of a traveller's needs, but eventually the value of the word was down-graded and acquired the connotation of a low-grade saloon, then was dropped from the language altogether.

A *popina* was a restaurant which could serve food and drinks to a customer but which did not offer any accommodation.

A *taberna* was comprehensive, meaning a shop in which all kinds of trades could be plied. To differentiate, the word was qualified with adjectives like *(taberna) libraria, unguentaria, vinaria,* or, as seen above, *cauponia.* Eventually the meaning of a drinking place (tavern) prevailed when the word was used without an adjective. A *taberna* would normally only offer wine, rarely food.

All efforts to determine what types of inns there are in Ostia are heavily handicapped by the bareness of the Ostian ruins. In Pompeii Kleberg found seventeen *hospitia* and three *stabula*. [17]

In Ostia there are only few places that can be classed as hotels, and of these only those with food or drink service shall be mentioned. One is the so-called Casa delle Volte Dipinte, which has been discussed above (no. 19). There it was stressed that the whole plan of the house, with the individual rooms marshalled along a central corridor on both floors, looks more like a hotel than anything else. The most persuasive detail was the existence of a kitchen and a bathroom-cum-latrine on each floor. The kitchens served the habits of the travellers who prepared their own meals. They also go against the idea that the Casa delle Volte Dipinte would be a bordello.[18] A supporting testimony to the hotel theory is the neighbour across the alley (III iv 1) which has been considered a *stabulum* by Becatti.[19] A comparison with similar Pompeian establishments confirms Becatti's idea. The most accessible example is the Hospitium Hermetis, of which Kleberg has given a plan and description (*Hôtels* 34-35). Feature by feature Becatti's *stabulum* and the Hospitium Hermetis match each other, except for the lack of a bar counter in the Ostian *stabulum*. Very conspicuous is the manure pit outside the entrance to the stable in Ostia. A further study of the *stabulum* is alien to the present subject, but it must be mentioned that Becatti's *stabulum* could make Casa delle Volte Dipinte a hotel by association, and vice versa. In Pompeii the hotels were clustered together in the same neighbourhood and hotel keepers behaved in the same way as the members of other professions in Roman cities (in a *vicus argentarius, unguentarius,* and the like).

The second example of a hotel is the Caupona del Pavone (no. 29). The bar did not open on to the street but was placed in the back of the building, internally and semi-privately. One had to pass through a long corridor with rooms on either side, an arrangement also found in the Casa delle Volte Dipinte, which is very different from private residences.

A third example, possibly, is no. 18, a large inn as inns go in Ostia; it served a three-wing, motel-like complex, which might be institutional or governmental (see discussion under no. 18 above).

The larger group of taverns in Ostia would be the wine-selling *tabernae* and the *popinae.*

A *popina,* an eating place with wine sale,[20] had a fireplace, a *focus,* for cooking, which of course would fill the room with smoke and cooking odours. Horace speaks of "uncta popina" (*Ep.* I 14, 21), "a greasy pub," which was not meant as flattery but which certainly must have been the truth; in *Sat.* II 4, 62 he speaks of *immundae popinae* ("foul pubs"); Martial speaks of "tepidae popinae" ("tepid pubs," I 41, 9); and, most unkind of all, Ausonius speaks contemptuously of low-class people and the uneatable pike in their restaurants: "fervet fumosis olido nidore popinis" (*Mosella* 124). The *popinae* had to put up with smoke and stench, a condition to which the Romans were accustomed as chimneys were not common until the Middle Ages. If a *popina* or *taberna* did not have a *focus*, it had a mobile *foculus*, the brazier, which presumably was the most widely used cooking equipment in shops as well as in private homes. The difference between a wine tavern and a *popina* is that in a *popina* there had to be room for people to sit or lie down at a table to eat. It is worth quoting Juvenal's *Sat.* VIII 173 ff., which gives a picture of Ostia: "mitte Ostia, Caesar,/mitte sed in magna legatum quaere popina/invenies aliquo cum percussore iacentem/permixtum nautis et furibus ac fugitivis" ("Send a messenger, Caesar, to Ostia, send a messenger, but look for the *legatus* in the big pub, and you will find him lying with some hit man, in company with sailors, thieves, and runaway slaves"). A different scene is *Copa* 5-6: "quid iuuat aestiuo defessum puluere abisse/quam potius bibulo decubuisse toro?" ("What is so pleasant about travelling over the hot and dusty road, why not rather lie down on the couch and drink?"), and, later, verses 29 to 30: "si sapis aestiuo recubans +nunc+ pro-lue uitro/seu uis crystalli ferre nouos calices" ("Be wise and lie down and wash the heat away with a cool glass, or would you rather drink of a new crystal tumbler?"). *Copa* was a summer scene with outdoor living, in the shade of the vine "pampinea . . . sub umbra" (verse 31). For indoor eating there were *triclinia* in Pompeian *popinae*.[21] But the *popinae* were not all that aristocratic; some had simple chairs and tables. Martial speaks of "Syriscus/in sellariolis uagus popinis/circa balnea" ("Syriscus, who tours the taverns with table service at the baths," V 70, 2-4). In Pompeii there is a picture of exactly this.[22] This latter way of eating is the habit of the common people, the apartment dwellers.[23]

One *popina* in Ostia is the tavern in Via di Diana (no. 3). On the wall of the main barroom is a picture of various kinds of vegetables and fruit; the room west of the barroom has a *focus*. Besides this there seems to have been plenty of space for chairs and tables in the barroom and the eastern room, and there was a great deal of space in the yard, which apparently, with its bench and fountain and its pantry, was part of the *popina*.

Another *popina* is the tavern of Alexander Helix (no. 32). The working area of the *popina* is concentrated in the northwest corner of the *taberna*, where the *focus* and the counter are located, and there is still more space left for tables and chairs. In addition, there is the eastern room (4,25 by 9,55 metres), which offered space for several small tables and chairs; the Romans needed no space for plates on a dinner-table.

It is the space that determines whether a *taberna* could be a wine tavern or a *popina*. A tavern like no. 6 in the Forum Baths and no. 24 in Annius's House could be *popinae* since they had other rooms than the barroom at their disposal. Some taverns had only one room for their use, but those with a fairly large room could accommodate many customers in the back of their locale. In this category belong the three taverns nos. 34 to 36 north of Alexander Helix's tavern. They are all 12,70 to 12,80 metres deep and 3,75 to 6,13 metres wide. Across from the Mithras Baths are two taverns, nos. 7 and 8, measuring 9,40 to 9,50 metres deep by 4,25 to 4,30 metres wide. Nos. 20 and 21 measuring 9,30 to 9,50 metres deep by 3,45 to 3,80 metres in width, no. 11 measuring 10,10 by 5,15 metres, and no. 4 measuring 9,50 by 5,84 metres—all these are big enough to have customer accommodation in the back of the room and are by no means smaller than many Italian restaurants today.

On the other hand there are *tabernae vinariae* that are too small to serve other purposes. Nos. 1 and 2 measure 4,85 to 5 by 4,45 to 4,85 metres, nos. 15, 16, 17, and several more do not seem to command enough room for other than simple tavern service with a fast snack.

There is not the material for a more detailed description, and this distinction between wine-serving taverns and *popinae* is at best a rather loose estimate.

The Taverns and the Emperor

At all times the Roman authorities were wary of the taverns, and occasionally they showed great hostility. Most conspicuous is the fierceness with which the emperors could turn against the taverns, a fierceness that has caused much surprise. It is all a consequence of the special Roman bias and the very narrow limit to what honourable people could do in public.

To give a few examples of class prejudice: Cassius Dio expresses the view that some *equites* should be admitted to the Senate even if they had begun their careers as low as centurions but that if they had served in the rank and file and had carried wood and charcoal it was such a disgrace that their admission was unthinkable (52, 25:6-7). Or, to show how morals in Rome have deteriorated, Juvenal (VIII 146 ff.) tells us that the consul Lateranus drove the *carpentum* himself, in the nighttime, to be sure, but the moon and the stars were witnesses, and, when his term was up, he would do it in broad daylight, unashamedly greet old friends with his whip, and afterward feed his horses. It was a crime for an honourable man to carry firewood and charcoal, to drive his own wagon, and to feed his horses. Another example: an honourable Roman could not be seen eating in public. Ammianus (28, 4:4) reports that this was one of the long neglected regulatives for restaurants, which was revised by *praefectus urbi* Ampelius, known to have been *praefectus* in 371-372.

But things could get worse still. As Juvenal tells it (VIII 158 ff.), Lateranus would also go to all-night *popinae*, to be welcomed by a Syrophoenician host. To top it all, when he was on his way later to his province, this man, to whom the defence of Armenia, Syria, the Rhine, or the Danube could be entrusted, this man could be found in an Ostian *popina* in company with sailors, thieves, fugitive slaves, murderers, and coffin makers, and he lay on a couch next to an assassin.

Cicero pontificates against Antonius (*Phil.* 13, 24) that, if Caesar had not taken care of him, "in lustris, popinis, alea, vino tempus aetatis omne consumpsisses" ("you would have spent all your life in brothels, saloons, gambling, and drunkenness!"); about two of Catiline's followers, he says: "Publicium et Munatium quorum aes alienum contractum in popina nullum rei publicae motum afferre poterat" ("Publicius and Munatius, whose debts, contracted in pubs and saloons, could not be wiped out by any political upheaval," *in Cat.* 2, 4). Worse things could not be said; a *popina* had the connotation of gambling, prostitution, and all vices.[24]

As a very persuasive example of the low esteem in which *popinae* were held by *honesti*, Ulpian's commentary in *Digesta* 4, 8, 21, 11 is worth quoting: in a case of arbitration in a legal dispute the arbitrator can summon the litigants, "sed si in aliquem locum inhonestum adesse iusserit, puta in popinam uel in lupanarium, ut Uiuianus ait, sine dubio impune ei non parebitur" ("but if he summons them to a disgraceful place like a *popina* or a brothel, as Vivianus says, they cannot be punished for refusing to obey").

Latin literature is full of descriptions of the dishonesty, the lack of morality, and, indeed, the murderous character of Roman *caupones*. There are a few stories about hosts murdering guests at night to get their money, or about a *caupo* murdering one guest in order to serve human flesh to other guests, or about the kinds of witchcraft practised in the *cauponae*. And so on. It would be superfluous to relate these rather well-known anecdotes, of which many are collected by Kleberg,[25] but it would be relevant to quote the codification in Roman law of this Roman prejudice. The stigma attached to the profession of the *caupones* diminished the civil rights of its members, as a few quotations will show. Constantine decrees in A.D. 336 that senators and other high-ranking citizens

> "maculam subire infamiae uel alienos a Romanis legibus fieri, si ex ancilla uel ancillae filia, uel liberta uel libertae filia, uel scenica uel scenicae filia, uel ex *tabernaria* uel *tabernariae filia*, uel humili uel abiecta, uel lenonis uel arenarii filia, uel quae mercimoniis publice praefuit susceptos filios in numero legitimorum habere uoluerint" ("will be marked with infamy or placed outside Roman law, if they want to acknowledge as legitimate their children by a slave woman, or a slave woman's daughter, or a freedwoman or a freedwoman's daughter, or an actress or

an actress's daughter, or a female innkeeper or a female innkeeper's daughter, or a low-class or vile woman, or a procurer's or a gladiator's daughter, or one who has sold merchandise in public," *Cod. Just.* V 27, 1).

In *Codex Justinianus* V 5, 7, the emperors Valentinian and Marcian say that senators and high-ranking men may marry poor girls, if they are born to *ingenui* parents, but they cannot marry *humilem et abjectam feminam*, which is explained as "ancillam, ancillae filiam, libertam, libertae filiam, scenicam uel scenicae filiam, *tabernariam* uel *tabernarii* uel lenonis aut arenarii *filiam* aut eam quae mercimoniis publice praefuit" ("slave woman, a slave woman's daughter, a freedwoman or a freedwoman's daughter, an actress or an actress's daughter, a female innkeeper or a male innkeeper's or procurer's or gladiator's daughter, or a woman who has sold merchandise in public").

But most telling is Constantine's law of 326 about *adulterium*, which says that no adultery was committed in cases where a woman who waited on customers in a *caupona* was involved, for those women, in the words of the law, "immunes a iudiciaria seueritate et stupri et adulterii praestentur, quas uilitas uitae dignas legum obseruatione non crediderit" ("are exempt from the severity of the law for rape as well as adultery whose low-class life makes them unworthy of the respect of the laws," *Cod. Just.* IX 9, 29:28).

The contempt in which the taverns were held was of course aggravated by the fact that three-quarters of the *caupones* were freedmen, close to the bottom of Roman society.[26] To this low esteem of the taverns were added the fear and disgust that the Romans nurtured against the guilds, or against any kind of organization. The reason: many guilds used taverns as meeting places, and when the guilds were used as fronts for political activities it caused the Senate, and later the emperors, to take severe reprisals against both, the taverns as well as the guilds.

The guilds were first prohibited in 64 B.C.: "senatus consulto collegia sublata sunt, quae aduersus rem publicam uidebantur esse" ("By decree of the Senate were abolished all guilds which appeared to work against the public interest").[27] In 58 B.C., Clodius had the prohibition cancelled, and he had numerous new *collegia* instituted: "collegia non ea solum quae senatus sustulerat restituta, sed innumerabilia quaedam noua ex omni faece urbis ac seruitio concitata" ("He not only reinstated the guilds that had been dissolved by the Senate, but also instituted numerous new ones, recruited among the riffraff and slave population of Rome"), says Cicero.[28] This was a clearly political move, and during the tumultuous years that followed it became obvious that the *collegia* when exploited politically could control the politics of the country. The gang wars, which characterized life in Rome, and which were commanded by Milo and Clodius during that period, were a memento to Caesar, Augustus, and the following emperors, who developed a maniacal fear of the guilds and had them under constant observation.

Caesar is said to have abolished all *collegia* except those long established: "cuncta collegia praeter antiquitus constituta distraxit" ("He dissolved all guilds, except those which had existed from old times");[29] Augustus revived his law, "collegia praeter antiqua et legitima dissoluit" ("He terminated all guilds except the old, legitimate ones"),[30] and outlawed those which had come into existence since Caesar's death. Tiberius was very restrictive, Gaius Caligula was rather conciliatory, and Claudius was very hostile to the guilds and abolished those which Gaius had permitted. He prohibited even the Jews' religious associations; Nero turned against the Jews.[31]

The same emperors who reacted so strictly to the guilds were usually ruthless with the taverns. We are told by Cassius Dio (60, 6:6-7) that Claudius abolished guilds which had been allowed by Gaius, and in order to attack the evil at its root he closed the taverns where the members of the guilds used to meet and drink. To get at the guilds the emperor understood that he also had to control the taverns. The viewpoint that guilds plus taverns equal riots and conspiracy is expressed in plain words by Philo, who says about Augustus that he ordered that the Jews alone should be permitted to assemble in synagogues. "These gatherings," he said, "were not based on drunkenness and carousing, but were schools of temperance and justice" (*legatio*, 311-12). Philo hands it all to us in a nutshell: the guilds would meet in the taverns to drink; drink made the guild brothers bold, irresponsible, and conspiracy-prone, which led to public unrest. The experience from the street fights in the middle of the first century B.C. taught the emperors to fear gang wars. So the closing of the guilds as well as of the taverns was nothing but a political move, and all the provisions to curb the activities of the taverns and inns and limit the services that the taverns were allowed to offer were introduced for the sole purpose of making them less attractive to the public.

Cassius Dio relates that the same Claudius who closed the taverns where the guilds met also ordained that cooked meat and hot water could not be sold in the taverns, at least in those that had not been closed. We might ask whether this prohibition would also include hotels. The wording of the Claudian law as told by Dio (l.l.) is rather brief and spare, and it is easy to say that we do not know. But on the other hand it was next to indecent for a respected Roman—and who cared about others?—to be seen eating in public. Since travellers in antiquity procured their own food and since, as was pointed out above (see no. 19), the hotel Casa delle Volte Dipinte has two of the three known kitchens in Ostia, it may very well be that meals could not be bought in Ostia (Rome) during times of restriction.

That the services of taverns were curtailed under Claudius is explained in Claudius's own words, although in an indirect way. When the Senate was discussing butchers and *vinarii*, Claudius said in the Senate chamber: " 'rogo vos, quis potest sine offula uiuere?' descripsitque abundantiam ueterum tabernarum, unde solitus esset uinum olim et ipse petere" (" 'Tell me, who can live without a bite to eat?' And he described the great variety offered in old taverns, where years ago he himself used to go for wine," Suet. *Claudius* 40, 1). It sounds as if Claudius deplores the restrictions imposed on the *tabernae vinariae*, and it indicates also that he might be inclined to offer food, for "who can live without a bite to eat"? It should be noted that Claudius speaks of the rich variety offered in the taverns "in the old days" (*ueterum tabernarum*), which indicates that those conditions did not exist at the time when he spoke. It should also be noted that the statement was made during a debate about butchers and *vinarii*, and that Claudius objects to the restrictions which have been imposed on the taverns so that one cannot have an *offula*, a snack, as in the past. This seems to indicate that the Senate was in favour of restraining the tavern owners, to the emperor's dismay. The butchers (or the butcher lobby) won out: whoever wanted meat could not have it served in the taverns but had to buy it from the butchers.

Suetonius quotes this incident to censure Claudius for speaking about an improper subject in an improper way, especially since the speaker was an emperor. But the facts of the matter are there, and the debate in the Senate could indicate that the restrictions on the *vinarii* were more the work of the Senate than of the emperor.

But besides the incident in the Senate, it is traditionally thought that Claudius had an economic problem as well as a supply problem on his hands (Dio 60, 17:8). Messalina and Claudius's freedmen are said to have sold not only citizenships and high military and civilian appointments but also everything else, so that a shortage of supplies developed. Claudius was then forced to summon the people to the Campus Martius and, from the platform, proclaim prices on merchandise—an attempt at price control. In addition to the motives described above he may have had other motives related to those attributed to Tiberius.

Although our sources about all of this are anything but abundant, we know that Claudius was not the first to limit the sale of food in the taverns. Tiberius is on record as having ordered the *aediles* to see that the *popinae* and *ganeae* did not even sell bakery products (Suet. *Tib.* 34, 1). It was part of an economic drive, and to show that he was serious about it he himself would eat left-overs from previous meals.

Nero continued Claudius's restrictions: he ordered that nothing but vegetables could be served in the *popinae* (Suet. *Nero* 16; Dio 62, 14:2). Vespasian maintains the same regulations (Dio 65, 10:3): only peas and beans could be prepared and served. It is remarkable that Claudius tried to get to the root of the socio-political problem as he saw it in the taverns; what was needed was to take the taverns out of the life of the Romans, change the habits of the Roman people, and re-educate them to live without taverns (Dio 60, 6:6-7).

Ostia may give us an indirect proof that the will of the emperors prevailed. The difference between the bar counters of Herculaneum-Pompeii and Ostia is indication enough. The

134.
Bar counter in Hercul-
aneum, *insula* II 6,
seen from inside the
bar. Part of the bar
counter has fallen away
and exposed the built-
in counter jars.

counter jars (fig. 134) that are so characteristic of Pompeian-
Herculanean bars have disappeared, and instead we see the
bar counter with the water basin. When exactly the Ostian-type
bar counter was introduced is unknown. The bar relief from
Isola Sacra (see pp. 187-88) gives a *terminus ante quem*. It comes
out of a Hadrianic grave, but it is questionable whether the
relief is of the same date. Calza points to the barmaid's hair-
style, which is the fashion toward the middle of the third century, a hundred years after Hadrian.[32]

The contents of the counter jars in Herculaneum complied
with Vespasian's legislation. In various jars the following were
found: grain in *insula* IV 10-11; beans and peas in *insula* V 6;
grain in an upstairs store-room over a bar in *insula* V 10; grain,
chick-peas, and beans in Insula Orientalis II 13.[33] But in no bar
was there any trace of meat, although bones were found in several homes outside the taverns.[34]

Vespasian's legislation had explicitly prohibited the serving of meat in the Roman bars and limited the menu to beans
and peas. Vespasian simply repeated the provisions which,
with minor modifications, had been handed down from Claudius through Nero. These laws would be meticulously
enforced in Ostia since it was so close to Rome. The status of
Rome was different from other places in the Empire in that all
laws to uphold peace and order were rigorously observed
there. These restrictive laws would, of course, make the taverns much less attractive to customers,[35] and from Claudius's

first attack on the taverns the new style of bars started to develop. The food jars disappear and the water basins, the prerequisite for the *conditum* and the *calda*, dominate.

Notes

1. Material in Kleberg, *Hôtels*, 16-17, 51-52.

2. *Ep.* 56, 2: "omnes popinarum institores mercem sua quadam et insignita modulatione uendentes."

3. Kleberg, *Hôtels*, 53.

4. *Ibid.*, 50.

5. Nos. 5, 9, 25, 30, 31, and 37 in the survey of taverns above.

6. G. Calza, *La necropoli del Porto di Roma nell'Isola Sacra* (1940), 203, fig. 107. A picture also in Meiggs, plate XXVI.

7. Thylander, *Études sur l'épigraphie latine*, 19. Calza, *Isola Sacra* (compare note 6), 204, dates the relief to the middle of the third century, because the hair-style of the barmaid is like that of Gallienus's empress Salonina.

8. VII, 61: "abstulerat totam temerarius institor. . . . Nulla catenatis pila est praecincta lagenis. . . . occupat aut totas nigra popina vias."

9. It seems that most *taberna* fronts in Ostia, Pompeii, and Herculaneum are arranged so that the storekeeper's door, that swung open on *cardines*, was on the right side of somebody entering, while the sliding shutters, which covered the counters, were on the left.

10. See *Polis and Imperium: Studies in Honour of E.T. Salmon* (1974), 176 and 178.

11. *NSc* (1915), 29.

12. See, for instance, Kleberg, *Hôtels*, 157, fig. 11.

13. More examples: Kleberg, *Hôtels*, 104.

14. Marquardt, *Privatleben der Römer* (reprint Darmstadt, 1964) II, 460-61. Apicius I, 1; Pliny, *n.h.* XIV, 108; for an imaginative use of *conditum: SHA Heliogabalus* 21, 6.

15. More on bar equipment: Kleberg, *Hôtels*, 114-15.

16. *Ibid.*, 26ff.

17. *Ibid.*, 33-35.

18. Raissa Calza, *Ostia*, 115.

19. *ScO* I, 137. Becatti expresses himself vaguely: "la cui destinazione era forse una stalla o rimessa con alloggio o ambiente di carattere industriale."

20. Isidorus, *Etym.* 15 2, 42: "poprina graecus sermo est quae apud nos corrupta popina dicitur. Est autem locus iuxta balnea publica, ubi post lauacrum a fame et siti reficiuntur."

21. Kleberg, *Hôtels*, 114.

22. *Ibid.*, figs. 13 and 16.

23. See p. 22 in this text.

24. *Much material is collected by Kleberg, Hôtels, 91ff.*

Ibid., 83ff.; In den Wirtshäusern, 20ff.

26. Kleberg, *Hôtels*, 77.

27. Asconius (Clarke), *in Pisonem 8;* see also de Robertis I, 83ff.

28. *in Pisonem 9;* see also de Robertis I, 109ff.

29. Suet. *Diuus Julius* 42, 3; see also de Robertis, I, 195ff.

30. Suet. *Augustus* 32, 1; Dio 54, 2.

31. Survey of the emperors' attitude toward the guilds: de Robertis I, 244-45; also his *Il diritto associativo romano*, 216-17.

32. See note 7 above.

33. Amadeo Maiuri, *Ercolano. I nuovi scavi*, 1927-58, vol. I, 432, 402, 251, 465.

34. Now in the Museo Nazionale, Naples. Compare J.J. Deiss, *Herculaneum* (New York, 1966), 3, 18, 156.

35. Kleberg, *Hôtels*, 54-55; *Wirtshäuser*, 43.

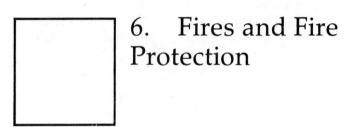

6.   Fires and Fire Protection

It is impossible to speak about fire in ancient Ostia without mentioning the Great Fire in Nero's Rome. The small fires that we can observe in Ostia started and were controlled in complete obscurity, and we owe to Nero's fire a description of Roman fire fighting. The Romans were just as helpless as all other generations, including the modern, when a major conflagration raged through a city.

   The fire of A.D. 64 is described by Tacitus and Cassius Dio, the former with some factual veracity, the latter in a tale which has the ring of the *rhetor* school. There is, however, from a much later time, a fire report that can serve as an illustration of the Roman disaster.

Fires in Constantinople

The report comes out of Constantinople of the nineteenth century. It is well known that so much of ancient civilization, which was suffocated in the West, survived in Byzantium. The old Roman baths, for instance, survived there and were returned to the West under the name of Turkish Baths. Similarly, ancient Roman fire fighting survived unchanged through the centuries. The following description of fires in Constantinople around the middle of the nineteenth century shows that neither in construction nor in fire fighting had there been many advances in eighteen hundred years.

The description is in the *Handbook for Travellers in Constantinople, Prusa, and the Troad* (London: John Murray, 1893, 9-10):

> Fires in Constantinople are of frequent occurrence and often very destructive, desolating whole quarters of the City. Great precautions are now taken both to prevent them and to check their progress. Arrangements are made to give the earliest possible notice to all parts of the City when and where a fire has broken out. For this purpose watchmen are stationed day and night on three commanding spots—the Galata Tower, in Galata; the Serasker Tower, in Stambul; and the high hill below Kandili, on the Asiatic side of the Bosporus. Cannon are fired from the last mentioned place to announce that a fire has broken out. A red balloon, lighted within, is raised at the same time to the top of a mast; at the Serasker Tower, balls, and at the Galata Tower flags are hoisted, showing by their number in what quarter the fire is. At these two posts there are firemen waiting, fast runners, who, the moment the fire is discovered, run to their different quarters to inform the regular watch, setting up the cry of fire, and the quarter where it has occurred. The fire-engines are in the hands of firemen who are paid by enjoying some special privileges; but the engines are small boxes, which are carried on the shoulders of four men; these run headlong, crying, Yangin Var, "Fire!" at the top of their voices. Hav-

ing reached the place of conflagration, they wait to be hired by the people whose houses are in danger. There is another set of firemen who prove eminently useful on such occasions. They are soldiers armed with axes and long poles, with iron hooks at the end. These tear down the wooden houses, and so isolate the fire, as effectually to put an end to its ravages. Still, a fire in Constantinople is an awful scene; 2000 houses and shops have been known to burn in a few hours. It is indeed impossible to describe the confusion and horror of the sight. Men, women and children escaping from their abandoned homes, each dragging or carrying on his shoulders whatever he happened to catch at the moment. The police are powerless for good. Evil-intentioned men rush into the houses and rob them, under the pretence of being friends of the family. They have often been known to spread the conflagration by carrying burning coals into the dwellings yet unreached by the flames. There is no doubt, however, that the narrowness of the streets, and the light inflammable materials of the houses, are the chief causes of these calamities; and it is a source of satisfaction to find that the streets are now widened after every fire, and that many stone houses are now erected in the place of the former wooden buildings. There is now a fire brigade, itfai alai, organized on a European model by Count Szecheny. It consists of three battalions of firemen, two at the Taksim Barracks, and one at the Seraskerat. It is well managed and has done good service during the last 10 or 12 years.

The close relation to ancient Roman fire fighting jumps to mind:

1. The fire engines, the boxes that the firemen are carrying on their shoulders, are, of course, the Roman *siphones* that are described by Vitruvius under the name of *Ctesibica machina* (X 7). They seem to have been common engines: there seem to have been two *sif(onarii)* in each cohort of the Roman *vigiles*, which may mean that each cohort had at least one *Ctesibica machina*.[1] It should be noted, too, that, after a major fire in Nicomedia, Pliny complains to Trajan that the city "nowhere has a publicly owned *sipho*" (Ep. X 33, 2).

2. The fire-fighters hurry up to the scene of the fire; there they wait to be hired by the people whose houses are in danger. This particular feature is a direct parallel to pre-Augustan Rome where Crassus's private fire brigade acted in the same manner, with the minor difference that Crassus wanted to buy the houses which were on fire—and then proceed to put out the fire.[2]

3. Fires are contained by demolitions: soldiers armed with axes and long poles with iron hooks at the end do the job, in the style of the *vigiles* of Rome. The *Digesta* I 15 prescribes that the *praefectus vigilum* shall patrol with his men at night with axes *(dolabrae)* and water buckets *(hamae)*; the *Digesta* 33, 7, 12, 18 lists *perticae* (poles) next to *siphones* (fire pumps); in one of the graffiti of the seventh cohort of the *vigiles* in Rome is the item VNC. COH.,[3] which Reynolds interprets as *uncinarius cohortis*. Tacitus tells how a fire in Rome was finally stopped on the sixth day at the foot of the Esquiline Hill: "sexto demum die apud imas Esquilias finis incendii factus, prorutis per immensum aedificiis" ("Finally, on the sixth day the fire was stopped at the bottom of the Esquiline Hill, after the demolition of buildings over a vast area," *Ann.* XV 40, 1).

4. The confusion and the horror of the sight is no different from the scene in Rome as described by Tacitus: "lamenta pauentium feminarum fessa aetate aut rudis pueritiae" ("the wailing of frightened women, old as well as young," *Ann.* XV 38, 5-6).

5. The reports of the criminal activities of those who deliberately set more fires and break into houses to loot, saying (in Constantinople) that they are friends of the owner, or (in Rome) that they are doing so under order, are close parallels (Tac. *Ann.* XV 38, 8).

6. The narrowness of the streets and the inflammable material are also quoted as aggravating factors by Tacitus: "incendium . . . anteiit remedia velocitate . . . et obnoxia urbe artis itineribus hucque et illuc flexis atque enormibus vicis qualis vetus Roma fuit" ("The fire . . . outraced the fire-fighters . . . and the city was an easy victim because of the narrow winding streets and twisted city blocks, such as old Rome was," *Ann.* XV 38, 4).

7. But now, the report goes on, the streets of Constantinople are widened after every fire, and many stone houses are replacing former wooden buildings—exactly as in Rome where construction was done; "dimensis uicorum ordinibus et latis viarum spatiis . . . ac patefactis areis" ("The streets were orderly laid out and made wide . . . and spaces opened up," Tacitus *Ann.* XV 43, 1), and where parts of the houses had to be built in Gabinian or Alban stone, while wood was banned in those places: "aedificia ipsa certa sui parte sine trabibus saxo Gabino Albanoue solidarentur, quod is lapis ignibus imperuius est" ("Certain parts of the buildings could not be built with wooden beams, but with solid Gabinian or Alban stone, which is fireproof," *Ann.* XV 43, 4).

8. Constantinople got a fire brigade, the *itfai alai,* while Rome got new regulations for fire fighting and fire prevention (Tac. *Ann.* XV 43, 4 *in fine*). Constantinople apparently had the same combination of private enterprise and public institution in fire-fighting as was characteristic of Rome. Constantinople with its firemen, who expect to be hired, the soldiers, who are ready to demolish, and the modern fire brigade *itfai alai* seems to duplicate the Roman combination of private efforts like Crassus's fire corps and public assistance (the *aediles,* [4] the *corpus vigilum*). The Roman approach is clear in Trajan's answer to Pliny when Pliny wanted to create a fire department in Nicomedia: do not create a politically dangerous organization, but supply the fire-fighting equipment and leave the rest to the private initiative of the property owners (Pliny *Ep.* X 34).

City-Roman Fire Legislation in Ostia

The Ostia that we can study is all post-Neronian and all built after the Great Fire, in accordance with the new fire regulations. Some of the Neronian rules have become redundant in the Ostia of the second century, because Ostia is developed a further step than New Rome. The prescription about the use of Gabinian and Alban stone is old fashioned in Ostia where the cement and rubble construction of the whole shell and all load-carrying elements have given more fireproofing and structural stability than what a combination of mud brick and stone could offer.

It is interesting that Nero, as far as we know, did not do anything to encourage the use of the rubble and cement technique, which under his successors, the Flavians, was used to build the biggest concrete building in the world up to that time, the Colosseum. Even in the Colosseum one observes a combination of stone blocks and cement, with travertine blocks constituting the main carrying element of the enormous bleachers. It was only after that time that the Romans had the experience and the mature technique to rely completely on cement alone for their building, with the Pantheon demonstrating the new building material's capacity for loads.

Ostia shows compliance with Nero's fire legislation. As a rule communal walls are banned (Tac. *Ann.* XV 43, 5); every house has its own walls and only where there is empty space on the one side of a house can it be separated from the neighbour's property by a single-ply common wall, which then belongs to the one who built it because he needed it. There are wide streets compared to the Roman streets that we are shown in old, pre-Neronian Rome. Important was the rule that everyone should keep water in his house or apartment. Already by Nero's time it is ordained that everybody should have means at hand to control fires, "subsidia reprimendis ignibus in propatulo," Tac. Ann. XV 43, 4. This would mean water (or vinegar, which also was popular, *Dig.* 33, 7, 12, 18), but it is very clearly expressed in the instructions for the *praefectus vigilum* (*Dig.* 1, 15, 3, 4): "that he shall remind all renters that they take care not to start fires through negligence, and that every one of them keep water in his apartment."

Other laws governed the distance that should separate public and private buildings. The *Codex Theodosianus* XV 38 says that public storehouses must be disconnected on four sides from private buildings, which may have to be torn down (A.D. 398); XV 46 prescribes that private buildings should be built fifteen feet from public buildings (A.D. 406). Earlier, Constantine had commanded that new residential construction should keep a distance of one hundred feet from state *horrea* (*Cod. Theod.* XV 1, 4, A.D. 326; 320).

This distance is of particular importance in a city like Ostia where *horrea* are so dominant. The provisions of the Theodosian Code are concerned with Portus, but they explain the *intercapedines* that exist in Ostia around the grain *horrea* for the protection of the *annona*. The provisions that are codified in the *Codex Theodosianus* are found implemented in Ostia from the first century; it is characteristic that the big Ostian grain *horrea* are isolated in this way. The *horrea* of Artemis (V x 18) and the *horrea* of Hortensius (V xii 1) are isolated from each other and from the unexcavated block of the Sabazeum (V xii 2). The *horrea* I viii 1 are separated by an *intercapedo* from two others: I viii 2 and 3. The Grandi Horrea are isolated in a block by themselves (II ix 3) in the same way as the Horrea Antoniniana (II ii 7). By adopting that practice of avoiding direct contact between buildings the Romans avoided many transfers of fires from one building to the next, and, in the case of a big fire, the advance of the fire through the city would be slowed.

Fire Hazards in Ostia

But even with all that fireproofing it is obvious that there were many fire hazards in Ostia. There was a lot of woodwork in those houses. It is only in few places that the separation between the ground floor and the second floor is constituted by a *concameratio*, a concrete vault. In most cases there were wooden floor-ceilings; holes in the walls or a ledge running all around the room supported the ends of the beams for the floor-ceilings, which were faced with mosaic on the floor side and with plaster and decoration on the ceiling side. Many houses had wooden stairs, although a great number of the apartment blocks had cement stairways to the various floors, as far as the remains permit us to judge. On the other hand, all stairs from the shops to their upstairs *cenaculum* were built in wood; only the first three to four steps and the landing were in concrete and masonry.

The amount of wood used in construction in Ostia cannot be verified now. However, there is no doubt that much of the

top floors was built in wood. Herodian tells about the street
fights in Rome in A.D. 238 (VII 12, 6). After the Roman mob had
attacked the Castra Praetoria, the soldiers counter-attacked and
set fire to the wooden balconies of the houses, and since many
houses were built in wood and were close to each other much
of the city burned down.

It is worth noting how Alexandria, in contrast to Rome, is
nearly fireproof: "nam incendio fere tuta est Alexandria," says
Bellum Alexandrinum 1, who goes on to explain that this is so
because wood is not used in the buildings in roofs or elsewhere. Walls and roofs are built in stone and cement: "aedificia
. . . structuris ac fornicibus continentur tectaque sunt rudere
aut pavimentis" ("The buildings are constructed in masonry
and vaults, and they are roofed over with mortar or cement
flooring"). This is an Italian's impression of Alexandria, which,
in a negative way, gives a picture of Rome.

Compared to Alexandria, Rome had great problems.
Vitruvius calls attention to the dangers of fires in the roof structures, because the roof beams are exposed at the eaves and liable to catch fire from the neighbouring houses. He tells how
Caesar observed the fire-resistant qualities of larch wood when
he was besieging the town of Larignum in the Alps, and Vitruvius remarks that this building material would be very useful in
houses—if not everywhere, certainly around the eaves of the
apartment houses. If larch were used in these places, the buildings would be safeguarded against fires from the outside: "ab
traiectionibus incendiorum aedificia periculo liberarentur"
("The houses would be protected from the danger of fires
jumping from one roof to the other," II 9, 16). The danger from
the roofs was compounded by the fact that there was a great
deal of light construction in the upper floors. In many cases the
solid houses of which we now can see the two bottom
storeys—three at the most—may have had a couple of storeys
built with *opus craticium*, with wood, reeds, and stucco (VII
3, 11). "I wish that these *craticii* had never been invented," says
Vitruvius, "for although they are fast to erect and save space,
they are like torches ready to start fires" (II 8, 20). What he
refers to in this case may be read into Gellius's description of a
great fire on the Cispius Hill: walking with Antonius Julianus

135.
The apse of S Saba demonstrates the late Roman building technique of covering the ends of the roof beams at the eaves in order to protect them from fires. It was common to build a ledge that was a combination of brick and corbels. For other examples, *see* Nash, *Pictorial Dictionary*, figs. 203, 777, 901, 1171, 1256, and 1328, and Boethius and Ward-Perkins, *Etruscan and Roman Architecture* (London, 1970) plate 269.

and his students he saw a towering, multi-storied apartment house engulfed by fire, and the neighbouring houses were already sending flames high into the sky ("Conspicimus insulam quandam occupatam igni multis arduisque tabulatis editam et propinqua iam omnia flagrare vasto incendio," XV 1, 2). Antonius Julianus advised his companions to fireproof wood by treating it with alum.

It is only in later times, well into the third century, that the Roman architects counter this fire hazard by building a brick moulding, supported by stone corbels, around rafter ends. Then the brick moulding and the stone corbels, not the rafter ends, support the eaves and the roof is completely encased in stone and roof tiles. No wood is exposed to flames (fig. 135).

Fire Protection by Demolition

It was often impossible for the Romans to cope with the speed with which fires developed. Unless a fire was caught in the very beginning, fire fighting was confined to demolition, which could contain the fire by depriving it of material to burn. Even modern cities with water-pressure systems are helpless when faced with major fires. The demolitions in Rome to some extent were given over to private initiative. The provisions of Roman law in this case are surprising, if indeed it was the law (*Dig.* 9, 2, 49, 1). Ulpian writes that Celsus argues that if somebody demolishes his neighbour's house in order to control a fire that seems to be approaching it, he is not liable to a damage suit if his action was motivated by a legitimate fear that the fire would reach his own house, and this was valid whether the fire actually got as far as his house or was extinguished before it reached it.

Evidence of Fires in Ostia

In Ostia there is no evidence of city-wide or even major fires. There is sporadic evidence of fires in the ruins. During the excavation signs were recovered that the bakery in Via dei Molini next to Casa di Diana (I iii 1) was burnt down at the end of the third century and never built again.[5] In a different part of the city the temple of the guild of the *stuppatores* was burnt down and left.[6] The Caseggiato del Sole (V vi 1) was also a fire victim. The evidence of fire, here as in other cases, is the presence of charcoal, from burnt wood and timber in the house, as charcoal will last forever. The Caseggiato del Sole was excavated in October 1939, and twice (8 and 11 October) the excavation diary makes remarks about the fire. The fire was confined to the Caseggiato del Sole, which seems to have been utterly destroyed. The house may be assumed to have been at least three storeys high. The walls were discoloured some by the fire, and after the fire much of the rubble was scooped together on the ground floor and the ground floor on Via del Sole was sealed off in *opus listatum*. The house was never rebuilt.

We see from *CIL* XIV 376, lines 18-19, "idem thermas quas Divus Pius aedificaverat vi ignis consumptas refecit," that P. Lucilius Gamala repaired the Baths (of Neptune), which had been built by Antoninus Pius but which had been damaged by fire; this repair must have been done under Marcus Aurelius.

It should be added that S4494 is a gravestone that commemorates a Pretorian soldier, to whom the City of Ostia gave a public funeral because he was killed while fighting a fire: "Militi cohor. VI Pr/Ostienses locum sepult/dederunt/publicoque funere efferun/decreverunt quod in incendio/restinguendo interit" ("To the soldier of the sixth cohort of the Pretorians the People of Ostia gave a grave site and decreed to give him a public funeral because he lost his life while fighting a fire").

Nero's *Porticus* as Fire Protection

A final fire protection were Nero's *porticus*. Tacitus mentions them, saying that Rome was rebuilt, "additis porticibus quae frontem insularum protegerent; eas porticus Nero sua pecunia exstructurum. . . . pollicitus est" ("and *porticus* were added to protect the façade of the apartment blocks; Nero promised that he would build those *porticus* with his own money," *Ann.* XV 43, 1-2). He does not give any reason for this imperial munificence, or any explanation of the purpose of the *porticus,* or why the emperor would pay for the *porticus* and for nothing else. Suetonius (*Nero* 16) reports that Nero made the Romans build *porticus* in front of *insulae* as well as *domus* so that fires could be controlled (*arcerentur*) from the balconies built on top of the *porticus*; he paid for their construction. So, according to Suetonius, the *porticus* with their balconies were made primarily to bring the fire-fighters up close to where the fires were.[7]

To understand fires in ancient Rome, and Ostia, one has to remember, first of all, that in case of a major fire the first place in a house to be struck was likely to be the roof with all its timber, as Vitruvius pointed out (see page 214). The roof would flame up and then collapse. The burning, charred timber would slide down and pile up in the street, a recurring event in antiquity as well as in modern times.

Under the circumstances, the height of the Roman houses went against Suetonius's claim that the balconies were designed for the purpose of fighting fires. Roman literature complains about towering, rickety houses that collapse, and Augustus limited the height of the buildings to seventy feet, which later was reduced to sixty feet by Trajan.[8] These standard measures concerned only the façades of the houses; what did not face the street was the private responsibility of the builder. Augustus's ordinance had already been repeated by Nero, "cohibitaque aedificiorum altitudine" ("having limited the height of the houses," Tac. *Ann.* XV 43, 1), and it seems to have been a law that was likely to be broken.

We have some material to verify this for Ostian buildings: of the approximately one hundred and seventy-five buildings that James Earnest Packer has studied about one hundred and fifteen may have been four storeys or over, fifty-eight to fifty-nine were presumably less than four storeys high; the over-all average for Ostia comes to 3,60 storeys.[9] If the fire-fighters were to combat a blaze from the top of the porticoes, they might still be two to three storeys below a burning roof. In Rome they would be worse off because the height of the houses in Rome exceeded those in Ostia.[10] Moreover, if they fought a roof fire from a balcony over a *porticus*, they were trapped and in danger of having the whole collapsing roof on their heads.

If they fought the fire by demolition they would hardly be helped by a *porticus*, and, as said, demolitions were what stopped major fires. It should be noted that the *fabri tignuarii*, the carpenters, the builders, were one of the three ancient guilds that constituted the later fire departments. The philosophy is, of course, that since they knew how to build they would also know how to unbuild or tear down. Pliny asked Trajan whether he could be permitted to start a *collegium fabrum* with one hundred and fifty members in Nicomedia, so that he could start a fire department; the city had been without any way of fighting a recent fire (*Ep.* X 33).

The duties of the *praefectus vigilum* (*Dig.* I, 15, 3, 3) comprise being on watch all night and patrolling with axes and fire buckets, the axes for tearing down, the buckets for extinguishing fires. The bucket brigade must have played a role in Roman fire fighting, in connection with the operation of the *sipho*. The *sipho* is mentioned as part of standard fire-fighting equipment in *Digesta* 33, 7, 12, 18, and Isodorus, shortly after A.D. 600, describes how fire-fighters in the East (*in Oriente*, meaning Constantinople?) come running with the *siphos* full of water

(*Etym.* XX 6, 9). He adds that *siphos* are also used to clean vaulted ceilings. The latter information indicates that their output must have been moderate, and there is no doubt that their usefulness was limited. But there is no doubt, either, that their usefulness would be enhanced if they were brought up on a high balcony of twenty to twenty-five feet, if there was a viable way of bringing water up to that level as well.

The *porticus* did not really bring the fire-fighters where action was required, and one could question the economy of the whole enterprise: one can think of various, much cheaper ways of bringing fire-fighters twenty feet up in the air than by building porticoes throughout an entire city. Suetonius's statement can be subjected to grave doubts, and a closer look at the Roman *porticus* to the extent that it can be studied today seems to prove that Suetonius is wrong. Only a minority of those *porticus* are of the type that has a balcony on top.

The ancient *insulae* with *porticus* that exist in Ostia and Rome mostly differ from the type that Suetonius writes about. Suetonius's *porticus* is added to the house (fig. 136), while the majority of those that can be studied in Rome and Ostia are built into the house so that the façade of the *porticus* and the façade of the house is one continuous surface and the pillars of the *porticus* support the whole façade wall of the house (fig. 137).

In Rome there are still a couple of houses with porticoed façades standing up to the fourth floor. One is the second-century house that is part of the church for SS Giovanni and Paolo. Actually, it is two adjacent houses on the old Clivus Scauri, but it is the western house that is of particular interest to us, because not only the *porticus* but also the walls of the *tabernae* can be studied in the basement of the church.[11]

The width of the six vaulted spans through which one entered the *porticus* is 2,79 to 2,94 metres. The pillars between the openings are 1,62 to 1,65 metres wide and 0,80 metre deep. The width of the *porticus,* the distance between the pillars and the *taberna* fronts inside the *porticus,* is 4,95 metres.

At the top of Via in Selci, the ancient Clivus Suburanus, is a later (early fifth century?) Roman house with portico whose façade is standing up to the fourth floor.[12] Four spans can be

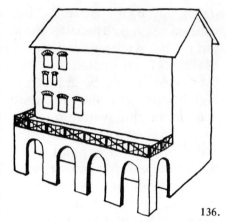

136.
Porticus according to Suetonius's concept.

137.
Porticus as at least two-thirds of *porticus* in Ostia (and Rome) were constructed.

138.
A pillar shares the load of the building with the pillar on either side and the inside wall of the *porticus*. One pillar supports the darkened area up through all the floors of the building.

136.

seen, of which three can be measured: 2,69, 3,91, and 3,94 metres. Here the pillars are 0,46 metre wide; their depth cannot be measured, neither can the inside walk, which is of little consequence here since the pillars of this portico are travertine and cannot count in the calculations that will be done later.

Turning to Ostia one encounters a different situation. There are few houses preserved up to the beginning of the third floor and, consequently, the porticoed *insulae* to that height cannot be studied. Most *insulae*, however, show only part of the first floor. Two of the best preserved are the Caseggiato del Serapide and Cas. degli Aurighi, both of which have porticoes surrounding their inside courtyards. In the Caseggiato del Serapide the spans between the pillars are 2,94, 2,69, and 2,77 metres, the width of the walk inside pillars is 2,36 to 2,49 metres, and the dimensions of the pillars are 0,89 to 0,90 metre by 0,61 metre. That house is estimated to have been five storeys high, and it is clear that the *porticus* was built into the house and that the pillars supported the full height of the walls around the courtyard.

The Casa degli Aurighi, too, has an interior *porticus* in the courtyard. There is a slight difference in the dimensions of the east side and the west side: on the east side the spans vary from 2,38 to 2,93 metres and the width of the *porticus* is 2,35 to 2,51 metres. The pillars are 0,74 to 0,75 by 0,95 metre. On the west side the spans are 2,35 to 2,49 metres, the width of the *porticus*

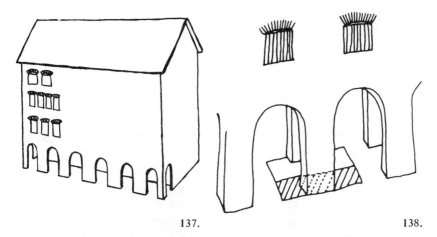

137.   138.

is 2,49 to 2,51 metres, and the pillars measure 0,72 to 0,89 by 0,90 to 0,95 metre. The Casa degli Aurighi was five storeys high, and the pillars supported the façade on the courtyard to the top. On the street a *porticus* had the dimensions of: span 2,74 to 3,35 metres; width 2,33 to 3,71 metres; and pillars 0,89 to 1,04 by 0,73 to 0,89 metre.

A third *insula* in Ostia, preserved up to the beginning of the third floor, is in Ostia's III Region xvi 6. Although this building collapsed, five arches of the fallen façade of the second floor and the beginning of the third floor stayed together and are laid out in Via della Foce. The house had four floors. The spans vary from 3,89 to 4,91 metres, the widths 2,59 to 2,67 metres, and the pillars measure 1,47 to 1,50 by 0,81 metre, with inside pilasters measuring 0,74 to 0,77 by 0,30 metre.

The key element in these *porticus* is, of course, the columns or pillars. The thicker the pillar the more weight it can support. A pillar in a *porticus* must share the load of the span with its neighbours on either side. Inside the *porticus* it shares the load with the inside wall of the house. The total load of the pillar is then a rectangle circumscribed by the façade of the *insula*, the lines indicating the middle between the pillar and its two neighbours, and, parallel with the façade, the half-way line between the façade and the inner line of the wall that is the limit of the *porticus* wall (fig. 138).

Simple reckoning will show that the proportion between the area of the pillar and its load area in the *insula* of SS Giovanni and Paolo is 1:10; in the Caseggiato del Serapide it is 1:10; in Casa degli Aurighi it is on the east side 1:7,9, on the west side 1:7,1, and on the street 1:10,5. The house in Via della Foce has the proportion 1:8,8.

In these four-to-five-storey houses the pillars, with the proportions of 1:7,1 to 1:10,5 between the areas of the pillars and the loaded area which they carried, were strong enough to support two to three upper storeys. If one goes into the ruined *insulae* of Ostia, of which only the ground floor is left, and measures the proportions between the areas and their loads, it would be a fair conclusion that the places where the proportions are 1:10,5 or less were *insulae* with engaged *porticus—porticus* whose pillars supported the façades of upper floors. However, where the same proportions are over 1:10,5 we know that at least some with the highest numbers were *porticus* added to the *insulae*, Suetonius's type of *porticus*.

In Ostia there are twenty-nine *insulae* with *porticus* that are accessible and measurable. Of these, ten are above the 1:10,5 ratio, while nineteen (65,5 percent) are below. In one of the former (II ii 6), many roof tiles were found on the ground.[13] In this *porticus* the proportion is 1:11,2; it is thought to be a two-storey *porticus* and it actually belongs in a different class from the others.[14] The *porticus* in Via degli Aurighi III ix 26 has a ratio of 1:19; these spindly pillars would only support a light load.[15] The testimony of the remains of Ostian *porticus* is that, conservatively expressed, two-thirds of them were without the Suetonian *solaria*. It proves Suetonius wrong since the purpose of the *porticus* could not be to create balconies from which fires could be fought.

It is interesting to note the difference between Suetonius's and Tacitus's wording: Suetonius says that "Nero . . . excogitavit . . . ut ante insulas ac domos porticus essent, de quarum solariis incendia arcerentur" ("Nero . . . got the idea that in front of apartment houses and *domus* there should be *porticus* from whose balconies one could fight fires," *Nero* 16, 1), while Tacitus speaks of "additisque porticibus, quae frontem insularum protegerent" (*Ann.* XV 43,1). Tacitus does not mention *domus*, only *insulae*, and this difference could derive from the fact that *porticus* were needed by the *insulae*, not by the *domus*.

Moreover, Tacitus does not speak of fire fighting like Suetonius: "de quarum solariis incendia arcerentur." There is no
special significance in the use of the verb *arcere* instead of
exstinguere, which is more common (*Thes. l.l.* VII, col. 863), as
the meaning is the same. Tacitus speaks of *frontem insularum
protegere*, cover in a protective way, but still the provision is a
direct result of the Roman catastrophe of A.D. 64 and it was considered a very vital enterprise, since the emperor would com-
mit the *fiscus* to pay for it.

The record is that in a fire the roof very often was the first
part of the house to erupt in flames, and it would soon collapse
and fall into the street like a large bonfire and block that street.
The descriptions of the fire (Tacitus, Dio) tell about people try-
ing to escape through one street, which was blocked by fire,
then attempting to go through a side-street only to find that it,
too, was blocked. Many people perished in that way. The *porticus* would save lives, since their pillars would keep the burning timber out of the sidewalk inside the *porticus* and give the
fleeing population a chance to get out. The *porticus* covered and
sheltered the Romans, and that is why the emperor would pay
for them.

Corpus Vigilum

Ostia very much felt the influence of the emperor, and fire
fighting, fire protection, and fire prevention must have been
highly regimented by the emperor. A fire corps was provided
by the emperor, under various forms, from Augustus on. In a
previous section was an example of his Pretorians as fire-
fighters (p. 216). This means that the highest authority, after
the emperor, would be the Pretorian prefect, under Augustus,
and later the prefect of the *vigiles* and his deputy in Ostia—
which again means that what was law in Rome was also law in
Ostia. The corps of the *vigiles* was started by Claudius (Suet.
Claud. 25, 2). From the time of Hadrian on we get some information about the organization of the service of the *vigiles* in

Ostia. Toward the end of that emperor's reign they moved into new quarters, the barracks of the *vigiles*, or Caserma dei Vigili.[16] The building was three to four storeys high.[17] In the middle, it had a rectangular courtyard surrounded by a portico, which probably went through all the storeys; in the four corners were stairs to the upper floors. On the ground floor were rooms with entrances from the portico on the north, east, and south sides; on the west side was a Caesareum. The main entrance is from the east, with ancillary entrances from the north and south. In the southeast and northeast corners of the courtyard were large water basins, in the southeast corner of the building a latrine. There is nothing to indicate where the equipment was kept or what the activities of the *vigiles* were in their station. That many people were going and coming in this building is shown by the deep wheel ruts in the pavement of the main gate. A similar station is known from the Forma Urbis.[18]

When this building was excavated, a great number of inscriptions were found. They show that Ostia was served by a detachment of Roman *vigiles* on a rotating basis. It seems that the regular strength of the detachment would be four centuries, for a total of over four hundred men,[19] and that in the rotation all seven cohorts were represented. They came down (*descenderunt* is the expression of the inscriptions) for a period of four months.[20] The Ostian inscriptions mention many of the strictly military titles, *praefectus, subpraefectus, tribunus, centurio, cornicularius, beneficiarius, optio, tesserarius, bucinator*, while some of the more technical charges are lacking, *sifonarius, uncinarius,*[21] *falcarius, aquarius.*[22]

A *seb(aci)arius* is mentioned in one inscription (S4530), a charge well known in Rome.[23] The title of *sebaciarius* was presumably held by the man responsible for the cresset torches that were fed with tallow (*sebum*). Torches were used by police and fire patrols at night.

Besides this there is no evidence of fire-fighting activities or, which is of greater importance to this study, fire protection or fire prevention undertaken by the *vigiles* of Ostia.

Notes

1. Reynolds, 89.
2. Plut. *Crassus*, 2e.
3. Reynolds, 89.
4. Mommsen, *Staatsrecht* (1887) II, 2, 1055.
5. *NSc* (1915), 242ff.
6. *ScO* II, 29 and 139.
7. For more material and a detailed discussion of the portico problem, see G. Hermansen, "Nero's Porticus" in *Grazer Beiträge* 3 (1975), 159-76.
8. Strabo V 3, 7; Aurel. Victor *Epit.* 13, 13.
9. James Earnest Packer, *The Insula of Imperial Ostia, MAAR* (1971) 80-90; see also his article "Housing and Population in Imperial Ostia and Rome" *JRS* 57 (1967), 80ff.
10. Compare *Grazer Beiträge* III, 171 with note 15.
11. See Nash, *Pictorial Dictionary* I, 357-58, figs. 432 and 434.
12. Nash, I 256, fig. 299.
13. *NSc* (1909), 231.
14. See Gismondi's illustration in Calza, "La Preminenza della 'insula,' " *Monumenti Antichi* vol. 23, tav. VI.
15. For measurements and tabulations, see *Grazer Beiträge* III (1975), 172-76.
16. *ScO* I, 133; Guido Calza in *Palladio* V (1941), 2-3; Meiggs 305-08, with references; Reynolds, 107ff.
17. See Gismondi's reconstruction in *Palladio* V (1941), 1.
18. Reynolds, 46.
19. Meiggs, 307.
20. S4499 ff.
21. Reynolds, 89.
22. Reynolds, 90.
23. Reynolds, 91.

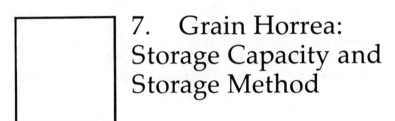

7. Grain Horrea: Storage Capacity and Storage Method

It has often been asked what the *horrea* space in Ostia meant to Rome. To what extent was it for the supply of Rome or for local consumption? It is safe to say that some of the *horrea* of Ostia, in the impressive line of *horrea* along the river, must have been built for the storage of grain alone. The biggest of all the excavated *horrea*, the Grandi Horrea, were definitely for grain storage: they were equipped with raised floors to allow air to circulate under the grain. The same kind of floor is found in the Horrea Antoniniana, of which only a fraction has been laid free but which may turn out to be the biggest of its kind in Ostia; also, there is the same kind of floor in the *horrea* I viii 2. Close to the river is the so-called Piccolo Mercato I viii 1; provisions for check boards (see below) are still preserved in some of its *cellae* and reveal the nature of these *horrea*. South of the Decumanus are Hortensius's *horrea* V xii 1, which have all the appearance of grain *horrea*. Whether they were is a moot point. Meiggs originally considered them grain *horrea*, but after a statement to the contrary by Rickman (Meiggs[2], 595) he gave it up. However, these *horrea* are protected from fire by *intercapedines*. They seem to lack *suspensurae*, but they may have been grain *horrea* even so, since *suspensurae* of brick are not the only solution to the problem of keeping grain dry (Rickman 293-94). For instance, are the *cellae* of the central block of the Grandi Horrea, some of which have check-board pilasters, any different from those of Hortensius's *horrea*?

Neither the *horrea* of the *mensores* nor the neighbouring *horrea* I xx 1 were set up for grain storage; Rickman believes that the latter *horrea* contained a market hall (71). To these must be added smaller and less important *horrea* in other parts of the city, but *horrea* are also used for many other purposes than storing grain. Finally, it is to be expected that more *horrea* will be excavated at the river west of the already excavated area, although not much space is left there. Still, west of Region III xvii the east wall of another *horrea* building has come out.[1]

What did this storage space mean to Rome, and would it be possible to arrive at a rough figure for the grain storage capacity in Ostia? The Grandi Horrea have sixty-four *cellae*, which in size vary from 4,5 by 7 metres to 4,5 by 17,5 metres to 5,5 by 10,5 metres. The storage capacity of the *horrea* depended on how high one piled the grain. The *cellae* offered the same type of storage as the common farm granaries on the Canadian Prairies, where it is standard procedure to build so that wheat can be stored to the height of eight feet (=2,44 metres). This height came naturally at a time when most of the work with the grain was done by hand, as in antiquity. If the Grandi Horrea, for instance, has all sixty-four *cellae* filled up to the 2,44-metre mark, they would hold 5660 metric tons.[2] If piled to the height of three metres, the storage capacity would be 6960 tons.

There is no doubt that, as a rule, the grain of the Romans was shipped in bulk and stored in bulk. This is clear from the provisions made by Roman law in cases where grain belonging

139.
Front end of a grain *cella*. Two pillars
on the inside of the door opening sustain
the check boards, which meet the pressure from the grain in the *cella* and permit
the door to move freely.

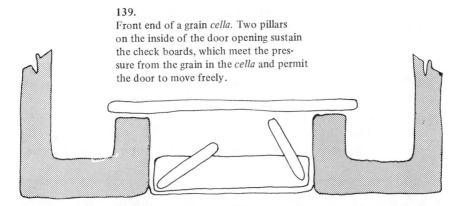

to different owners were dumped in the same ship's hold without partitions or other kinds of separation (*Dig.* 19, 2, 31).[3] It is
also clearly demonstrated by a wall painting in Domitilla's catacombs in Rome, where two *naves codicariae* are shown while
they are being unloaded. One sees here the loose grain in the
holds of the boats.[4]

This bulk handling had the consequence of the grain being
measured at every step of the operation, and there was a great
need for grain measurers. As well, it deserves to be noted that
many *cellae* of the *horrea* were set up for the storage of loose
grain and for filling to greater heights than 2,44 metres or eight
feet. Thirty-seven *cellae* of the Grandi Horrea, all the excavated
cellae of the Horrea Antoniniana, some of the *cellae* in the *horrea*
I viii 1 and I viii 2, and some *cellae* in the *horrea* at Claudius's
portico in Portus[5] still have preserved the inside door pillars
that would hold the check boards, so that the loose grain would
be kept back from the door and the door could move freely (fig.
139).

In modern times loose wheat is piled with the mechanical
help of elevators or augers or blowers. In antiquity it was han-
dled by many small men, who could not reach up high inside a
granary but who could carry sacks on their backs or on their
heads (as in the loading operation on the Isis Giminiana, Testaguzza 226), climb ladders, and walk on movable planks on
top of the grain pile. In the *horrea* at Claudius's portico at
Portus (Testaguzza 211) the height of the *cellae* would permit

the grain to be stored to about four metres at the back, and here it would be necessary to climb ladders and walk on planks. The grain level at the front depended on the height of the door opening. These *horrea* have *suspensurae* floors and are grain magazines and nothing else. Even though some of the *cellae* are seven metres high, as was the case in the Piccolo Mercato I viii 2,[6] it is doubtful that the grain was piled higher than three metres. The limiting factor was the height of the doors. The window above the door or the loophole in the back of the *cella*, if any, could not possibly have been covered. The window would be the only access to a filled and boarded-up granary, and the bottom of the windows were the absolute top limit of grain storage. This is the case in the Piccolo Mercato, where the sills of the window openings above the doors are well below the four-metre mark.[7]

What has been discussed is the ground-floor storage capacity. There were, however, upstairs floors in some *horrea*. The north wing of the Commodan alteration of the Grandi Horrea has a first floor served by two ramps. The walls of the wing are ninety to one hundred and ten centimetres thick. Similar dimensions are found in the *horrea* in Portus that are laid free and accessible.[8] These walls are strong enough to support an upper story with a heavy load of stored grain. The other *horrea* with staircases are Piccolo Mercato I viii 1 and *horrea* I viii 2, but it is doubtful how much grain could have been stored there. A fifty-three to fifty-four centimetre wall (*horrea* I viii 2)[9] may have been too thin to support the weight of a five-by-eight-metre cella stored with wheat to the height of three metres, which is ninety-two tons, nor does the Piccolo Mercato with sixty-centimetre walls[10] seem able to support the 137 tons in an upstairs *cella* five by twelve metres, especially since the ground floor *cella* had walls that were seven metres high. It seems unlikely when compared to many walls in Ostian buildings that had been reinforced by pillars under load conditions which must be considered much lighter. If those upstairs rooms had grain in them, it must have been a reduced load.

To give a round figure: the Grandi Horrea, with a storage potential of 6960 metric tons if each *cella* were filled to the three-metre mark, cover an area of 7200 square metres. Horrea

Antoniniana, with a front of ninety-seven metres on the Decumanus, may have gone to the same depth as the Grandi Horrea
and would then measure 9700 square metres. *Horrea* I viii 2 are
2020 square metres. Piccolo Mercato I viii 1 is 4370 square
metres. Those are the evident grain *horrea,* with a total area of
23,290 square metres. For our calculations another ten thousand square metres may be added from three sources: from
upstairs storage space; from new excavations further west; or
from the already excavated *horrea* which do not obviously look
like granaries, bringing the total up to some 33,300 square
metres, a figure that may be realistic when one considers that
the total area of excavated *horrea* now stands at 46,035 square
metres.[11] Whereas the 7200 square metres of the Grandi Horrea
have a potential of 6960 tons, the whole 33,300-square-metre
storage potential would be about 32,190 tons.

For these calculations the whole area of the *horrea* buildings has been used as a basis. The proportion between the area
of any whole *horrea* building and the area of the *cellae,* the real
storage space, is reasonably constant, with variations of
between 10 and 15 percent.[12] This procedure is necessary in
cases like the Horrea Antoniniana, where the overall area can
be estimated but where only few *cellae* are excavated.

The grain import from Egypt and Africa is recorded as
being sixty million *modii* a year,[13] equal to three hundred and
ninety thousand tons. This figure is highly suspect; it is based
on a combination of statistics from the times of Augustus and
Vespasian, which means that it applies to a time much earlier
than the period discussed here. If, however, it is fairly correct,
the 32,190 tons that could be stored in Ostia would be 8,25 percent of the yearly grain import to Rome from Egypt and Africa
in the first century A.D.

In the course of time, storage facilities, on a much larger
scale than in Ostia, were developed at Portus.[14] Although
space was more restricted than in Ostia, as remarked by
Meiggs (162), the space given to *horrea* and other import facilities was more conspicuous than in Ostia. The capacity of the
individual *horrea* in Portus was bigger than that offered by their
Ostian counterparts: the Severan (Lugli), or Marcus Aurelian,[15]
horrea at the basin between the two harbours has twenty-nine

cellae 5,9 by 11 metres and fifteen *cellae* 5,9 by 15 metres for a total of 3210 square metres on each of the two storeys or 6420 square metres in all. Filled with grain to the three-metre level it would hold 14,500 tons, to the four-metre mark nearly 19,400 tons. It may be fair to assume that the Romans also went on using some *horrea* space at Puteoli,[16] which according to Seneca was the port of the Alexandrian fleet (*Ep. 77*, 1-2).

What Ostia could mean for the food supply of Rome can only be expressed in a very loose estimate to establish a level. The 32,190 tons that could be stored in Ostia equalled the old-style *frumentatio* of over eighty-four thousand recipients in a year, if the grain was distributed at the old rate of five *modii* a month per person.[17] The figure of 32,190 tons is an ideal capacity that, when dealing with a commodity on the move, could hardly ever have been achieved in real life. Ostia, of course, can only have been a station on the way to Rome, and Ostia's capacity as grain supplier would depend on the turnover: how fast the grain was in and out of Ostia. The ideal was, of course, to get as much grain as possible to Rome at once, but when the influx of grain came faster than the transport facilities could bring it out of Ostia, or if there was a grain glut in the cities' *horrea*, the surplus would have to be stored in Ostia. While the import to Ostia depended on the weather and season, the traffic from Ostia to Rome could go on the year around.

The short navigation season would hardly allow for more than two round trips between Alexandria and Rome,[18] and closer to home the traffic from Africa, Sicily, Sardinia, and other locations was running concurrently. The Alexandria fleet travelled in convoy, which meant that the fleet did not weigh anchor until everybody was loaded up. This meant that the first had to wait for the later ones, and during the voyage the slowest boats would set the pace; the same seems to have been repeated on the home-bound trip, after a protracted lay-over time for some of them.[19] By modern standards the whole movement was slow—the *codicarii* took three days to make one trip from Ostia to Rome.[20] If, then, the slow-down of navigation in winter is considered, it might not be prudent to estimate an annual grain flow into the Ostian *horrea* of more than three times their capacity. That would, ideally, mean a grain flow of some ninety-five thousand tons during the year, about 25 percent of the alleged import to Rome of three hundred and ninety thousand tons from Egypt and African in the first century A.D. Some of these ninety-five thousand tons must have been consumed in Ostia by the local population, seasonal workers, travellers, and visitors. P.A. Brunt (382-83) estimates that each *frumentatio* ration fed two persons, so that ninety-five thousand tons would be the diet of nearly half a million people a year. If grain rations for fifty thousand persons were retained for local consumption, nearly four hundred and fifty thousand Romans could, theoretically, benefit from the granary capacity of Ostia.

As already pointed out, the utilization rate of the *horrea* could not be a hundred percent. When fast action was needed, the *cellae* would only be two-thirds full, because the last third— the top third—would require just as much time as the lower two-thirds. Moreover, there was always need for empty space for manoeuvring, if the grain was damp and would heat or if there were signs of vermin infestation beginning. The remedy and standard procedure would be to move the grain; sometimes it would have to be shifted around over and over again. This need would increase with the size of the granary *cellae* and the height to which the grain was stored. [21]

Presumably there must have been the necessary space in Ostia and Portus, especially after Septimius Severus, if one can believe the report in his Vita that at his death he left a stockpile of seven years' grain supply to the Romans (SHA *Sept. Severus* 8, 5). It is unlikely that it should be understood literally, for what would seven-year-old grain be like in old Rome?

The problem of keeping Rome supplied with bread proved to be a rather precarious task, and it is hardly necessary to quote examples of the many times when the supplies were running so low that the emperor or the city prefect faced a rioting population. Hence the administration's great nervousness about the grain supply.

There are very few sources at our disposal that shed light on the grain import before the fourth century. At that time the City of Rome is almost exclusively dependent on Africa for her grain supply. [22] After 330 all grain shipments from Egypt had been directed to Constantinople to supply that city. Most of the grain for other parts of Italy appears to have been grown locally.[23] The wheat crops of Italy had decreased for centuries and as a result much land had gone out of culture. Indeed, the situation was so bad that the emperors had given important tax incentives to those who would bring unproductive land back into production.[24] During a journey in Italy in 375 Symmachus writes to his father about the deplorable state of Roman agriculture and ends with the words: "namque hic usus in nostram venit aetatem, ut rus quod solebat alere nunc alatur" ("For in our time it has become customary that the farm land that used to feed us all now must be fed").[25] Another detail worth noting is that in 364 Valentinian I and Valens prohibited *adaeratio* being accepted instead of grain delivery *in specie*—that is, to pay money instead of paying taxes in kind was prohibited—the emperors wanted the grain.[26]

Rome was vulnerable whenever the shipping of grain from Africa was interrupted. During Gildo's insurrection in Africa, Stilicho manages to import grain from Spain, Gaul, and Germany and is praised for it by Claudian.[27] That is another clear proof that Rome looked to Africa for her bread. One particular event deserves to be mentioned: Ammianus reports that Rome in A.D. 383 suffered a famine,[28] which the Romans countered by expelling strangers, in particular the scholars, but they let actors and three thousand dancing girls remain. Symmachus blames the famine on the failure of the African grain import,[29] to which Ambrosius of Milan has the commentary that the crops that year had been good,[30] and only the City of Rome needed imported grain; the city could have been helped if it had asked for grain from those Italians whose sons were expelled from Rome!

The frequent shortages of food and outright famines show that Severus's supply pattern with its heavy reserves did not prevail. The Romans seemed to live from hand to mouth. When Alaric laid siege to Rome the first time, he arrived in October of 408.[31] He shut off all supplies to the city, occupied Portus at the mouth of the Tiber, and seized the grain boats that had arrived from Africa and those that came in later. After a short time the bread ration in Rome, the *erogatio panis*, was halved, then reduced to one-third, and famine set in, followed by disease. After a few weeks the senate began to negotiate with Alaric, and then Alaric let grain be brought from Ostia to Rome and the farmers from the surrounding country were allowed to hold market for three days outside the gates of Rome. The peace was most likely negotiated by the middle of January 409, so Rome's hardships could not have lasted much more than three months. [32]

This incident shows how limited were the supplies kept in Rome even after Gildo, when there had been no particular hindrance to the grain traffic. The events during the periods that have been discussed above expose the weakness of the City of Rome: her supply lines were now too long, the means of transportation too primitive and slow for the task and too much at the mercy of the weather, and the system would only work when Rome was strong enough to secure peace on the sea and in Africa.

Notes

1. All Ostian *horrea* are described and their use discussed in G.E. Rickman, *Roman Granaries and Store Buildings* (Cambridge, 1971) 15ff.

2. The slightly rounded figures used in this and the following calculations are: one *modius* equals 8,5 litres; with an average bushel weight for wheat of sixty imperial pounds, the modius weighs 6,5 kilograms. Compare Anne P. Gentry, *Roman Military Stone-built Granaries in Britain* (Oxford, 1976), 23ff. The *cellae* of Grandi Horrea: twelve *cellae* average 4,5 by 9,5 metres; eight *cellae* average 4,5 by 12 metres; eight *cellae* 4,5 by 7 metres; seven *cellae* 5 by 10 metres; seven *cellae* 5 by 7 metres; six *cellae* 5,5 by 10,5 metres; six *cellae* 4,5 by 10 metres; six *cellae* 5 by 10,5 metres; and four *cellae* 4,5 by 17,5 metres; about Grandi Horrea, see Calza in *NSc* (1921), 360ff.

3. I owe this reference to Lionel Casson, who discusses it in his *Ships and Seamanship*, 200.

4. Tengström, plate VI, and reference to Wilpert's publication of the painting, 101. When the painting is viewed in the catacombs today, the fine reddish points that indicate the wheat kernels are best seen in the boat to the right.

5. Testaguzza, 211 top.

6. Rickman, 20.

7. See Rickman's plates 1 and 2, where the four *cella* fronts are shown; the *cella* vaults have been restored, but the bottoms of the original windows can easily be discerned in the photographs.

8. Testaguzza, 192 and 211.

9. Rickman, 29.

10. Rickman, 20.

11. Becatti in *ScO* I, 170.

12. The proportion between yard and storage space is: in *horrea* I viii 1 (Piccolo Mercato) 1:1, 39; in *horrea* I viii 2 1:1, 58; in Grandi Horrea 1:1, 43.

13. Aurel. Victor, *De Caes. Epit.* 1, 6, combined with Josephus *Bell. Jud.* II, 383 and 386.

14. Testaguzza, 185-91; Meiggs, 162-63, 167-69.

15. Bloch, *Bolli laterizi*, 280.

16. Meiggs, 57.

17. This rate is from the first century B.C. (Brunt, 382), and our information from later times is frustratingly inadequate. *Frumentatio* was later replaced by *erogatio panis*, bread instead of grain, but details of the system are lacking. An edict of 369 (*Cod. Theod.* 14 17 5) prescribes that each Roman citizen shall receive thirty-six Roman ounces of bread a day free of charge, which seems to indicate that previously they had to pay for them.

18. Casson, 136ff.

19. Irenaeus's letter in Hunt and Edgar, *Select Papyri* (London, 1934) no. 113; compare Casson, 237.

20. Tengström, 59, with quotation from Philosotratus.

21. Tengström, 71, has expressed concern about the time-consuming measurement by means of a *modius,* but such procedure would not be necessary when grain was laid down in *cella* whose inside dimensions were known. A simple measurement of the grain level with a yardstick would immediately tell how many *modii* were in the bin.

22. Prudentius, *Contra Symmachum* II, 937-39; Claudian, *De bello Gild.* I, 60-65.

23. There is, however, some evidence of fiscal wheat allocations by Constantius I (Constantine?), Constans, and Constantius II to Puteoli, by Julianus to Terracina, and by Gratian to Capua, Symmachus, *Rel.* 40, 2-5.

24. *Cod. Just.* XI, 59 1 (Aurelian and Constantine); *Cod. Theod.* XI, 16.9 and 12 (A.D. 359 and 380).

25. Symmachus *Ep.* 1, 5.

26. *Cod. Theod.* XI 1, 8: *nemini aurum pro speciebus urbis Romae liceat exigere de futuro.*

27. Otto Seeck, *Ges d. Untergangs d. Antiken Welt,* 2d ed. (Stuttgart, 1920), V 287 with notes.

28. XIV 6, 19 (Seyfarth) with note, 262-63.

29. *Ep.* II 6, 2; 7, 3; 52; IV 74.

30. *De off. min.* III, 49: "Et certe arriserat anni fecunditas, invectitio urbs sola egebat frumento. Potuisset iuvari, si peteretur ab Italis frumentum, quorum filii expellebantur."

31. Otto Seeck, o.1. (note 26) V 392, with note, 593-94.

32. Seeck, o.1., 393-96, with notes.

Appendix:
The Guilds of Ostia

1. Grain shipping and related services
The shipowners of Ostia
Weight controllers
The guild of the grain measurers of Ostia
Grain measurers of Ceres Augusta
The guild of assistant and receiving grain measurers of Ostia
President of the guild of the nautical grain measurers of Ostia
The guild of the assistant grain measurers of Ostia
The guild of the assistant measurers
The president of the nauticals
The president II of the receivers
The very old guild of the receivers in Ostia and Portus

2. *Commerce*
Bankers
Money changers
Grain merchants
Oil merchants
Merchants of the wine forum
The most magnificent guild of wine importers and merchants
Fishermen-fishmongers

3. *Transport*
Cab drivers
Bargemen
The five guilds of the boatmen of Ostia
The order of the guilds of registering, assistant boatmen of
  Ostia
The order of the guild of the boatmen of the assistant lighters of
  Ostia
The guild of the operators of skiffs and ferryboats at Lucullus's
  crossing
The guild of the civilians' crossing
The guild of the marblemen's crossing
The guild of Lucullus's crossing
The guild of the skiffmen at the Rusticelian crossing
The curators of seagoing vessels
The operators of light barges

4. *Trades*
Lime burners
Shipwrights
Carpenters
Fullers
Furriers
Painters, painter brothers
Bakers
Ropemakers
Caulkers
Divers

5. *Civil Service*

Wax tablet scribes, book scribes

Lictors and messengers

Heralds

Public service corps of freedmen and slaves

Lictors and public slaves who are organized in a guild

Lictors, messengers, honour recipients and freedmen of the Colony, and public slaves, who are guild brothers

Civilian employees from the Forum and the weight control

6. *Cults*

Hastiferi

Cannophori

Dendrophori

Augustales

Worshippers of Jupiter the Protector

Worshippers of the Lares and the statues of our Lords the Augusti from the Rusticelian estates

The priests of Volcan

The priests of the invincible Sun Mithras

The Arulensic brothers

The Herculean brothers

The brothers of the five regions of the Colony of Ostia

The order of the guild brothers who contributed money to enlarge the temple

Glossary

The page numbers denote key references.

adaeratio Payment of taxes in cash instead of grain contribution in the Later Empire.

aedicula An altar built as a niche, framed by pilasters or small columns; a small chapel.

aedilis A Roman official charged with surveillance of streets and the market-place, in the early years also responsible for fire-fighting.

ager publicus Public land.

album A list of guild members, arranged after rank, with the patron(s) and the officers at the top.

ancones Drinking vessels used in taverns (p. 191).

angiportus   A narrow passage either through a house from street to backyard or in between houses. Often a blind alley.

annona   The supply of foodstuff for Rome, especially the wheat; also name of the authority which was responsible for it under the direction of the *praefectus annonae*.

aquarius   A waterman in the corps of the vigiles; details of his exact duties are unknown.

atriensis   A domestic slave, butler.

atrium   See *domus*.

balnea   The public baths.

basilica   A public building; a columned, rectangular hall, used primarily as seat of the courts.

beneficiarius   A lance corporal or adjutant in the corps of the vigiles.

biclinium   A dining couch for two persons; also a dining ensemble of a table with a biclinium on either side (compare *triclinium*).

bipedalis   A square brick measuring two by two feet; used in bonding courses or, occasionally, as pavement.

bucinator   A hornblower, member of the corps of the firefighter.

calda (calida)   Hot water, a necessary ingredient of conditum.

calix (pl. *calices*)   Goblets (p. 191); *crystalli calix* crystal goblet.

cannophori and *dendrophori*   Worshippers of Magna Mater and Attis.

cardo   1. The main street running N-S and meeting the E-W running Decumanus at right angles. 2. A door peg: Roman doors did not have hinges, but would swing on two pegs, one at the bottom and one at the top of the door frame. In Ostia there are numerous doorsteps with cardo holes.

carpentum   A two-wheeled, horse-drawn wagon, used for travel and city driving.

casa stretta   (Ital.) A narrow Roman house, built on the hereditary, archaic, small building lot; the narrowness of the house would be very obvious if the house was several storeys high.

case a giardino   (Ital.) Apartment houses in park-like surroundings.

caseggiato (Ital.) a large, complex apartment house, as distinct from *insula*. The distinction is modern.

Casette-tipo (Ital.) Houses of standard building type (p. 25).

Castra Praetoria The barracks of the Praetorian guard in north-east Rome.

Castrum The fortress, built 338 B.C. and constituting the core of Ostia. Large parts of its wall are preserved.

caupona A hotel-restaurant (p. 192).

cava aedium Courtyards in a house (*atrium*, peristyle).

cenaculum, coenaculum The Roman term for apartment.

cenatorium A banquet room.

centurio A subaltern Roman army officer, originally commanding a hundred-man unit (*centuria*); also a *vigiles* officer.

cibaria Foodstuff.

cippus(-i-) A boundary stone (p. 6).

cisiarius(-i-) A driver of a *cisium*. The stand of the *cisiarii* was on the Piazzale della Vittoria, right inside the Porta Romana.

cisium A light two- or four-wheeled, horse-drawn vehicle, used for the taxi service between Ostia and Rome.

clipeus A decorative shield, often used as basis for a painting; a medallion.

codicarius(-i-) An operator of the river barges that transported grain from Ostia to Rome (see *navis codicaria*).

collegium A guild. There are three kinds of guilds: religious, professional, and funeral guilds (*see* next entry).

collegium funeraticium A funeral guild whose only purpose was to provide a decent funeral for its members.

concameratio(-nes) A vaulted ceiling.

conditum The common social drink in Rome, consisting of wine and hot water (*calda*) with honey and pepper (*piperatum*) or other spices (p. 190).

congiarium A measure holding three and one-quarter litres.

conventus A meeting (of a guild).

coquus A cook.

cornicularius An adjutant of an officer of the *vigiles*.

corpus A guild; a corporation.

corpus vigilum   The corps of the militarily organized fire-fighters, who also provided the police service at night.

crystalli calix   A crystal goblet.

cubiculum   Means a room, but was used increasingly to denote a bedroom. For the sake of clarity, a bedroom could be called *cubiculum noctis et somni* (a room used at night for sleep) or a *cubiculum dormitorium* (a dormitory room).

cucullus   The hood of a Roman travel cloak.

cultor   A worshipper; name used for members of certain guilds, especially the funeral guilds. A guild was a religious association dedicated to the cult of the patron god of the guild (p. 60).

curia   The town hall where the town council, the *decuriones*, met and where the town records were kept.

cyathus   A small tumbler (p. 191).

decuria   A division of a guild (p. 57).

dendrophori   See *cannophori*.

deversorium   A hotel (p. 192).

diaeta   An apartment (p. 20).

dolabra   A fire axe, with a cutting edge on the one side and a pick on the other.

dolium   A huge storage jar with a capacity of approximately one thousand litres; *dolium defossum* was dug into the ground to provide a cooler storage for wine and oil.

domus   The traditional one-storey Roman house, consisting of two halves: closest to the street, after the entrance hall *(vestibulum)*, is the *atrium*, which is a hall surrounded on all sides by rooms. In the middle of the floor is the *impluvium*, which is a basin designed to catch the rain coming in through a hole in the roof (the *compluvium*). Opposite the entrance is the *tablinum*, the living-room of the house. Behind the *tablinum* is the other half of the house, the peristyle *(peristylium)*, which is a garden surrounded by a colonnade. Off the colonnade are various rooms, among which often a dining-room *(triclinium)*.

edictum perpetuum   The *praetor urbanus* issued every year a law-book containing all the laws which he would apply to all suits brought before him. The yearly changing edictum of the successive praetors was edited under Hadrian in a permanent form and called *edictum perpetuum*.

equites   The knights, the class of wealthy businessmen, ranking second after the senators.

erogatio panis   The distribution of bread (see *frumentatio*).

exedra   The living-room in the Roman apartment, corresponding to the *tablinum* of the *domus* (pp. 21-23).

fabri tignuari   Carpenters, housebuilders.

falcarius   A soldier of the corps of the vigiles; a sickle bearer?

falernum   A famous wine from *ager faliscus* in Campania.

familia   The members of a Roman household, free as well as slaves. In time the meaning of slavehold became prevalent; *familia publica* were the slaves owned by the city.

fasti   The public records of officials and main events during their terms of office, written on marble tablets and posted permanently in a public place. Many fragments of Ostia's *fasti* have been found, the oldest from the middle of the first century B.C.

focus(-i-)   A fireplace for cooking (p. 131).

foculus(-i-)   A brazier.

forma urbis   A plan of Rome, chiselled on marble slabs and showing streets and ground plans of houses and public buildings, at the beginning of the third century A.D.

frida (frigida)   Cold water.

frumentatio   The grain distribution by the *annona* authority to privileged Roman residents, later replaced by *erogatio panis*.

fullonica   A fuller's shop, where cloth was fulled and clothes were laundered. A cleansing agent was well-seasoned urine, whose offensive smell infested the neighbourhood.

furca   A meat fork (p. 191).

ganea   A very low-class restaurant.

hama   A fireman's water-bucket.

hastiferi   The worshippers of Bellona.

honestiores   Members of the upper class, who enjoyed a preferential treatment by the law but whose freedom of behaviour was limited by prejudice.

horrea   A storage magazine.

hospitium   A hotel (p. 192).

humiliores   The lower class without privilege before the law (compare *honestiores*).

hypocausis   A furnace for heating the *hypocaustum*. It was placed in a small room next to those that should be heated.

hypocaustum   The hollow space under a floor through which heated air from a furnace can pass and heat the floor and room above it.

impluvium   See *domus.*

in antis   An architectural temple plan in which columns are placed in line with and between the front of the cella walls. Often these wall ends were decorated with pilasters, the *antae.*

inquilinus   A tenant of an apartment or a *taberna.*

institor   A waiter (in a tavern) or a sales clerk.

insula   An apartment house (pp. 17-20).

intercapedo   An empty space as a fire-guard between buildings in Ostia, especially to protect the *horrea* (pp. 212-13).

isolato   (Ital.) The name of Ostian city blocks; the subdivisions of the *regiones.*

lacus   A major water basin fed by the public water system. A utilitarian construction to supply water to the *inquilini* of Ostia. Half of the *lacus* in Ostia are covered (compare *nymphaeum*).

lictor   The name of the attendant to Roman magistrates, from consul down, carrying *fasces,* which were bundles of rods, held together with a red strap, with an axe added if the magistrate could execute people. The *fascis* was the symbol of the magistrate's power, the *lictors* his protectors.

linter   A light boat, equipped with oars or sail.

macellum   The meat market, food market.

maenianum   A balcony (p. 21).

magister cenarum   The master of a guild's banquet, arranging it and presiding over it.

marina lavacra   The bathing and swimming establishments at the seashore.

medianum   The "room in the middle" of a Roman apartment (pp. 21-22).

navicularii   The shipowners.

navis codicaria   One of the many river barges into which grain from overseas vessels was trans-shipped and which then was towed to Rome on the Tiber by slaves and oxen, all pulling at a hawser attached to the mast of the *navis codicaria*.

nyphaeum   A fountain in a decorative and elaborate setting (see *lacus*).

oecus   A greek word meaning room; on its use, see p. 19.

optio   A sergeant, adjutant.

opus craticium   A light wall built of wood, reed, and stucco (p. 214).

opus incertum   A Roman cement wall faced with tufa blocks of different sizes and showing flat surfaces of irregular pattern.

opus listatum   See *opus vittatum*.

opus mixtum   A Roman cement wall faced with brick and *opus reticulatum* in alternating sections.

opus reticulatum   A Roman cement wall faced with small tufa blocks with a square surface, so that the face of the wall looks like a net (Lat. *rete*).

opus sectile   A wall and floor covering made of marble slabs, often multicoloured and cut in artful patterns.

opus spicatum   A pavement made of brick set on edge in a herringbone pattern.

opus vittatum   A Roman cement wall faced with courses of brick and tufa block in bands. Sometimes called *opus listatum*.

palaestra   An exercise yard for ball-playing and gymnastics always in connection with public baths.

patronus   A high-ranking person who undertook the patronage of a guild, a town, and the like.

peristyle   See *domus*.

pertica   A pole, presumably with a hook at the end, used for fire fighting (p. 210).

piperatum   See *conditum*.

pistor   A baker.

popina   A restaurant, *popina sellariola* is a restaurant providing tables and chairs (pp. 131-32, 192-94).

porticus   A colonnade.

praefectus vigilum   The commander of the fire corps.

praetor urbanus   Roman official, in rank just below the consul, in charge of the civil jurisdiction and the law courts of the city of Rome.

quaestor iuvenum   The treasurer of the guild of youth.

quinquennalis perpetuus   The president for life (see also *sevir augustalis*).

regio I-V   There is inscriptional evidence that Ostia was organized in five regions. The modern division of Ostia into five regions (see Introduction, fig. 2) is a practical provision with no backing in the tradition as to the boundaries or the numbers attributed to them.

scapha   A light rowing boat used for transport of goods and passengers.

schola   The meeting place of a guild.

sebaciarius   An attendant to the cressets used by the *vigiles*. The name derives from the tallow *(sebum)* that was the fuel of the cressets.

senatus frequens   A well-attended senate meeting.

servi soluti, vincti   Slaves that are free *(soluti)* or chained *(vincti)*.

sevir augustalis qq.   One of the six members of the guild instituted for the cult of Augustus (and following emperors). The number of the members grew well beyond the original six. The initials *qq. (quinquennalis)* denote a president. The *Augustales* were mostly freedmen, and the membership was highly prestigious.

sextarius   A measure holding 0,27 litre.

sifonarius   The operator of a *sifo*, also written *sipho*.

sigma   A dining table in the form of a new moon or the Greek letter sigma, C.

sipho(-nes)   The fire pump of the *vigiles* (p. 210).

sportula   A gift, often of food, distributed to guild members at certain guild celebrations, most frequently on the anniversaries of deceased members.

stabulum   A hotel (p. 192).

stibadium   Another name for a *sigma*.

stuppa   Oakum.

stuppatores Caulkers.

subscalare The narrow room under a flight of stairs on the ground floor, having the sloping underside of the stairs as a ceiling.

subpraefectus vigilum The vice-commander of the *vigiles.*

suspensura A floor suspended on small brick pillars so that air could circulate under it.

taberna A one-roomed shop in which any kind of trade could be practiced; eventually *taberna* acquired the meaning of *taberna vinaria,* a wine shop.

tabernarius A tavern-keeper.

tablinum See *domus.*

tabula ansata A rectangular signboard frame with a small handle-like extension on either side; a popular design in the second century A.D. (example, fig. 76).

tempio collegiale (Ital.) A guild temple.

tesserarius The carrier of the password, corps of the *vigiles.*

tetrastylum An *atrium* with four columns.

thermopolium A Greek term for a wine shop, which without much justification has been used about Ostian taverns.

tribunus An officer of the corps of the *vigiles,* listed between *subpraefectus* and *centurio.*

triclinium A dining couch for three persons; also a combination of a dining table and three *triclinia. Triclinium* is also simply a dining-room.

trulla A wine ladle (p. 191).

uncinarius A fire-fighter; a member of the demolition team, equipped with a hook (p. 224).

unguentarium An ointment bottle.

urna A water pitcher (p. 191).

vasa Crocks (p. 191).

veru A spit (p. 191).

vestibulum See *domus.*

vigiles See *corpus vigilum.*

vinarius A wine seller, compare *taberna vinaria* (p. 200).

vitrum A wine glass (p. 191).

zotheca An alcove (p. 22).

Index of Names
and Subjects

Index of Sources

A. Classical Authors

B. Inscriptions

Bloch: **2**, 57; **6**, 76; **9**, 58; **31**, 63; **33**, 72, 73; **40**, 80; **41**, 80; **43**, 63; **49**, 59; **54**, 59; **68**, 93; **73**, 32, 56, 72, 73.

Corpus Inscriptionum Latinarium: **II** 5929, 57; **IV** 1096, 146; **IV** 1097, 146; **IV** 1115, 146; **VI** 1741, 57; **IX** 2689, 191; **X** 787, 95; **XIV** 2, 57; **10**, 58; **25**, 59; **32**, 58; **33**, 59; **34-37**, 59; **40**, 59; **45**, 59, 69; **51**, 56; **99**, 56; **101**, 58; **118**, 59; **119**, 59; **123**, 67; **154**, 56; **161**, 57; **168**, 58; **169**, 58, 73; **170**, 58; **172**, 56; **214**, 145; **246**, 59; **250**, 58; **251**, 58; **252**, 58; **255**, 58; **256**, 58; **280**, 59; **281**, 59, 69; **284**, 59; **285**, 59; **289**, 56; **298**, 73; **303**, 57, 58; **309**, 56, 58; **341**, 58, 59 (bis); **346**, 58; **347**, 58; **352**, 58, 59; **353**, 58; **363**, 58; **364**, 58; **373**, 59 (bis); **374**, 58; **375**, 59; **376**, 58, 59, 216; **403**, 58, 59; **409**, 56 (bis), 57, 58, 59, 66, 82, 116; **425**, 58; **2793**, 23; **3603**, 56, 72; **4140**, 56; **4142**, 56, 57, 58; **4144**, 58; **4234**, 57, 58 (bis); **4616**, 58; **S4301**, 59; **S4448**, 82; **S4459**, 58; **S4494**, 216; **S4499**, 224, n.20; **S4509**, 145; **S4526**, 145; **S4530**, 224; **S4549**, 1, 58 (bis); **S4549**, 2, 58, 84; **S4549**, 43, 58; **S4550**, 58; **S4552**, 82; **S4553-56**, 58; **S4561-63**, 59; **S4569**, 58, 62, 108; **S4570**, 59; **S4573**, 58; **S4613**, 58; **S4648**, 56; **S4699**, 58; **S5327-28**, 58; **S5356**, 59; **S5374**, 59.

Unpublished Ostia: Inv. 7906, 58, 65, 115.